T0330043

Public Banks in the Age of Financialization

ADVANCES IN CRITICAL POLICY STUDIES

Series Editors: Frank Fischer, *Rutgers University, New Jersey, USA*, Holger Strassheim, *Humboldt University, Berlin, Germany*, Steven Griggs, *De Montfort University, UK* and Laureen Elgert, *Worcester Polytechnic Institute, USA*

The Advances in Critical Policy Studies series offers scholars and practitioners an innovative and interdisciplinary forum to further the understanding and analysis of public policy. Critical policy studies as a field of inquiry has emerged as an effort to understand policy processes not only in terms of apparent inputs and outputs, but more importantly in terms of the interests, values, and normative assumptions that shape and inform the practices of policy-making. Led by distinguished series editors, and supported by an esteemed international advisory board, this series brings together critical approaches to policy studies and invites scholars to engage actively with the interpretive interplay between normative and empirical perspectives, as well as qualitative and quantitative methodological issues. The audience for the Advances in Critical Policy Studies series is global, and books in the series will appeal to those interested in public policy analysis, political theory and analysis, governance, discourse and deliberation, interpretive analysis, policy practices, and methodological issues.

Titles in the series:

The Two Faces of Institutional Innovation
Promises and Limits of Democratic Participation in Latin America
Leonardo Avritzer

Public Banks in the Age of Financialization
A Comparative Perspective
Edited by Christoph Scherrer

Public Banks in the Age of Financialization

A Comparative Perspective

Edited by

Christoph Scherrer

Executive Director, International Center for Development and Decent Work, University of Kassel, Germany

ADVANCES IN CRITICAL POLICY STUDIES

Edward Elgar
PUBLISHING

Cheltenham, UK • Northampton, MA, USA

Published by
Edward Elgar Publishing Limited
The Lypiatts
15 Lansdown Road
Cheltenham
Glos GL50 2JA
UK

Edward Elgar Publishing, Inc.
William Pratt House
9 Dewey Court
Northampton
Massachusetts 01060
USA

A catalogue record for this book
is available from the British Library

Library of Congress Control Number: 2017941896

This book is available electronically in the **Elgar**online
Social and Political Science subject collection
DOI 10.4337/9781786430663

ISBN 978 1 78643 065 6 (cased)
ISBN 978 1 78643 066 3 (eBook)

Typeset by Servis Filmsetting Ltd, Stockport, Cheshire
Printed and bound in Great Britain by TJ International Ltd, Padstow

Contents

List of figures   vii
List of tables   viii
List of contributors   ix

Introduction   1
Christoph Scherrer

PART I   JUSTIFICATIONS FOR PUBLIC BANKS

1. Beyond the market failure argument: Public banks as
    stability anchors   13
    Ana Rosa Ribeiro de Mendonça and Simone Deos

2. Back to the future of alternative banks and patient capital   29
    Kurt Mettenheim and Olivier Butzbach

PART II   PUBLIC BANKS AS STABILITY ANCHORS: CASE
          STUDIES

3. Facing the 2008 crisis: Brazilian Central Bank and public
    banking system as Minskyan 'big banks'   53
    Simone Deos and Ana Rosa Ribeiro de Mendonça

4. Federal public banks in Brazil: Historical overview and role
    in the recent crisis   67
    Simone Deos, Camilla Ruocco and Everton Sotto Tibiriçá Rosa

5. Public banks and recent anticyclical policies: A comparison
    of the experiences of Brazil and Chile   83
    Ana Rosa Ribeiro de Mendonça and Brunno Henrique Sibin

PART III   PUBLIC BANKS AND DEVELOPMENT

6. The role of the Brazilian Development Bank (BNDES)
    in Brazilian development policy   101
    Adriana Nunes Ferreira and Everton Sotto Tibiriçá Rosa

7. Public banks and financial intermediation in India: The
    phases of nationalization, liberalization and inclusion   116
    Pallavi Chavan

8. Governance of development banks under uncertainty   136
    Tamilla Tagieva

PART IV   POLITICAL ATTACKS ON PUBLIC BANKS IN
          EUROPE

9. Savings banks and *Landesbanken* in the German political
    economy: The long struggle between private and public banks   155
    Daniel Seikel

10. Marginalizing the German savings banks through the
    European Single Market   176
    Halyna Semenyshyn

PART V   KEEPING PUBLIC BANKS ACCOUNTABLE TO THE
          PUBLIC

11. Governance makes a difference: A case study of the German
    Landesbanken Helaba and WestLB   195
    Xeniya Polikhronidi and Christoph Scherrer

12. Changing structure of non-performing loans: The case of
    Indian public banks   212
    Meenakshi Rajeev

13. The stakeholder governance of microfinance   230
    Magdalena Dieterle

14. The challenge of keeping public banks on mission   243
    Christoph Scherrer

Index   257

Figures

5.1 Credit evolution: BancoEstado and banking system,
2005–13   89
5.2 Loans: Public vs private banks, Brazil, 2002–14   91
6.1 Composition and evolution of contributions of BNDES
funding, 2003 to 2014   111
7.1 Structure of the Indian banking system, 2015   117
7.2 Private and public banks in India, 1969–2015   118
7.3 Intensity of public banking business per capita, 1969–2015   124
8.1 Task environment of state development banks   139
10.1 Market share for loans to businesses and self-employed
persons, by banking group, 2009   180
11.1 The multi-paradigm perspective on the study of
organizational governance   200
12.1 Sector contribution to NPA in percentage of total NPA,
2004–13   220

Tables

2.1	Banks as financial firms versus banks as institutions for patient capital	35
2.2	Operations performance of cooperative, commercial and state banks in North America and EU-15, 2006–12	41
2.3	Capital quality of cooperative, commercial and state banks in North America and EU-15, 2006–12	43
2.4	Asset quality of cooperative, commercial and state banks in North America and EU-15, 2006–12	44
5.1	Assets, loans and market share of public banks: Brazil and Chile, 2014	86
11.1	The major influencing factors on the governance of Helaba and WestLB	208
12.1	NPA by total advances ratio for selected countries and selected years	217
12.2	Bank group wise NPAs of Indian commercial banks, 2002–09	218
12.3	NPAs of state commercial banks recovered through various channels, selected years	223

Contributors

Olivier Butzbach is Researcher in Political Economy at the University of Campania 'Luigi Vanvitelli', Naples, Italy. He holds a PhD in Political Science from the European University Institute (Florence). His research focuses on the comparative history, political economy and performance of not-for-profit banks – especially savings banks and cooperative banks, in France, Italy and the United Kingdom. He is co-editor, with Kurt Mettenheim, of *Alternative Banks and Financial Crisis* (Pickering and Chatto, 2014).

Pallavi Chavan is an economist with research interests in Indian banking, agricultural credit, financial inclusion, and gender and finance. She holds a PhD in Economics and has been a recipient of the Central Bank Research Fellowship offered by the Bank for International Settlements, Basel, Switzerland in 2015. Some of her latest publications include: 'Bank lending and loan quality: The case of India', *BIS Working Papers No. 595* (2016, co-authored with Leonardo Gambacorta); 'Bank credit to small borrowers: An analysis based on supply and demand side indicators', *RBI Occasional Papers* (2014–15).

Simone Deos, PhD in Economics, is Assistant Professor of Economics at the Institute of Economics (IE), University of Campinas (Unicamp), São Paulo, Brazil, teaching both undergraduate and graduate courses in political economy, macroeconomics and monetary economics. At the moment she runs the Graduate Program in Economics at the same institution (IE-Unicamp). Her research has concentrated on financial instability, financial regulation and public finance for development. Recent English publications include: 'Banking-system transformations after the crisis and their impacts on regulation', *The Journal of European Economic History*, **44**(2) 77–111, 2015 (co-authored with Olívia Mattos and Ana Rosa Ribeiro de Mendonça).

Magdalena Dieterle is an economist and political scientist. She is currently teaching at Bremen University of Applied Sciences, Germany. She is an expert in microfinance. Her research interests include political economy and questions of inequality, stakeholder governance, gender, development, varieties of capitalism and financial institutions.

Adriana Nunes Ferreira, PhD in Economics, is Assistant Professor and Researcher at the Institute of Economics – University of Campinas, São Paulo, Brazil. She researches and publishes in the fields of macroeconomics, political economy and labour relations. She is currently directing a research group focused on the analysis of the Brazilian financial system and its relationship with macroeconomic and developmental policies.

Ana Rosa Ribeiro de Mendonça, PhD in Economics, is Assistant Professor of Macroeconomics and Banking at University of Campinas, São Paulo, Brazil. She is a researcher at CERI, the Center of International Economics Studies in Paris. Her areas of interest include banking regulation and public and development banks. Recent papers in English include: 'Challenges for Brazilian development: Investment and finance'; 'Notes on development banks and the investment decision: Finance and coordination'; 'Facing the crisis: Brazilian central bank and public banking system as Minskyan "big banks"'; and 'The crises in the financial regulation of the finance capitalism: A Minskyan analysis'.

Kurt Mettenheim is Professor in the Graduate Programs of Public Administration and Government at the Escola de Administração de Empresas de São Paulo, Fundação Getulio Vargas, FGV-EAESP, Brazil. Formerly University Lecturer in Brazilian Studies at the University of Oxford, he has taught at Columbia University, the University of Pittsburgh, and the Universities of São Paulo and Brasília. Recent publications include *Monetary Statecraft in Brazil, 1808–2014* (2016), *Federal Banking in Brazil: Policies and Competitive Advantages* (2010), and, is editor, with O. Butzbach of *Alternative Banking and Financial Crisis* (2014). Dr Mettenheim has conducted research on banking and microfinance in Brazil as a Fellow of the University of California, Irvine Institute for Money, Technology and Financial Inclusion and was resident and host of the international conference 'Alternative Banking and Social Inclusion' at the Rockefeller Foundation Bellagio Center.

Xeniya Polikhronidi studied global political economy at the University of Kassel and has a finance degree from the Goethe University in Frankfurt, Germany. Currently she is working as an analyst in a risk management division in a German private bank.

Meenakshi Rajeev is the Reserve Bank of India Chair Professor in the Institute for Social and Economic Change, Bangalore, India. She graduated from IIT Kanpur and received her PhD degree from the Indian Statistical Institute, Kolkata. She has published on a variety of research topics from both theoretical as well as empirical perspectives in national and international journals. She has visited and taught in a number of universities in the USA, Europe and India. Her recent publications include her book, co-edited with Sugata Marji, titled *Emerging Issues in Economic Development*, Oxford University Press, 2014.

Everton Sotto Tibiriçá Rosa, PhD, is Professor of Economics at the Federal University of Goiás, Brazil, and a member of Citizen Debt Audit-Brazil (Goiás Group). He received his PhD in Economics from the Institute of Economics of the University of Campinas, Brazil. His research interests include monetary economy, institutional/evolutionary economics and history of economic thought. He has published articles in indexed journals, and in annals of national and international scientific events.

Camilla Ruocco, PhD, studied economics at the University of Campinas, Brazil, and has concentrated her research in particular on the role of federal public banks during the recent crisis in Brazil. She worked as a consultant at McKinsey & Company for almost three years and now works as a project manager in the educational field.

Christoph Scherrer, economist and political scientist, is Professor of Globalization & Politics and Executive Director of the International Center for Development and Decent Work at the University of Kassel, Germany and Adjunct Member of the Political Science Graduate Program at Rutgers, The State University of New Jersey, USA. Recent English language publications include: *Combating Inequality: The Global North and South*, Routledge (2015, co-edited with A. Gallas, H. Herr and F. Hoffer), and *Financial Cultures and Crisis Dynamics*, Routledge (2014, co-edited with B. Jessop and B. Young).

Daniel Seikel, PhD in Political Science, is Senior Researcher at the Institute of Economic and Social Research (WSI) at the Hans-Böckler-Foundation, Düsseldorf, Germany. His main area of research is European integration, especially integration through law and European economic governance. His PhD research on liberalization of the German public banking sector was published in 2013 ('Der Kampf um öffentlich-rechtliche Banken. Wie die Europäische Kommission Liberalisierung durchsetzt' [The fight for public banks. How the European Commission enforces liberalization], Campus. One of his most recent publications is 'Flexible austerity and supranational autonomy. The reformed excessive deficit procedure and the asymmetry between liberalization and social regulation in the EU', *Journal of Common Market Studies*, **54**(6), 1398–416, 2016.

Halyna Semenyshyn is a PhD student and a graduate of the Master Program in Global Political Economy at Kassel University, Germany. She received a scholarship from the Stiftung der Deutschen Wirtschaft (sdw).

Her research interests include banking and finance, financial crisis, and European politics.

Brunno Henrique Sibin is a PhD student in Economics at the University of Campinas, São Paulo, Brazil, with Master's and Bachelor's degrees in Economics from the same university (2017 and 2014). His research interests include macroeconomics and public banks.

Tamilla Tagieva is a PhD student and a graduate of the Master Program in Global Political Economy at Kassel University, Germany. She receives a scholarship from the German Academic Exchange Service (DAAD). She writes about international development banking. Her research interests include international development, modernization theory, sociology of organizations, finance of small and medium-size enterprises (SMEs) and value chain finance.

Introduction

Christoph Scherrer

In recent decades, the financial sector has undergone a major shift from 'boring banking' (Krugman, 2009) to 'financialization' (Krippner, 2005). While boring banking was characterized by simple deposit and loan transactions, the term financialization captures the trend toward securitization of loans (and other financial products) to be traded on secondary markets. It has led to the development of complex financial instruments such as derivatives, the intensification of international capital flows and an increasing share of corporate profits going to the financial sector (Nölke et al., 2013). While in the period of boring banking (the post-war period until the mid-1970s) the banking system was stable, with the onset of financialization financial markets have become volatile. The volatility of the financial system has destabilized many economies, with detrimental effects on employment, working conditions and social security schemes (Herr et al., 2014).

The severity of the recent financial crisis starting in the United States in 2007 has led to calls for a more sound financial system and subsequently to more strict regulation of banks in the United States, in Europe and other places. Critics of financialization, however, have found that the reforms fall short of what is necessary for a stable financial system since the core of financialization – securitization – has remained virtually untouched (Helleiner, 2014; Scherrer, 2016). Therefore, some critics have called for strengthening alternative banks, which are banks owned by cooperatives or by public entities such as municipalities or state governments. These banks are said to be more prudent in their risk-taking, more long-term oriented and in general more attuned to the public good; most importantly, they have weathered the crisis rather well (Butzbach and Mettenheim, 2014).

While cooperative banks have received rather scant attention, banks owned by municipalities, state governments or other public entities (referred to here as public banks) were the target of much criticism before the crisis of 2007. The International Monetary Fund spearheaded the critique of public banks. On its advice, many countries privatized the public banks in the 1990s (Marston and Narain, 2004). The IMF continued this critique into the 2000s. For example, in its Financial System Stability Assessment, the fund recommended that Germany facilitate market-oriented restructuring by allowing private banks to take over public savings banks (IMF, 2003, p. 4). In academia, adherents of the principal–agent theory provided the scientific rationale against public banks. Lacking the discipline of the market, public banks are either misused by their owners (principals) for political purposes or by their management (agent) for aggrandizement (La Porta et al., 2002).

During the crisis, policy elites changed their perception of the state's role in financial markets. Many banks were nationalized and the government infused new capital or provided large-scale loans and guarantees (Contessi and El-Ghazaly, 2011). It seemed as if the delegitimization that the private banks had suffered from their reckless behavior would relegitimize public banks. The government crisis measures, however, turned out to be ad hoc crisis interventions. They were not done with the intention of rebuilding the public banking sector (ibid.).

The call for expanding and strengthening public banks went unheeded. The question is whether this neglect is justified or a product of interest constellations and ideological blinders. This book is intended as an exploration of the role public banks could play in stabilizing the financial system and in serving the 'real' economy with financial services. It aims at understanding how public banks fared in the current crisis. Do public banks serve as stability anchors in financial markets? Do public banks provide the much-needed finance for development? Against the background of the prevalent critique of public banks as politicized, badly managed financial entities, contributions to this volume will ask the following questions: Does the governance structure differ between the sound and the reckless public banks? What kind of governance keeps public banks accountable to the public? To these questions the book provides answers. It combines theoretical treatment of the issues raised with empirical investigations.

The empirical analysis will focus on three very different countries that share one similarity, namely the presence of a significant public sector in banking: Brazil, Germany and India. In 2013, the share of public banks was about 51 percent in Brazil (EMIS, 2014, p. 6), 40 percent in Germany (Bankenverband, 2014, p. 6) and 75 percent in India (see Chavan, Chapter 7 in this volume). Given the significant differences among these countries, this volume will not compare their public sectors in a strict sense. Rather, the differences are used to elucidate certain specific functions, performances and challenges of public banks. The case of Brazil allows for the study of a function seldom attributed to public banks, namely stabilizing the financial sector via anticyclical policies. As such anticyclical policies were pursued under the Lula presidency (2003–10), one can analyze the degree to which they were successful in stabilizing the economy and whether they came at the expense of deteriorating quality in bank loan portfolios. Brazil is also home to one of the world's largest development banks, BNDES. An analysis of its performance since the early 1950s promises insights into the factors driving its activities and influencing its performance.

Germany, as one of the places where public banking began, lends itself to an analysis of the early motives for public banks and their subsequent performance. Since Germany remains one of the very few countries among the more economically advanced countries with a large public banking sector, it is a good place to look at the role and performance of public banks in mature financial markets. Despite or because of their overall good record, they have come under attack from private banks using the competition policy doctrine of the European project of a single market in the 1990s and recently the post-crisis regulation proposals in the form of a Banking Union. These attacks are a good opportunity to explore the political vulnerability of public banks. Since not all German public banks were performing equally well, a comparison between successful and failing banks allows for insights into the factors that determine performance. Since the less well-performing banks in particular had jettisoned any reference to a public mandate besides increasing the competition in financial markets, the German public banks are good study objects for the issue of mission creep, that is, why public banks might lose sight of their public mandate and what could be done about it.

Since the broad-based nationalization of private banks in the late 1960s, India has been a country with one of the largest public banking sectors. It is therefore a good place to study the achievements and challenges of a largely publicly controlled financial system. India is also a country with historically high levels of unbanked households. The issue of financial exclusion and what public banks can contribute to increase the levels of inclusion can thus be discussed. Its banking system also allows us to study an important challenge for public banks, namely non-performing loans.

The main insights gained from these case studies can be summarized in the following way. Beyond supporting their regional economies by providing patient money and expertise, public banks can stabilize the business cycle through their long-term orientation and short-term mobilization of liquidity for countercyclical investment and consumption. They also increase the level of financial inclusion by reaching out to low-income households. As even mature financial markets do not provide these kinds of services, public banks are also valuable for economically advanced countries. Despite or because of their social functions, public banks perform on average better than their private counterparts in these countries, even measured in terms of traditional managerial objectives such as

profitability and cost efficiency. In sum, public banks can perform important functions for an economy without having to rely on risk-prone financial instruments. Strengthening the role of public banks in the financial
system could contribute significantly to stabilizing it.

Yet, public banks are also prone to mission creep. They are sometimes
misused for narrow, self-serving political purposes, for aggrandizing their
management or by powerful debtors. To safeguard public banks against
losing sight of their original mission, neither changes in the incentive structure for their management nor institutional fora for public deliberations
will suffice. In addition, it is necessary for management's as well as politicians' perception of the mission of public banks to change. This calls for a
much broader debate about the role of the public sector and the limits on
private actors. It calls into question the underlying concepts and practices
of financialization, starting with academia and not stopping at Wall Street.

SUMMARY OF CHAPTERS

The book is divided into five parts. The first part, 'Justifications for Public
Banks', contains two contributions that provide reasons for the existence
of public banks – the one more theoretical and the other more historical.
The title of the first contribution (Chapter 1) already hints at an overlooked
raison d'être for public banks: 'Beyond the market failure argument: Public
banks as stability anchors'. Ana Rosa Ribeiro de Mendonça and Simone
Deos from the Universidade Estadual de Campinas (Unicamp) in Brazil
argue that limiting public banks to filling the gaps left by private banks –
the standard argument in economics – neglects a very important dimension
of public banks, that is, their capacity to act countercyclically and thereby
stabilize access to credit during economic downturns. Taking a cue from
Hyman Minsky, they point to the immanent volatility of financial markets
dominated by private actors. In order to counter destabilizing tendencies,
the presence of institutions with a logic of action that differs from that of
the market is necessary. As public banks are not primarily concerned with
profitability, they can play this role. To a certain extent, their presence in
the market is an automatic stabilizer because public banks provide credit
with long maturation. In times of crisis, they can also be used for discretionary intervention, that is, opening up new credit lines.

In their contribution, 'Back to the future of alternative banks and
patient capital' (Chapter 2), Kurt Mettenheim from the Getulio Vargas
Foundation in Brazil and Olivier Butzbach from the University of
Campania 'Luigi Vanvitelli' in Italy explore the genesis of alternatives to
private banks, that is, savings banks, cooperative banks and development

banks in the nineteenth century. They interpret the establishment of alternative banks as social reactions of self-defense in Karl Polanyi's sense. The strengths of these alternative banks are rooted in what they call patient capital. Financial investments can be called patient when they are not made in expectation of short-term profits but in anticipation of more substantial returns in the future. Patient capital actually provides alternative banks with a competitive advantage, for which the authors provide proof in the form of an extensive statistical analysis of historical data as well as data from 2006 to 2012. The success of alternative banks in recent years helps them argue that although reforms have marginalized alternative banks in liberal market economies, liberalization produced back-to-the-future modernization of patient capital practices at alternative banks in coordinated market economies.

In the second part of the book, 'Public Banks as Stability Anchors: Case Studies', the previously theoretically underpinned claim that public banks can counteract the volatility of financial markets is empirically explored through the behavior of public banks in Brazil and Chile during the financial crisis of 2008. The first contribution, 'Facing the 2008 crisis: Brazilian Central Bank and public banking system as Minskyan "big banks"' (Chapter 3), by Simone Deos and Ana Rosa Ribeiro de Mendonça, picks up on Hyman Minsky's concept of a 'big bank', that is, the central bank as a lender of last resort, which together with big government stabilizes the economy. According to the authors, the provision of liquidity in order to avoid the financial crisis can be performed by a group of public banks in coordination with the central bank, thereby jointly playing the role of big banks. Empirically, they show that the impact of the 2008 crisis on the Brazilian economy was rather limited because the Brazilian Central Bank together with the public banks supplied sufficient liquidity for non-financial agents. Specific institutional characteristics of the Brazilian financial system have allowed these big banks to react promptly to the crisis.

The second contribution to this part of the book, 'Federal public banks in Brazil: Historical overview and role in the recent crisis' (Chapter 4), by Simone Deos and her co-authors Camilla Ruocco and Everton Sotto Tibiriçá Rosa (Unicamp), complements the first by providing a historical overview of two important Brazilian public banks, Banco do Brasil and Caixa Econômica Federal. It also details their anticyclical interventions during the crisis, which did not lower the quality of their respective portfolios. Only the shift to restrictive macroeconomic policies well after the crisis in 2014 has offset the expansion of public credit. The authors draw lessons from this: the anticyclical credit instruments have to be better coordinated with macroeconomic and currency policies.

The last contribution to the issue of public banks as stability anchors

(Chapter 5) is written by Ana Rosa Ribeiro de Mendonça and Brunno Henrique Sibin (Unicamp). 'Public banks and recent anticyclical policies: A comparision study of the experiences of Brazil and Chile' analyses the parallels between the crisis response of the Brazilian public bank Caixa Econômica Federal (Caixa) and its Chilean counterpart BancoEstado in their different political and economic environments. Both banks acted anticyclically, but encouraged by the strong pro-growth orientation of the Brazilian government and enabled by the institutionalized access to compulsory savings funds, Caixa continued the expansion of lending even after the crisis had been overcome. This procyclical behavior is a sign that Caixa's mandate went beyond the function of a stability anchor.

Part III, 'Public Banks and Development', takes a look at one of the major functions of public banks, namely the support of economic development. Its first contribution (Chapter 6), 'The role of the Brazilian Development Bank (BNDES) in Brazilian development policy', by Adriana Nunes Ferreira and Everton Sotto Tibiriçá Rosa (Unicamp), traces the history of one of the largest development banks in the world, Banco Nacional de Desenvolvimento Econômico e Social. In its various phases since the 1950s, the history of BNDES has mirrored the vision of development held by the leaders of the Brazilian economy. It moved from support for industrialization based on import substitution to relieving private companies of their foreign-denominated debt, to facilitating privatization and finally to carrying out industrial policy initiatives. While it undoubtedly contributed to economic growth in Brazil, the country has yet to fulfill the original vision of development with an endogenous technical progress and social justice.

The second contribution (Chapter 7) to the issue of development, 'Public banks and financial intermediation in India: The phases of nationalization, liberalization and inclusion', written by the Indian economist Pallavi Chavan, looks at one of the biggest public banking sectors in the world, also from a historical perspective. Besides supporting employment-intensive sectors such as agriculture and small enterprises, Indian banks are charged with reaching out to a great number of people without bank accounts, especially in rural areas, since the broad-based nationalization of banks in the late 1960s. Until the financial liberalization phase in the 1990s, branch outreach increased rapidly and bank credit became much more accessible in agriculture. The expansion of public banking was accompanied by a striking increase of national savings and investments. However, the policy of financial liberalization brought about a reversal in most of these accomplishments. The policy of financial inclusion and low interest-bearing loans to address agrarian distress resumed after 2005, but also included bulky loans to infrastructure and core industrial sectors with a higher propensity for default. Rejecting the call for privatization, she asserts the need not only to preserve the public character of these banks by way of recapitalization given their role in financial inclusion but also of a professional and transparent management of these banks.

The last contribution under the heading of development explicitly deals with the topic of good governance of development banks: 'Governance of development banks under uncertainty' (Chapter 8) written by Tamilla Tagieva from the University of Kassel in Germany. The contribution makes use of the sociological literature on organizations to answer the question of how a development bank can fulfill its public mandate of promoting industrialization under the conditions of uncertainty typical for many countries trying to catch up economically. With references to the internationally active German development bank KfW the author comes to the conclusion that development banks can successfully pursue their mission, even under conditions of uncertainty, if their board includes stakeholders beyond the government, if they can diversify their sources of capital, and if they strengthen their own knowledge in creating and learning capacities. These measures could increase their input as well as output legitimacy and thereby strengthen their standing in society.

The fourth part of the book, 'Political Attacks on Public Banks in Europe', picks up on the political vulnerability of public banks with the example of German public banks. Its first contribution (Chapter 9), 'Savings banks and *Landesbanken* in the German political economy: The long struggle between private and public banks', is written by Daniel Seikel from the Institute of Economic and Social Research (WSI) at the German Hans-Böckler Foundation. It introduces the reader to the traditional structure of the German banking system, the role of the public banks therein, and the relevance of this structure for the German production regime. It then traces the conflict between private and public banks as the latter increasingly competed for the same business. The conflict stalemated in the national arena until the European Single Market project was launched. This offered the private banks the opportunity to bypass the strong opposition in Germany. As European competition law presumes that all actors act like profit-maximizing private investors, the state liability guarantee for German public banks was considered to be an unfair competitive advantage. Under the dictates of the European Commission, this guarantee had to be withdrawn by the year 2005.

This part's second contribution, 'Marginalizing the German savings banks through the European Single Market' (Chapter 10), picks up where one timeline ends and another begins. Its author, Halyna Semenyshyn from the University of Kassel, addresses the questions of how and why the German public banks are once again threatened by the European Single

Market project despite the good performance especially of the municipal savings banks during the crisis of 2008. The Banking Union as envisaged by the European Commission will force savings banks to abandon their own joint liability schemes in favor of a more expensive European Union scheme. This disregard for alternative banking models stems from the continuing predominance of neoclassical economic thinking within the European Commission, despite its delegitimization in the crisis of 2008 and the fact that after the privatization wave of the 1990s, the German public banks were left with few allies among the European member states. But it is also the result of the massive losses incurred in another section of German public banking: the regional state banks or the *Landesbanken*. Their failure to adapt to the loss of the state liability guarantee placed the whole public sector on the defensive.

In the book's last part, 'Keeping Public Banks Accountable to the Public', the recurring issue of the previous parts – the public mandate – is covered from different perspectives by four contributions. In the first contribution (Chapter 11), 'Governance makes a difference: A case study of the German *Landesbanken* Helaba and WestLB', Xeniya Polikhronidi and Christoph Scherrer from the University of Kassel take aim at the German regional state banks, the *Landesbanken* mentioned in Part IV. By comparing an ambitious but ultimately failing *Landesbank* (WestLB) with a more prudent and so-far successful *Landesbank* (Helaba), they analyze the impact of governance structures on the performance of public banks. By applying a multi-theoretical perspective, they find that the governance of these banks differed remarkably in terms of processes, which may explain the different fate of these *Landesbanken* to a large extent. While both banks suffered a major crisis in the 1970s, the owners of Helaba learned their lesson and set up a governance structure characterized by strict control and monitoring mechanisms. They also upheld the commitment to a public mandate. At WestLB, this commitment was dropped and the governance structure left management with a very high degree of autonomy.

The problem of Indian public banks with non-performing loans, already mentioned in Part III, receives special attention in the contribution by Meenakshi Rajeev from the Institute for Social and Economic Change in India: 'Changing structure of non-performing loans: The case of Indian public banks' (Chapter 12). In her historical account of non-performing loans on the books of banks, the early years after nationalization are characterized by neglect of the problem. Only after the liberalization of the banking sector did the banks start to take serious measures to reduce the number of non-performing loans, whereby the public banks were as successful as their private counterparts. However, in the recent decade the problem resurfaced when the share of loans to large corporations increased. Based on field interviews, Rajeev identifies a number of reasons for non-payment, some of which pertain to the low collateral recovery rates in the courts, and others to the insufficient bank monitoring of borrowers. In contrast, self-help groups enhance the loan recovery rate in the poorer sections of society.

The third contribution (Chapter 13) on governance looks at alternative banking models in the form of microfinance institutions: 'The stakeholder governance of microfinance'. Its author, Magdalena Dieterle from Bremen University of Applied Sciences in Germany, argues that stakeholder-based financial institutions with supportive governance structures and local ownership (whether explicit or implicit) can offer more healthy and stable growth, even in times of crisis, for the institutions, their customers, and the communities in which they are based. This claim is based on a look at the history of microfinance that goes back to Irish loan funds and an analysis of today's microfinance institutions, especially those with a sense of client ownership.

Finally, Christoph Scherrer explores what leads public banks to disregard their public service function and how one can prevent this disregard in his contribution, 'The challenge of keeping public banks on mission' (Chapter 14). Again taking the German public banks as an example, it briefly describes their 'mission creep' in the form of financialization. Guided by the theory of hegemonic discourse, he interprets mission drift as part of neoliberal hegemony. This leads him to be skeptical about technocratic organizational solutions to the problem. From his discourse and analytical point of view, awareness about the public mandate seems to be of utmost importance. If the key actors of public banks are not aware of the public mandate and do not identify with the public mandate, then staying within the public mandate cannot be expected. Therefore, he argues that one needs to start with the general debate about the content of the public mandate and how public banks can contribute to it.

REFERENCES

Bankenverband – Bundesverband deutscher Banken e.V. (2014), *Zahlen, Daten, Fakten der Kreditwirtschaft* [Figures, Data and Facts of the Credit Economy], Berlin: Bankenverband.

Butzbach, O. and K. Mettenheim (eds) (2013), *Alternative Banking and Financial Crisis*, London: Pickering & Chatto.

Contessi, S. and H. El-Ghazaly (2011), 'Banking crises around the world. Different governments, different responses', *The Regional Economist*, Federal Reserve Bank of St. Louis, April, 10–16.

European Institutional Investor Group (EMIS) (2014), *Banking Sector Brazil*, accessed 30 June 2017 at https://www.emis.com/sites/default/files/EMIS%20Insigh t%20-%20Brazil%20Banking%20Sector%20Report.pdf.

Helleiner, E. (2014), *The Status Quo Crisis: Global Financial Governance After the 2008 Meltdown*, Oxford: Oxford University Press.

Herr, H., B. Ruoff and C. Salas (2014), 'Labour markets, wage dispersion and union policies', *International Journal of Labour Research*, **6**(1), 57–74.

International Monetary Fund (IMF) (2003), *Germany: Financial System Stability Assessment, IMF Country Report 03/343*, Washington, DC: IMF.

Krippner, G.R. (2005), 'The financialization of the American economy', *Socio-Economic Review*, **3**(2), 173–208.

Krugman, P. (2009), 'Making banking boring', *New York Times*, 10 April.

La Porta, R., F. Lopez-de-Silanez and A. Shleifer (2002), 'Government ownership of banks', *The Journal of Finance*, **57**(1), 265–301.

Marston, D. and A. Narain (2004), 'Observations from an International Monetary Fund survey', in G. Caprio, J.L. Fiechter, R.E. Litan and M. Pomerleano (eds), *The Future of State-owned Financial Institutions*, Washington, DC: Brookings Institution Press, pp. 51–71.

Nölke, A., M. Heires and H.-J. Bieling (2013), 'Editorial: The politics of financiali-zation', *Competition and Change*, **17**(3), 209–18.

Scherrer, C. (2016), 'The U.S. management of the financial crisis – a study of hegemony', in A. Truger, E. Hein, M. Heine and F. Hoffer (eds), *Monetary Macroeconomics, Labour Markets and Development*, Marburg: Metropolis, pp. 257–67.

PART I

Justifications for public banks

1. Beyond the market failure argument: Public banks as stability anchors[*]

Ana Rosa Ribeiro de Mendonça and Simone Deos

During the 1950s and 1960s, in a political and economic scenario still heavily influenced by the so-called 'Keynesian consensus', many economists advocated for direct state participation within banking systems, a view often shared by policymakers. In the following decades, there was a drastic change in the understanding of the state's proper position in the economy within the scope of the new neoliberal policies codified in the Washington Consensus, which led to a widespread process of privatization. This wave of privatization resulted from a growing perception on the part of governments that the state's role in financial institutions tended to hinder, rather than stimulate, financial development (Jeanneau, 2007). However, despite the widespread privatization process observed in the 1990s, bank assets controlled by states still proved significant (Yeyati et al., 2007).

For the period 1998–2004, there was a global trend, with the exception of some Asian economies, of reduction or, at least, stabilization in the ratio of state-owned bank assets over total bank assets. This downturn mirrored the great privatization wave of the 1980s and 1990s, in tune with the widespread perception that public financial institutions perform poorly, as demonstrated by their systematically lower indicators as compared to private banks (Novaes, 2007).

However, in 2008 and 2009, in the face of an intense crisis in the financial systems of most countries, the debate surrounding public banks was revived, and one can identify a shift in the view on the role they should play. On the one hand, the renationalization of major private financial institutions in countries with mature financial systems, such as the United States and the United Kingdom, was part of the agenda. On the other hand, the way in which public financial institutions intervened to confront and minimize detrimental consequences of crisis, as in Brazil, Germany

[*] The authors are grateful to Brunno Henrique Sibin for his help with this chapter.

and China, drew attention to a new vector of action for these entities. Concurrently, the unquestionable leading role private institutions played in creating the extremely fragile financial environment that enabled the crisis stimulated the development of new proposals of action on the part of public institutions (Lapavitsas, 2009).

A large part of the literature surveyed understands that the role to be played by public institutions is coupled with the perception of a certain immaturity, or incompleteness, in the development of banking systems and markets. In this sense, public financial institutions are justified as a way of bridging gaps left behind by the private sector in their provision of credit, or lack thereof, to some economic segments and/or geographical areas, and even in the provision of some other types of financial services. We call this perspective of analysis the 'conventional view', and consider it quite narrow.

In contrast, we believe that these institutions can, and indeed must, play an important role even in economies with a highly developed private sector, that is, in economies with 'mature' financial systems. They prove crucial both in addressing segments not adequately serviced by the private sector – but remain relevant for the local, sector or national economies – and to contributing to the implementation of financial policy. Besides this more 'isolated' action, which we believe is performed not only to minimize market failures and gaps, but also to create non-existent markets, public institutions should act in other spheres. These include: (1) competition regulation in markets and the creation of new markets; (2) anticyclical performance to both avoid the development of a highly fragile system (in the Minskyan sense), and to act during moments of great fragility in financial systems by establishing an informal safety net and/or guaranteeing the maintenance of credit operations.

The purpose of this chapter is to critically consider ideas that permeate the conceptual debate on the role of public financial institutions. Thus, the key questions underlying this discussion and guiding the literature review concern the need for these institutions in economies with different characteristics, central or peripheral economies, and concurrently relates to such institutions' embeddedness in the political economy and their performance profiles. A reflection on the role of these institutions has to take into account the historical moment, the institutional framework, or the economic and financial structure in which such institutions exist. Indeed, this role cannot be separated from the institutionality of each financial system, especially concerning their form, development and regulatory framework. Moreover, one must consider the origins, structure, governance, logic of action and regulation to which public financial institutions are subject. The disregard of these specificities impoverishes the theoretical exercise of reflection and even detaches it from reality, at least from context-specific realities. To this one must add the frequently explicit ideologization of arguments, which makes this discussion a far from trivial exercise.

The role actually played by public financial institutions, and that which they could play, stands as the *leitmotif* for the present analysis, and we try to conduct it based upon an understanding of uncertainty and instability as central concepts. Following this introduction, the first section discusses different views on the role of public banks, mainly within the credit market. The second section evaluates the broader role played by such institutions, based on a post-Keynesian approach. Last, final remarks are presented by way of conclusion, asserting the significance of the discussion surrounding resource allocation in credit markets and deducing the corresponding need for state presence, we defend the position that public banks should be used to reduce the inherently cyclical behaviour of markets.

PUBLIC BANKS AND RESOURCE ALLOCATION IN CREDIT MARKETS

Over the past several decades, there were moments when the question of public financial institutions was discussed in academic circles, among policymakers, and even by society in general. Throughout this debate, lines of argumentation were primarily built around the role these institutions play in the credit market and, more specifically, their mechanisms and decisions related to credit allocation. A closer examination of almost all such arguments reveals that this debate was largely predicated upon the concept of market imperfections, especially credit market imperfections, leading to an opposition between those who posit the relevance of 'market failures' and those who rather indicate that of 'government failures'. Advocates of public financial institutions understood their intervention as necessary in order to allocate credit to those economic sectors and/or segments that would otherwise remain unserved (Stiglitz, 1994), while critics of these institutions who founded their analyses upon the concept of government failures argued that public bank credit allocation would result in distortions and even higher costs for the economic system (Caprio et al., 2004; Hanson, 2004).

However, it is important to emphasize that the perception of gaps in the credit allocation process is also present among authors who do not build on the concept of perfect markets. When constructing arguments, they refer to the need for intervening in credit markets, especially in contexts where the private sector cannot guarantee adequate mechanisms to finance spending decisions, mainly on investments that prove crucial for generating income and employment in capitalist economies.

In order to better understand these various positions, this section is organized as follows. First, we will present different lines of argumentation based on the perception of 'market failures' and the presence of externalities, referring to a perspective in which the best allocation for scarce resources is central – we call it the conventional view. Next, we will discuss arguments that assert the necessary role of the state's presence within credit markets, building on the belief that it is important to guarantee financing for certain spending categories.

Market Imperfections and State Intervention

The conventional arguments highlighted above require further evaluation and will thus be discussed in greater depth next. First, however, it is worth underlining that the *leitmotif* of this discussion is not historical time, that is, the moment in time in which such arguments were brought forward, but, rather, the polarity between those who defend and those who attack the direct presence of the state – as owner – in the banking sector. Before entering into this discussion, we must make some remarks on the general rationale of state intervention in financial markets, derived from this conventional approach, which itself stems from neoclassical thought centred upon ideas of market perfection/imperfection and the generation of externalities.

Yeyati et al. (2007) attempt to parse the set of ideas underlying this rationale for state intervention in financial markets. The first group of ideas points to the need for intervention in order to guarantee the soundness and safety of the financial system, noting the inherent fragility of financial institutions, particularly of banks. The first vector of this fragility is evident within the problem of maturity transformation, as financial institutions raise funds in the short run and maintain illiquid and long-term assets. In addition to the issue of maturity transformation, these authors stress other characteristics inherent to banking institutions that generate negative externalities – such as bank runs and bankruptcy – and demand intervention. As institutions with high leverage ratios, banks tend to adopt less conservative behaviour than that expected by depositors, demanding intervention from outside the market. The logic underlying this set of ideas is founded upon the justification for prudential regulation, that is, for regulation that guarantees soundness of and trust in the banking system. We emphasize that the central point of this argumentation lies in the special characteristics of banking institutions that generate far-reaching negative externalities when such institutions operate jointly in the market, thus requiring state intervention.

The second group of arguments stresses the need for intervention as a way of reducing market imperfections derived from costly and asymmetric information, especially in the banking business, which carries out information-intensive operations. This asymmetry is present both in the relationship between credit suppliers and demanders, which can lead to credit rationing, and in operations between depositors and deposit-collecting institutions. In this context, asymmetric information creates imperfect markets, as the results obtained are suboptimal in terms of both price and quantity.

A third set of arguments for state intervention is based on the opportunity for financing socially relevant projects, with the belief that they produce positive externalities despite being less financially profitable. In this case, the market is not an appropriate mechanism for resource allocation because 'private lenders may have limited incentive to finance projects that produce externalities' (Yeyati et al., 2007, p. 220). Alongside this argument is the view that private banks may operate in ways that frustrate expansionary and/or anticyclical monetary policies, regarding either volumes negotiated or prices charged, since they fail to internalize the fact that they would help steer the economy out of an undesirable trajectory if they responded positively to such policies. In these cases, state intervention solves the coordination problem and makes the expansionary monetary policy more effective.

Finally, the fourth group of arguments for intervention is tied to the need to promote financial development and provide competitive banking services to agents who are seen as less attractive to private capital. The advocates of this form of intervention argue that guaranteeing access to banking services may lead to financial development with positive externalities, including growth and poverty reduction (Burgess and Pande, 2005). Another argument posits the presence of public banks as a means of guaranteeing competitive behaviour in otherwise collusive markets.

Public Banks: The Conventional Controversy

A question that arises from the arguments listed above – which, at different levels, justify the need for intervention – is related to the form the intervention assumes. The total or partial ownership of banking institutions is but one of many possible forms, together with prudential regulation, functional regulation and direct subsidies. However, a careful reading of the arguments above points out that, to a greater or lesser degree, the public ownership of institutions is an appropriate form of intervention. In other words, intervention through financial institution ownership is an effective way of minimizing credit market failures, while dealing with cases in which externalities, positive and negative, are highly significant. It is further justified by financial underdevelopment and the tendency towards collusion, factors that indicate less competitive markets.

A more comprehensive and critical understanding of the nature of this line of argumentation can be found in Chang:

> The point here is that, using a purely neoclassical logic, one can justify an enormous range of state intervention ... Thus seen, whether a neoclassical economist is an interventionist or not depends more on his/her political preference rather than the 'hard' economics that he/she practices. (Chang, 2000, p. 7)

Next, we present different lines of argumentation concerning the appropriateness of public financial institutions within the market, given the existence of market failures. An emphasis on certain consequences of their poor performance distinguishes these arguments from those already discussed. However, all arguments are ultimately rooted in the concepts of market failures and the generation of externalities since they are predicated on the perception that it is the role of public banks to allocate credit to sectors and segments that the market otherwise fails to provide for adequately. In this sense, they form what we have called the conventional view, which we consider extremely narrow.

The social view emphasizes that the public sector's role, and more specifically the role of public banks, is to compensate for market imperfections that leave 'socially profitable' investments without financing (Yeyati et al., 2007). Therefore, the emphasis is on a deficiency generated by markets that do not finance socially important investments.

In turn, the view that financial institutions are not capable of performing as development agents in the market is the critique that underlies the development view (Stiglitz and Uy, 1996). This line of argumentation stresses the need for intervention in specific situations stemming from the poor functioning of existing markets or even from the non-existence of such markets, and thus represent an obstacle to development. Among these situations it is worth highlighting capital scarcity, general public distrust, and endemic fraudulent practices among debtors (Yeyati et al., 2007). The state's direct intervention via the ownership of financial institutions enables it to raise resources and allocate them to projects of interest, such as long-term strategic projects, which may mitigate failures that hinder the functioning of the private stock market. Therefore, projects that are interesting from a social point of view, but not appealing to private capital, or that are too large for the amount of private capital available, could still be financed, contributing to further development (Stiglitz and Uy, 1996). It must be emphasized that this line of argumentation is essential to the social view, which manages to bring these two positions closer together. The argument in favour of the presence of public financial institutions contends that they facilitate financial and economic development, since they allow for increased accumulation and productivity. A conclusion derived from this line of argumentation is that public banks are more appropriate in less developed economies, marked by the presence of less or little organized financial institutions and markets.

Also focusing on the problem of market failures and the generation of externalities in the banking sector, but noting a slightly different consequence, Rocha (2003) presents another 'line of defence' for state-owned financial institutions. Her central argument is that the state's absence in the provision of banking services, besides implying little commitment to universalizing these services, would limit investments in important segments of the production chain, such as infrastructure, research and development. The latter, fundamental to increasing productivity, are riskier, since their chances of failing are higher, perhaps indicating insufficient or even non-existent resources for segments that provide higher productivity gains.[1]

This situation could be alleviated by the presence of public financial institutions, which can allocate credit to segments that provide productivity gains, since such institutions would: (1) be more willing to promote the internalization of positive effects and externalities; (2) not be subject to the same risks, given that state ownership and, consequently, state guarantee signify the impossibility of insolvency;[2] (3) regard the social value of credit for essential sectors more than the risk of operations. According to Rocha (2003), another positive externality generated by the presence of public institutions is the enhancement of trust in the system.[3] Thus, the generation of positive externalities could be divided into two orders of arguments. The first, also present in the so-called 'development view', is that, given its characteristics, credit provided by public banks would exert positive impacts on growth. The second is that the presence of these institutions would improve the reliability of the banking system. It is worth stressing that, according to Rocha (2003), public banks should seek to maximize social welfare, rather than focusing on profit maximization.

Contrary to the argumentation explained above, the 'political view' is quite critical of the existence of state-owned financial institutions, based primarily on the issue of their objectives and efficiency. On the one hand,

---

[1] Rocha considers uncertainty as a result of the association of macroeconomic conditions, debtor's credit worthiness, adverse selection and moral risk.

[2] The idea that permeates this line of argumentation is that the state would not allow one of its institutions to go bankrupt.

[3] It is not possible to disregard the potential that this presence could generate moral risk and adverse selection.

politicians' intent to pursue their personal objectives permeates state ownership of financial institutions, potentially conflicting with resource allocation to socially efficient uses. Controlling public banks politically, politicians would be able to create employment, as well as generate subsidies and other benefits as means to obtain electoral, but not 'economic' or 'social' advantages (LaPorta et al., 2002). On the other hand, such institutions would finance politically interesting, but otherwise inefficient projects. Projects not financed by the private sector may still be socially uninteresting, and additionally could decrease productivity, contrary to what the externalities/development position advocates (ibid.). Besides, public institutions could crowd out private companies by taking on their roles and resources. Therefore, the conclusion is that government failures prove to be a greater risk than market failures. According to this diagnosis, and considering scenarios in which public financial institutions are already present, the best prescription is privatization.

Another line of argumentation is deduced from the so-called 'agency view', which, according to some authors, can be understood as 'intermediary'. On one side, there is the social and development view, pointing to the benefits of direct intervention, and, on the other, there is the political view, indicating the deficiencies derived from intervention. In the middle of this spectrum stands the agency view (Novaes, 2007; Yeyati et al., 2007). The 'intermediary' nature of this view results from synthesizing this polarity through the idea that the service (credit allocation) could be rendered, in principle, either by a public agent or by a private agent hired by the state. The answer would depend on the nature of the contract made between them.

As for banks, the problem, which would point to the inappropriateness of the state's direct presence, stems from a lack of quality in the interaction between agents – public institution administrators – and the principal – governors and policymakers, who stand as democratic representation (Pinheiro, 2007). A poor relationship between agent and principal may result 'in weak administrative incentives that may cause corruption, technical inefficiency and poor allocation of resources' (Pinheiro, 2007, p. 162).

From the debate presented above, we deduce that, in essence, all discussion surrounding state intervention, particularly as the owner of financial institutions, is built on the concepts of market failures (or imperfections) and the generation of externalities.

Public Banks: The Non-conventional Controversy

Another order of arguments – called here the 'non-conventional' – found in the literature, and that in some way serves as a foundation for government intervention in credit markets, is based on the belief in the importance of financing mechanisms that guarantee crucial decisions, especially on investment, and that are not frequently provided by private agents. It is worth emphasizing that some of the arguments brought forward by the authors discussed here refer to government intervention, which does not necessarily mean intervention through public banks. However, we believe that these arguments contribute convincingly to a reflection on the role these institutions play. Moreover, it is important to stress that the arguments are based on specific institutional contexts, which might explain the proposed forms of intervention, but certainly does not preclude a broader reading of the intervention process itself.

Minsky et al. (1996) write from the perspective that the key role of a financial structure is to guarantee the accumulation of capital in order to promote production capacity growth and wealth generation within an economy. In this sense, they defend that whenever banking activities are not adequately performed by those institutions already active in the market, there is room for government intervention, mainly via credit supply and though saving and payment mechanisms for given segments of the population – such as low-income individuals, ethnic minorities and small business in particular.

Thus, one can observe that the defence of intervention is predicated upon the existence of gaps in service supply for given segments and regions, especially within the credit market. This position highlights the importance of financial services, particularly financing mechanisms to guarantee decisions on expenditures, income generation and, consequently, economic development:

> Capital development of the country, in general, and of depressed regions, in particular, requires a broad range of financial services in order to raise effective demand and revitalize the regional and national economies. In other words, 'capital development' is the primary concern . . . this includes the provision of financial services to all segments of the economy, including consumers, small and large business, retailers, developers, and all levels of government. (Minsky et al., 1996, p. 387)

The form of intervention considered in the above passage is the creation of Community Development Banks within the US financial system. This form (and not another) was probably proposed due to the institutionality and structure of that particular system.

Torres Filho (2007) develops a line of argumentation justifying the presence of public development banks based on a broader debate surrounding state intervention in credit markets.[4] He builds on the

---

[4] Certainly, when compared to the analysis by Minsky et al. (1996), the structural and

observation that intervention occurs worldwide, albeit with different purposes, and acts in three areas: monetary policy, credit regulation and credit allocation (or earmarking).[5]

Intervention in the credit market in the form of regulation takes place as the enforcement of norms, mechanisms and public institutions to preserve the proper functioning of the financial market. As for monetary policy, determining shorter-term interest rates, it directly or indirectly influences credit demand and supply.

The direct intervention in credit allocation, differing from the other forms, does not focus on the market as a whole. Rather, it aims to generate or reallocate resources to sectors, regions or specific types of borrowers, such as micro, small and medium-sized companies. However, aware of the fact that this debate has an important and irremovable institutional dimension, Torres Filho demonstrates that the degree of intervention and its instruments vary considerably among countries.

One possible form for intervention, typical of the United States, is the provision of instruments that guarantee credit of private origin. However, this allocation may well assume another form, that is, through public banks, as seen in Brazil.

The aim of this section was to present and analyse a list of the most commonly debated arguments regarding public banks. As we have already pointed out, the discussion of public banks, regardless of the side one takes in respect to the need for their presence, focuses on their role either as institutions capable of minimizing market failures or, according to the non-conventional view, as institutions that can fill market gaps, given the crucial role of financing for certain spending decisions.

The authors ascribing to the non-conventional view have raised a fundamental issue, emphasizing the distinct hierarchy of certain categories of expenditures and the corresponding need to reduce the uncertainty that surrounds them, and hence deducing the need for the presence of the state. However, we intend to go further into this debate and present another set of ideas, complementary to this one, which helps to develop a more comprehensive – and appropriate – argumentation about the need for public banks.

---

institutional context of the present analysis is quite distinct, since Torres Filho's final objective here is to reflect on the Brazilian case.

[5] Within the scope of this chapter, our focus is on credit allocation.

FINANCIAL STABILITY AND PUBLIC BANKS

The role of public banks can, and must, go beyond that of facing deficiencies in the process of credit allocation. Considering Minsky's theoretical contribution as central, the purpose of this section is to discuss the role that can be played by public banks in the context of an economy marked by financial instability and the generation of inequalities.

Minsky is among the most important authors of the post-Keynesian theoretical approach. During the moment of the eruption of the international financial crisis, Minsky's work was transformed into a reference not only within the academic mainstream, but also often in major newspapers.

It is remarkable that an author as important as Minsky has broken through theoretical and ideological barriers and begun to emerge in almost trivial debates. Nonetheless, this phenomenon did not happen without sacrificing much of the theoretical richness found in his ideas. We must underline that in contrast to the media debate, the central question in Minsky is not characterizing a moment – the alleged 'Minsky moment', marking the start of a more open crisis process in financial markets with dire consequences for the 'real side' of the economy. Rather, the crucial contribution of his scholarship lies in his illumination of the precise nature and dynamics of a capitalist economy. At last, Minsky is not the theoretician of a moment, but of a movement, the movement of the capitalist economy with developed financial markets, which, as opposed to the postulate of the neoclassical thought, does not tend towards equilibrium. In Minsky's words:

> In a world with capitalist finance it is simply not true that the pursuit by each unit of its own self-interest will lead an economy to equilibrium. The self-interest of bankers, levered investors, and investment producers can lead the economy to inflationary expansions and unemployment-creating contractions. Supply and demand analysis – in which market processes lead to equilibrium – does not explain the behavior of a capitalist economy, for capitalist financial processes mean that the economy has endogenous destabilizing forces. Financial fragility, which is a prerequisite for financial instability, is, fundamentally, a result of internal market processes. (Minsky, 1986 [2008], p. 280)

It is important to stress the meaning of this passage, which is far from trivial. The author points to the fact that, in a developed capitalist economy – that is, one with developed financial systems – the expected result from the agents' endless search for their own interests is not equilibrium. It is quite the opposite – disequilibrium and instability. In addition, Minsky shows that the heart of this instability may be found in the unbalanced behaviour of financial markets, and that such disequilibrium does not result from a 'failure' introduced 'from the outside'. On the contrary, disequilibrium is endogenous; it is in the nature of the system itself. To Minsky, instability is the counterpart of a system that seeks continuous expansion. Finally, it should be clearly stated that, to Minsky, a capitalist economy with developed financial systems does not tend to an optimizing equilibrium.

From this point on, the issue to be discussed is how such instability is, or should be, faced. In other words, how is it best mitigated on the one hand and what leads to its intensification on the other? The author's answer is that institutions, created within societies during certain economic and political conjunctures, play this crucial role.

Minsky's analysis of the behaviour of capitalist economies, emphasizing their inherent tendency to generate fragility and instability, allows for a different perspective on the discussion about public banks, opening space to reflect on their performance in much more general – and appropriate – terms than those based on failures, or even on market gaps, especially in the process of credit allocation. We contend that the importance of and the need for such institutions as public banks are better evaluated from this point of view. For public banks can, and must, be considered in the context of institutions capable of contributing to higher efficiency in the service provided to given segments of the financial (or credit) markets, and also able to assure more stability in the financial system and the economy as a whole:

> Decentralized markets are fine social devices for taking care of the particular outputs and prices of an economy, but they are imperfect devices for assuring stability and guaranteeing efficiency where large expensive capital assets are used in production. But most important, capitalist market processes that determine the prices of capital assets and the flow of investment introduce strong destabilizing forces into the system. Once we achieve an institutional structure in which upward explosion from full employment are constrained even as profits are stabilized, then the details of the economy can be left to market processes. (Minsky, 1986 [2008], p. 329)

Minsky's perspective is radically opposed to that of the mainstream, asserting the destabilizing role of markets and the (potentially) stabiliz-ing role of institutions created not by markets, but by governments. Therefore, the presence of institutions with a logic of action that differs from that of the market is necessary in order to counteract destabiliza-tion. Besides pointing to the need for intervention in key markets, he holds the view – logically derived from his analysis of the economy's unstable dynamics – that deep and long-lasting recessions are not observed today as a consequence of the important role played by governments:

> Big Government is the most important reason why today's capitalism is better
> than the capitalism which gave us the Great Depression. With Big Government,
> a move toward a deep depression is accompanied by a large government deficit
> that sustains or increases business profits. With profits sustained, output and
> employment are sustained or increased. (Minsky, 1986 [2008], p. 330)

The central stabilizing role of the state in modern capitalist economies in
many economies, takes the form of active public banks, which in some
cases could be called 'big government banks', as they are integral parts of
the government structure.

Andrade and Deos (2009) make an effort to conceptualize public banks
from a Keynesian-Minskyan theoretical perspective not limited to the
conventional idea of public banks as institutions that act to correct market
failures. The authors also criticize the use of this concept within the discussion surrounding the need for and appropriateness of public banks.
They argue that, more than correcting failures, such institutions structure
markets in which the private sector is reluctant to act.

For Andrade and Deos, a public bank is characterized as an institution
that performs activities that exceed the traditional, but important, role of
providing long-term development and credit lines to segments politically
defined as priorities and that the market does not serve properly. Public
banks go, or should go, beyond this point when (1) defining new financial
products and/or new conditions for existing products, so as to induce the
market to operate on new foundations, engaging in financing politics in a
broad sense; (2) operating in the market to change its 'natural dynamics',
clearly procyclical, as a privileged means to convey the impacts of decisions made within the scope of monetary and credit policies; (3) taking
action in the credit market to minimize uncertainty, especially in moments
when it is exacerbated, since in such circumstances there is a natural and
defensive 'shrinking' of private credit. The latter occasion for public bank
action is very close to conclusions drawn from the Minskyan discussion. The authors observe that, when playing its role as a public bank,
an institution should not be primarily concerned with profitability. They
demonstrate that, if profitability is the institution's main concern, this may
indicate that its public role is not being adequately fulfilled.

In Mollo (2005), we also find a broader analytical perspective on the
role of public banks, following in Keynes's and Minsky's footsteps. Mollo
discusses unstable monetary and financial dynamics that enlighten the
reflection on the need for public banks and on their role in general. For her,
parallel to the development of financial markets and increasingly liquid
instruments, there is an increase in the speculative dimension of the system
and in its instability. In this sense, she points to the need for state regulation, which we can understand in a broad sense, either involving indirect

intervention, such as prudential regulation, or direct intervention, including the use of public banks.

Besides highlighting the endogenous aspect of financial instability, Mollo stresses another interrelated dimension, concerning the increase in social, sector, and/or spatial (regional and even national) inequalities as consequences of the market logic. The need for regulation/intervention to reduce inequalities does not derive from an 'absence' of the market. On the contrary, it is the outcome of its full functioning, and the state's role is to break with its logic. Thus, it is necessary to design discretionary policies, redefining actions in the monetary and financial domain, both to guarantee investment financing, promoting employment and income growth, and to counteract instability and inequalities.

The message conveyed by the authors analysed in this section is that the role of public banks can, and must, go beyond the role traditionally discussed, that of acting to resolve deficiencies in the credit allocation process, stressed by what we have called the 'conventional view' and 'nonconventional view'. Here, we advocate that these institutions can, and must, be used to face issues such as the instability and inequalities generated by the normal functioning of the market.

CONCLUSION

Following the intense crisis experienced in central and peripheral financial markets at the end of the first decade of the 2000s, a shift occurred in the debate on the role of public banks away from the previous two decades of extremely negative assessments, especially within some multilateral institutions.

Written in this context, our purpose here was to reflect on the various perspectives and concepts that permeate the debate on the role of public financial institutions. It is worth observing that the boundaries for a reflection on the 'general' role of these institutions are circumscribed by an analytical exclusion of the historical moment, the institutional framework, and the economic and financial structure in which they perform. We should stress that ignoring these specificities impoverishes the exercise of theoretical reflection, and even detaches it from context-specific realities.

The literature review indicates that most authors who discuss public banks understand that the role to be played by these institutions is coupled with a perception of some immaturity, or incompleteness, in the development of banking systems and markets. In this sense, public financial institutions are justified as a way of correcting the failures or filling the gaps left by the private sector as it fails to meet the credit demands of given economic segments and geographical areas, and to provide certain types of financial services. We have noticed that such a position is held by authors whose work is based on a conventional (neoclassical) theoretical approach and those who adopt a heterodox approach, all firmly tied to the perspective of effective demand.

The discussion about resource allocation in credit markets is truly fundamental, especially considering the importance of financing spending decisions that generate income and employment, further emphasizing the existence of a hierarchy among spending categories as well as a need for reducing the uncertainty that surrounds them. These critical issues all point towards the need for an active state presence within markets. However, we have sought to go beyond this dimension and present another set of ideas, complementary to this one, which help to build a more comprehensive – and, in our opinion, more appropriate – argumentation about the need for public banks.

For such purpose, we started from a Keynesian-Minskyan theoretical approach and concluded that public banks can, and must, be used to reduce the inherently cyclical behaviour of markets, acting to slow both their contraction and expansion by applying an alternative logic. At the same time, public banks should be used to reduce sector or regional inequalities generated and reinforced by the market. Finally, the key role played by government banks, perhaps deemed 'Big Government Banks', to face severe situations of instability and the generation of inequalities that result from the normal functioning of the markets should now be beyond question.

BIBLIOGRAPHY

Andrade, R. and S. Deos (2009), 'Trajetória do Banco do Brasil no período recente (2001–2006): Banco Público ou Banco Estatal', *Revista de Economia Contemporânea*, **13**(1), 47–79.

Burgess, R. and R. Pande (2005), 'Do rural banks matter? Evidence from the Indian social banking experiment', *American Economic Review*, **95**(3), 780–95.

Caprio, G., J. Fiechter, M. Pomerleano and R.E. Litan (eds) (2004), 'Introduction', in *The Future of State-Owned Financial Institutions*, Washington, DC: Brookings Institution Press.

Chang, H.-J. (2000), 'An institutionalist perspective on the role of the state: Towards an institutionalist perspective', in L. Bulamarqui, A. Castro and H. Chang (eds), *Institutions and the Role of the State*, Cheltenham, UK and Northampton, MA, USA: Edward Elgar Publishing, pp. 3–26.

Hanson, J. (2004), 'The transformation of state-owned banks', in G. Caprio, J. Fiechter, M. Pomerleano and R.E. Litan (eds), (2004), *The Future of State-Owned Financial Institutions*, Washington, DC: Brookings Institution Press, pp. 13–49.

Jeanneau, S. (2007), 'Evolving banking systems in Latin America and the Caribbean: Challenges and implications for monetary policy and financial stability', *BIS Papers No. 33*, Basel: Bank for International Settlements.

La Porta, R., F. Lopes-de-Silanes and A. Shleifer (2002), 'Government ownership of banks', *The Journal of Finance*, **57**(1), 265–301.

Lapavitsas, C. (2009), 'Systemic failure of private banking: A case for public banks', *Research on Money and Finance Discussion Paper No. 13*, London: Department of Economics, School of Oriental and African Studies.

Marston, D. and A. Narain (2005), 'Observations from an International Monetary Fund survey', in G. Caprio, J. Fiechter, M. Pomerleano and R.E. Litan (eds), *The Future of State-Owned Financial Institutions*, Washington, DC: Brookings Institution Press.

Micco, A. and U. Panizza (2006), 'Bank ownership and lending behavior', *Economics Letters*, **93**(2), 248–54.

Minsky, H. (1986 [2008]), *Stabilizing an Unstable Economy*, New York: McGraw Hill.

Minsky, H., D. Papadimitriou, R. Phillips and R. Wray (1996), 'Community Development Banks', in D. Papadimitriou (ed.), *Stability in the Financial System*, London: Macmillan, pp. 385–99.

Mollo, M. de Lourdes (2005), 'Por uma dinâmica monetária e financeira menos excludente' [For a less excluding monetary and financial dynamics], in J. Sicsú, L.F. Paula and M. Renaut, *Novo Desenvolvimentismo: Um Projeto Nacional de Crescimento com Equidade Social*, Barueri: Manole/Konrad Adenauer.

Novaes, A. (2007), 'Intermediação financeira, bancos estatais e o mercado de capitais: A experiência internacional' [Financial intermediation, state banks and the capital market: International experience], in A. Pinheiro and L. Oliveira Filho (eds), *Mercado de Capitais e Bancos Públicos: Análise e Experiências Comparadas*, Rio de Janeiro/São Paulo: Contra Capa Livraria/ANBID.

Pinheiro, A.C. (2007), 'Bancos públicos no Brasil: Para onde ir' [Public banks in Brazil: Where to go], in A. Pinheiro and L. Oliveira Filho (eds), *Mercado de Capitais e Bancos Públicos: Análise e Experiências Comparadas*, Rio de Janeiro/ São Paulo: Contra Capa Livraria/ANBID.

Rocha, M. (2003), *Privatização no Sistema Bancário e o Caso do Banespa* [Privatization in the Banking System and the Banespa Case], Belo Horizonte: FACE/FUMEC.

Stiglitz, J.E. (1994), 'The role of the state in financial markets', in *Proceedings of the World Bank Annual Conference on Development Economics*, Washington, DC: The World Bank.

Stiglitz, J.E. and M. Uy (1996), 'Financial markets, public policy, and the East Asian miracle', *World Bank Research Observer*, **11**(2), 249–76.

Torres Filho, E. (2007), 'Direcionamento de crédito: O papel dos bancos de desen-volvimento e a experiência recente do BNDES' [Direction of credit: The role of development banks and the recent experience of BNDES], in A. Pinheiro and L. Oliveira Filho (eds), *Mercado de Capitais e Bancos Públicos: Análise e Experiências Comparadas*, Rio de Janeiro/São Paulo: Contra Capa Livraria/ ANBID.

Yeyati, E., A. Micco and U. Panizza (2007), 'A reappraisal of state-owned banks', *Economía*, **7**(2), 209–47.

2. Back to the future of alternative banks and patient capital

Kurt Mettenheim and Olivier Butzbach

This chapter explores how savings banks, cooperative banks, and development banks, referred to here as alternative banks, were founded as social reactions of self-defense in the nineteenth century. It also explores how they thereafter accumulated patient capital, but suffered political capture in the early twentieth century and, unexpectedly, realized competitive advantages as liberalization and new technologies changed their industries in the late twentieth and early twenty-first centuries. Theories of banking and institutional foundations of competitive advantage help explain this anomaly for contemporary approaches that define banks as profit-maximizing financial firms. Evidence from history, balance sheets, and results of 36 means test indicators for 7581 commercial banks, 1693 cooperative banks and 70 government banks from 2006 to 2012 are consistent with recent evidence that alternative banks make better banks. Although reforms have marginalized alternative banks in liberal market economies, liberalization has produced 'back-to-the-future' modernization of patient capital practices at alternative banks in coordinated market economies, as well as in developing and emerging countries.

Theories of banking and institutional change, balance sheet evidence, and comparison of bank performance explain how patient capital helped cooperative banks and savings banks grow from social reactions of self-defense[1] in the nineteenth century into two of the three pillars of banking systems (private banks being the third pillar)[2] in twenty-first century coordinated market economies. Concepts and theories from banking studies and political economy clarify how patient capital at alternative banks has sustained better business models than profit-maximizing financial firms,

---

[1] In Polanyi's sense (1944), despite his treating labor unions, central banks, and protectionism as social reactions of self-defense rather than alternative banks.

[2] The expression 'three pillars' (Schmidt et al., 2014) actually underestimates alternative banking because government special purpose banks (as a fourth 'pillar') continue to provide around 10 percent of domestic credit and finance in many coordinated market economies.

despite the latter remaining paradigmatic in financial economics and contemporary banking theory. Patient capital at alternative banks is related to six institutional foundations of competitive advantage in banking: lower cost of capital; lower agency costs; relationship banking; economies of scale; longer time horizons; and intertemporal risk mitigation. Alternative banks thereby produce more sustainable returns to cover deposit flows, liquidity risk, credit risk, returns on savings, and long-term investments toward social missions or public policy.

ALTERNATIVE BANK RESILIENCE IN THE FACE OF LIBERALIZATION

Although bank change since liberalization will require further study, a compelling anomaly has arisen. Liberalization in coordinated market economies has not produced convergence toward private banking, but instead different trajectories shaped by various hybrid reform strategies, private banks, and the focus of this chapter: a 'back-to-the-future' return to patient capital traditions at alternative banks with stakeholder governance and social or public policy missions. This differs from expectations about convergence toward private, market-based banking and impatient capital in comparative capitalism, financial economics, and banking studies; expectations shared by the vast majority of private bankers, the financial press, bank regulators, and international financial institutions (Deeg, 2010).

Expectations about convergence are grounded in contemporary banking theory that defines banks as private firms able to tap capital market efficiencies to deliver investment and banking services cheaper and more directly to customers (Berger et al., 2010; Bhattacharya et al., 2004). If contemporary banking theory is correct, then it follows that patient capital and other traditional banking practices are no longer needed. Critical studies of market-based banking (Hardie and Howarth, 2013) also tend to see private, money center banks as having largely replaced traditional banking. Whether positive in the sense of expecting deregulation to modernize the industry, or critical in the sense of fearing that liberalization may unravel longstanding institutions (Allen and Gale, 2000; Hall and Soskice, 2001), researchers in comparative political economy, financial economics, and banking studies concurred, until recently, that the trend was *away* from patient capital (Schmidt et al., 2002).

The decline of long-term equity holding and long-term loans (Culpepper, 2005; Jackson and Vitols, 2001) may continue, but evidence about patient capital at alternative banks suggests, at minimum, important exceptions.

Financialization studies also report increased short-term profit impera-
tives in banks and firms (Erturk et al., 2007; Jones and Nisbet, 2011; Van
der Zwan, 2014). However, these studies underestimate the importance of
alternative banks as patient capital providers (Carnevali, 2005). New regulatory frameworks have also been proposed to ensure long-term lending
(Bank of England, 2014; G30, 2013; Kay, 1991), while new industry associations such as the Long-Term Investors Club pursue similar goals.

And alternative banks are not the only managers of patient capital.
Aglietta (2009) focuses on three (non-bank) financial institutions that
manage long-term patient capital. In 2009, liabilities in official peren-
nial funds and reserves for public pensions totaled $2.8 trillion, while
private pension funds ($21.6 trillion) and insurance companies ($18.6
trillion) totaled $40.2 trillion. On the asset side, these institutions held
$30.2 trillion without liability commitment (patient capital), $8.6 trillion
in defined contribution pension funds (patient capital), $19.3 trillion in
mutual fund holdings (mixed), and $2.3 trillion in hedge funds and private
equity (impatient capital). In 2014, the International Investment Funds
Association reported $30.8 trillion in total mutual fund assets. Institutional
investors in advanced economies, especially the United States, remain the
largest. In 2007, US institutional investors held $24.2 trillion; this is seven
times the value of assets held by UK institutional investors ($3.4 trillion),
over ten-fold levels in Germany ($2.2 trillion) and France ($2.5 trillion),
and half the OECD total ($40.3 trillion). Pension funds predominate in
liberal market economies, while insurance companies predominate in
coordinated market economies; both have come under pressure to adopt
impatient capital practices (Bank of England, 2014).

This chapter focuses not on institutional investors but on large alternative banking groups in coordinated market economies that remain
two of three banking pillars. Alternative bank industry associations in
Europe reported a total of $13.1 trillion in assets held by member banks in
2013–14. Savings banks in the euro area held $5.6 trillion in assets in 2014
(EASB, 2014). Cooperative banks held $3.1 trillion in assets in 2013, and
special purpose banks in the euro area held a further $4.4 trillion in assets
in 2014 (EAPB, 2013).

Evidence and theory suggests that patient capital helps make alternative banks better banks. This runs counter to private bank models that
remain dominant in research and bank regulation. This chapter explores
past ideas from epistemic communities in social and public banking and
historical and balance sheet evidence to clarify how patient capital works at
alternative banks. Institutional foundations of competitive advantage have
made (and continue to make) it possible for alternative banks to provide
long-term investments for strategic sectors, social groups and public policy

(Zysman, 1983). On the meso and macro levels, this helps avert capital drain and credit rationing (Bressler et al., 2007; Stiglitz and Weiss, 1985). Patient capital at alternative banks also ameliorates business cycles by helping to avert the formation of asset bubbles during upswings, and by ensuring credit flows and finance during downturns (Schclarek, 2014). In sum, patient capital at alternative banks helps sustain higher levels of growth, helps fund and coordinate public policy, and sustains access to credit, finance and banking services.

Traditionally, private banks and capital markets retained upmarket clients in prosperous urban areas. Alternative banks accumulated patient capital for bankless groups while expanding from simple retail savings and loans to offer more complex, wholesale services such as payments, insurance, mortgage securitization, and capital market operations. In the late eighteenth century, municipal savings banks were founded to provide savings and payment services to communities not served by private banks. Cooperative banks were founded to help farmers without access to credit amidst economic crisis and the 1848 revolutions. Government mortgage banks were created in the late nineteenth century to finance agriculture, small firms, and local public entities, notably securitizing mortgages to accelerate lending. Development banks financed large-scale, long-term projects for industry and infrastructure that private banks refused to fund.[3]

In the late nineteenth century, independent local and regional savings banks and cooperative banks created second-tier financial groups that reduced costs, increased scale, and improved monitoring and control over local banks (Guinnane, 2002). Alternative banks used patient capital strategies to manage balance sheets and match long-term investments with liabilities secured through deposit guarantees and the greater trust of clients and the public in general (Grössl et al., 2013). A historical perspective suggests precisely the reverse causal order supposed by theories of financial repression and crowding out: alternative banks responded to demand for patient capital from groups left bankless by private commercial banks. Alternative banks and patient capital can therefore be seen as Polanyian reactions of social self-defense that helped (and continue to help in coordinated market economies) reverse market failures, credit rationing, capital drain, financial instability, and financial exclusion.

---

[3] 'The existing commercial banks were unable to provide industry with long-term finance for two main reasons. First, they were unwilling to bear the inevitable risks associated with the financing of new enterprises. Second, they lacked the specialized skills required to deal with the higher risk long-term investments' (Aghion, 1999, p. 3).

ALTERNATIVE BANKING AND PATIENT CAPITAL

English dictionaries often assert that the word 'bank' refers to the benches of medieval moneylenders (i.e., impatient capital). However, Bergier (1979) confirms MacLeod, Thornton, and other classical political economists who trace the English word to German derivations of the Italian word '*monti*' (pawn savings banks), and therefore traditions of patient capital. Indeed, savings banks and cooperative banks trace their social missions back to ancient church fund management (Bogaert, 1966). Unfortunately, the two major intellectual traditions of the nineteenth century, Marxism and liberalism, both *opposed* the accumulation of patient capital at alternative banks. Engels did consider cooperative banks as critical institutions for transition to socialism.[4] However, the radicalization of Marxist movements led to viewing workers who joined cooperative banks or sought to accumulate savings as traitors seduced by bourgeois individualism or errors of utopian socialism and elite philanthropy (Peabody, 1908). Liberal economists also saw (and continue to see) patient capital at alternative banks as unnecessary dead weight that should be put to more effective use by more efficient private banks and capital markets.[5]

Contrary to its critics, the causal logic of patient capital at alternative banks provides competitive advantages over private banks and retains complementary relations with many other dimensions of political economy. To explore historical and statistical evidence about complementary relations across these domains, it is important to recognize four different theoretical approaches to patient capital at alternative banks. The first is social banking.[6] Savings banks and cooperative banks were founded to help citizens and farmers not served by private commercial banks. Development banks were founded as institutions for national or regional public policy. From the perspective of political economy, these banks were not designed to maximize profits, but instead to reach bankless groups and realize social or public policy missions. Savings banks and cooperative banks should

---

[4] Hilferding succeeded in placing alternative banks at the center of the 1925 'Heidelberger Programm' of social democracy, but hyperinflation, fascism and war prevailed instead (Hoffrogge, 2011).

[5] Even a progressive political economist such as Charles Gide believed that private, money center banking should replace traditional patient capital practices at savings banks: 'The function of a savings bank, in fact, is not to serve as an institution for investing money. Its business is to enable people to put money aside and even to build up a little capital. But when this capital has been formed, if the depositors wish to invest it – that is to say, to make a profitable use of it – they have merely to withdraw it: the role of the savings bank is ended, and it rests with other institutions such as we have already studied in dealing with banks and credit establishments, to take charge of it' (Gide, 1906, p. 510).

[6] For a review of social banking history, see Mettenheim and Butzbach (2014a).

therefore be evaluated by the degree to which they help excluded groups to accumulate savings and obtain credit, finance and other banking services. Similarly, special purpose banks should be evaluated by how they contribute to policy missions.

The second theory about patient capital at alternative banks is that of political capture (Lowi, 1964). Although savings banks and cooperative banks were founded with social missions, once these institutions accumulated capital and large market shares in banking and finance, they attracted the attention of political forces. Savings banks and cooperative banks were used by prime ministers to bypass parliamentary budget control and finance colonial acquisitions and war. Totalitarian movements and governments also captured alternative banks during the first half of the twentieth century. However, after 1945, cooperative banks, savings banks and special purpose banks helped finance recovery, and coordinate policies in welfare states. Since the liberalization of European banking in the 1990s, they have also remained two of three banking pillars in coordinated market economies.

The third theory about patient capital at alternative banks is that of banking theory.[7] Fundamentals from banking theory explain how patient capital helped alternative banks to manage balance sheets better than private banks, both in the past and since liberalization (see next section for detail). These include asset and liability management, corporate governance, challenges arising from balance sheet mismatch, credit risk, liquidity risk, and maturity transformation, and further concerns about agency costs, transaction costs, and information problems.

The fourth theory about patient capital at alternative banks involves institutional foundations of competitive advantage (Hall and Soskice, 2001). Heterodox theories of the firm broaden the limited and biased definition of banks as profit-maximizing financial firms to better explain the performance and behavior of alternative banks. Because of greater trust among clients, consumers and depositors, alternative banks are able to manage liability risk and avert runs on deposits better than private banks. Because of their presence in social and political networks and public policymaking, alternative banks retain further competitive advantages in relational, retail and wholesale banking. The central offices of special purpose banks provide powerful cost advantages over private banks forced to retain expensive networks of branch offices and large numbers of employees. Savings banks and cooperative banks remain small, independent, local and regional institutions. However, they nonetheless reduce costs, achieve scale

---

[7] By banking theory we mean contemporary theories of credit intermediation and banking, consolidated in works such as Bhattacharya et al. (2004) and Berger et al. (2010).

Table 2.1   *Banks as financial firms versus banks as institutions for patient capital*

	Financial Firms	Institutions for Patient Capital
Theory	Efficient markets	Long-term investment
Capital theory	Liquid capital	Patient capital
Governance	Shareholder	Stakeholder
Mission	Profit maximization	Profit sustainability
Business model	Manufacture assets	Balance assets and liabilities
Strategy	Maximize leverage	Moderate leverage
Risk management	Value at risk or risk model	Relationship banking & soft information
Theory	Financial intermediation	Uncertainty and institutional theory
Method of study	Econometrics	Historical-institutional
Expected change	Convergence	Persistent variety

and scope, and improve risk control and management by sharing wholesale banking, finance, and insurance groups.

These four theoretical approaches help explain the historical emergence and 'back-to-the-future' modernization of patient capital at alternative banks in coordinated market economies as well as many developing and emerging countries.

POLITICAL ECONOMICS OF ALTERNATIVE BANKING

Traditionally, banks were seen as deposit-taking, loan-making institutions for which assets, liabilities, governance, risk management, and performance differed from other types of firms. Since the 1980s, contemporary banking theory has redefined banks as financial firms that intermediate directly between clients, money markets, and investment funds (Berger et al., 2010; Bhattacharya et al., 2004). Table 2.1 summarizes ten differences between contemporary banking theory and practices of patient capital at alternative banks. Contemporary banking theory emphasizes shareholder governance, profit maximization, the manufacture of assets on capital markets, strategies of low capital reserves and high leverage, quantitative methods of risk management on efficient markets, and financial intermediation theory to predict convergence toward private, market-based banking. In contrast, patient capital at alternative banks involves stakeholder governance, the production of sustainable returns over time, higher capital reserves and lower leverage to balance assets and liabilities, as well as soft information and relationship banking, and theories of uncertainty and institutional change to predict persistent variety in banking rather than convergence.

Studies of alternative banks indicate six institutional foundations of competitive advantage that are related to patient capital: stakeholder governance; two-tier organizational structures; long-term profit sustainability orientations; relationship banking embedded in politics, society and public policymaking; greater trust; and lower cost of capital (Butzbach and Mettenheim, 2014). Case studies and comparisons of savings banks since liberalization and transition to new regulations such as International Financial Reporting Standards (Ramanna, 2013) and Basel Accord capital reserve guidelines (Lall, 2012) also indicate that these institutions have realized competitive advantages over private banks (Ayadi et al., 2010; Schmidt et al., 2014).

Over time, alternative banks elaborated on institutional solutions to manage agency risks, transaction costs, liability risk, and other matters at the core of banking theory and political economy. Balance sheets, annual reports, public documents, and secondary studies of these banks suggest the following observations. Retail networks and relational banking in local communities provide savings banks and credit cooperatives with powerful competitive advantages. However, independent local and regional savings banks and cooperative banks also created second-tier, joint operations for giro payments and wholesale banking services to reduce costs, increase scale and manage risks (Guinnane, 2002). The social missions of savings banks and cooperative banks sustain socially oriented corporate cultures and long-term profit sustainability orientations that help manage risk and avert losses in capital markets.

Special purpose banks retain different institutional foundations of competitive advantage: less staff and lower operational costs. Access to official savings and other sources of capital at low or zero cost also permits special purpose banks to direct credit to strategic economic sectors at below market rates. After the 2007–08 crisis, the advantages of these institutions[8] led the UK and US governments to found special purpose banks for green investments and infrastructure finance, albeit much smaller banks than in coordinated market economies.

Special purpose banks also multiply money for public policy to alleviate fiscal constraints. A core idea in post-Keynesian monetary theory is that

---

[8] In 2009, cost–income ratios for special purpose banks in Germany (33.0) remained far below private banks (79.9), foreign banks (69.0), savings banks (67.2), and cooperative banks (69.1) (Bundesbank, 2017).

banks are uniquely able to multiply money. It follows that development banks and special purpose banks are uniquely able to multiply funds for public policy. Instead of allocating funds directly for policies, governments may instead hold funds as capital reserves (or official savings funds as long-term deposits) in special purpose banks to multiply money for public policy, provide long-term credit and finance below market prices, exercise leadership in bank consortia, and improve contractual control over policy implementation.

A HISTORICAL-INSTITUTIONAL BALANCE-SHEET APPROACH

In the late eighteenth and early nineteenth centuries, savings banks grew out of municipal savings agencies and philanthropic initiatives first in Northern Germany, then quickly throughout Europe. Cooperative banks were founded by Raiffeisen and Schultze-Delitzsch movements amidst economic crisis, hunger, and the 1848 revolutions to share risk and provide credit to farmers not served by private banks and urban savings banks. After the Credit Mobilier spurred capital in France to accelerate industrialization and infrastructure construction in the 1820s, national and regional governments across continental Europe founded development banks (Aghion, 1999; Cameron, 1953).

During Polanyi's period of liberal market supremacy (1834–73), eight types of financial institutions emerged as social reactions of self-defense to accumulate patient capital and acquire large market shares in domestic banking and finance. Private commercial banks continued to focus on trade, commerce and capital markets. However, savings banks, development banks, emission banks, insurance companies, cooperative banks, payment banks, mortgage banks, and construction banks were founded to reach groups not served by private banks. These eight types of banks and financial institutions under national liberalism in 1900 provide a rich legacy of largely lost theories, practices, and epistemic communities in social and public banking.

The following sections briefly review the origin and accumulation of patient capital and competitive advantages by savings banks.[9] The five other types of financial institutions in 1900 (emission banks, insurance firms, payment banks, mortgage banks, construction banks) have largely

---

[9] Development banks and special purpose banks are not discussed here as other chapters focus on these institutions. For cooperative banks, see Mettenheim and Butzbach (2014b, p. 12).

been incorporated by the three types of banks under consideration (private banks, savings banks, cooperative banks). Emission banks were transformed into central banks, but many emission bank functions were also retained as second-tier operations in regional and local savings banks and cooperative banks. Insurance companies grew independently, but also as joint ventures between savings banks and cooperative banks. Payment banks were also founded as joint ventures between savings banks and cooperative banks. Mortgage banks and construction banks originated as government banks, but also became part of wholesale financial groups of cooperative banks and savings banks, or were privatized to operate on capital markets only to fail after the 2007–08 crisis.[10]

Savings banks were created across Northern Europe and North America in the late eighteenth and early nineteenth centuries (Mura, 1996; Vogler, 1998). Early savings banks were often philanthropic or benevolent associations connected with churches. Later, savings banks were created within municipal entities or as corporations backed by public guarantees.[11] District savings banks were created in Prussia and then throughout German states by pooling local government guarantees. Mutual savings banks in the United States and savings trusts in the United Kingdom also accumulated patient capital during the latter nineteenth century and early twentieth centuries to constitute half of domestic banking and credit markets, specializing in home mortgages (US Census Bureau, 1949, pp. 266–71). However, the United States and the United Kingdom privatized or demutualized alternative banks after 1970, shifting these institutions from the mainstream to the margins.

Balance sheet and organizational data help clarify the causal logic of patient capital at alternative banks. From 1839 to 1913, Prussian savings banks (*Sparkassen*) grew from 85 to 1765 regional and local institutions with 5268 branch offices and 14 million savings accounts holding 13 billion marks. The evolution of liabilities and assets illustrates the contours of traditional patient capital balance sheet management. Account balances (liabilities) from 1870 to 1914 reflect the gradual inflow of deposits that covered interest payments and withdrawals. Reserves also were composed of cash or government bonds rather than market positions as in contemporary banking theory and practice.

The changing composition of assets at Prussian *Sparkassen* also suggests the gradual evolution of patient capital practices as these institutions

---

[10] DEPFA is an illustrative case study. A federal German mortgage bank, it was privatized in 1991 and became a global public finance bank in the late 1990s, only to fail in 2007.

[11] In 2005, the last of these guarantees fell under EC competition rulings (Schmidt et al., 2014, p. 119).

acquired larger scale. From 1870 to 1914, urban mortgages increased from 25.9 to 42.6 percent of assets, outpacing rural mortgages that declined from 28.5 to 16.3 percent of total assets, while securities and business investments increased slightly, and promissory notes declined from 17 to 3.9 percent of assets (Deutsche Bundesbank, 1976, p. 64).

Sparkassen were designed with social missions and retained corporate mandates to contribute to the improvement of the lower and middle classes.[12] Two concerns about social banking emerged in the early twentieth century. First, the influx of large deposits was seen as usurpation of savings banks by the upper classes and capitalists in search of safe, often guaranteed deposits. Second, the investments of savings banks often strayed from lending to the lower classes, becoming instead important sources for public finance and small and medium enterprises.

To test for capture, Hans Seidel calculated the average deposit values at *Sparkassen* from 1850 to 1913 (195.4 to 909.4 marks) to find out if increases reflected the gradual accumulation of compound interest or, instead, if increases in deposit would suggest capture (Büschgen, 1983, p. 199). The high-end average of 909.4 marks is in fact just *below* the 925.82 marks that would have accumulated exclusively from annual compound interest at 2.5 percent between 1850 and 1913. If clients had deposited an average of 20 marks in additional savings per year between 1851 and 1913, this would have brought the average per capita balance in savings accounts to 3916.3 marks, which is well above the 909.4 marks reported by savings banks in 1913. The evidence presented by Seidel suggests that *Sparkassen* continued to serve workers and farmers and averted capture by larger depositors from upper classes and capitalists, which would have increased liability risk and betrayed the social missions of savings banks.

PATIENT CAPITAL AND ALTERNATIVE BANK PERFORMANCE

The above sections have explored the institutional foundations of alternative bank performance in terms of banking theory and organizational evolution in history. This section uses statistical evidence from Bankscope data to compare the performance of savings banks and cooperative banks with private commercial banks. The evidence is consistent with other

---

[12] Prussian savings bank regulations in 1838: 'It must be remembered that the institution is intended primarily for the needs of the poorer classes, in order to extend to them the opportunity for depositing small savings. Any deviation from this policy must be avoided' (Seidel, 1908, p. 350).

econometric studies, finding that alternative banks perform better than private banks according to standard measures of banking and economic growth (Andrianova, 2012; Ayadi et al., 2009, 2010). This section reports the results of means tests for 9344 banks in Europe and North America based on 36 bank performance indicators from the Bankscope balance sheet database. Although cooperative banks and government banks are not necessarily designed to maximize profits, alternative banks nonetheless perform *as well as or better* than private commercial banks in 35 of 36 measures in terms of bank operations, capital quality, asset quality, and liquidity.[13]

In terms of operations, alternative banks: (1) maintain lower, more competitive cost–income ratios; (2) retain more cash from returns because of lower requirements to pay dividends; (3) produce more net interest revenue on equity; and (4) maintain lower net interest margins that suggest advantage in competitive markets. Alternative banks reported lower non-interest expenses, similar pre-tax income levels, and similar returns on assets compared to private commercial banks (see Table 2.2).

In terms of capital performance, cooperative banks hold less capital funds than private commercial banks as a lower percentage of deposits and short-term funding, liabilities, net loans and total assets. However, state banks hold almost twice as much capital as private commercial banks as a percentage of deposits and short-term funding, liabilities, net loans and total assets (see Table 2.3). Similar results were obtained for data on equity in comparison to custodian and short-term funding, liabilities, net loans, and total assets. Cooperative banks hold less equity than private banks while state banks hold much more. However, Basel Accord Tier 1 capital measurements remain biased toward market-based banks and impatient capital practices at private banks (Lall, 2012), such that market positions, contrary to the core idea and intent of the BIS Basel Accords, count as capital reserves.

In terms of asset quality, alternative banks: (1) equal or better private commercial banks in terms of the value of impaired loans on their balance sheets as a percentage of equity and gross loans; (2) hold lower fund levels as loan loss provisions (in terms of gross loans/net interest revenue and gross loans/impaired loans); and (3) hold similarly lower levels of unreserved impaired loans (in terms of equity; see Table 2.4).

The result of the above statistical difference of means tests for 36 indicators of bank performance suggests that alternative banks perform equal to or better than private banks. And this holds for averages of the 2006–12

---

[13] Bankscope data combine local and regional government savings banks with special purpose banks.

Table 2.2 Operations performance of cooperative, commercial and state banks in North America and EU-15, 2006–12

		2006	2007	2008	2009	2010	2011	2012	Mean
Cost to income ratio									
EU-15	Cooperative	65.6	69.5	71.0	69.2	69.5	68.4	68.0	68.7
	Commercial	63.7	64.1	70.0	70.5	71.5	80.0	74.1	70.6
	State	49.0	50.8	63.6	52.8	59.0	55.8	60.9	56.0
N. America	Commercial	63.2	66.9	75.2	73.4	69.4	66.4	65.5	68.5
Dividend payout									
EU-15	Cooperative	28.9	29.6	33.9	26.5	23.1	23.1	22.0	26.7
	Commercial	55.2	53.1	61.7	53.4	52.4	51.7	61.1	55.5
	State	39.9	40.5	40.2	31.5	38.8	25.4	51.9	38.3
N. America	Commercial	47.8	58.5	40.9	24.8	30.9	37.1	47.8	41.1
Net interest margin									
EU-15	Cooperative	2.8	2.8	2.7	2.6	2.6	2.6	2.5	2.6
	Commercial	2.5	2.6	2.5	2.2	2.2	2.2	3.2	2.5
	State	1.8	1.8	1.7	1.5	1.4	1.5	1.5	1.6
N. America	Commercial	3.8	3.8	3.6	3.6	3.9	3.8	3.7	3.7
Non-interest expenses/average assets									
EU-15	Cooperative	3.2	3.0	2.9	2.8	2.7	2.6	2.6	2.8
	Commercial	3.4	5.0	4.4	4.3	4.5	4.2	4.1	4.3
	State	2.1	2.1	2.3	2.3	2.4	2.6	2.3	2.3
N. America	Commercial	5.1	5.2	5.5	6.0	5.2	4.2	4.1	5.0

Table 2.2 (continued)

		2006	2007	2008	2009	2010	2011	2012	Mean
Pre-tax op. income/average assets									
EU-15	Cooperative	0.8	0.7	0.6	0.6	0.7	0.8	0.8	0.7
	Commercial	1.4	1.3	0.6	0.5	0.5	0.4	0.3	0.7
	State	1.3	1.3	0.3	0.8	1.1	0.7	0.9	0.9
N. America	Commercial	2.3	2.2	0.5	−0.2	0.7	1.2	1.6	1.2
Return on assets									
EU-15	Cooperative	0.6	0.5	0.4	0.3	0.4	0.3	0.3	0.4
	Commercial	1.3	1.3	0.4	0.3	0.2	0.1	0.4	0.6
	State	1.0	1.2	0.1	0.4	0.7	0.3	0.5	0.6
N. America	Commercial	1.5	1.4	0.3	−0.2	0.5	0.7	1.1	0.8

Note: Means calculated from Bankscope samples of 797 commercial banks, 1716 cooperative banks and 70 state banks in 15 states of the European Union, and 6784 commercial banks in North America. We were unable to separate savings banks from special purpose banks in Bankscope sample of 70 state banks.

Source: Bankscope database, Bureau van Dijk.

Table 2.3 Capital quality of cooperative, commercial and state banks in North America and EU-15, 2006–12

		2006	2007	2008	2009	2010	2011	2012	Mean
Basel 1 ratio									
EU-15	Cooperative	17.2	18.9	15.9	15.4	15.1	14.0	13.8	15.8
	Commercial	14.1	13.8	14.8	17.3	16.6	17.3	30.5	17.8
	State	11.2	10.9	13.0	12.5	14.9	16.2	16.1	13.5
N. America	Commercial	20.4	19.0	19.6	22.1	22.6	23.6	19.9	21.0
Capital ratio									
EU-15	Cooperative	17.8	17.3	16.5	16.4	17.0	17.3	17.4	17.1
Commercial		16.7	17.2	16.1	17.3	20.0	20.7	21.1	18.4
State		15.0	14.7	16.6	15.5	17.9	20.2	19.9	17.1
N. America	Commercial	21.8	20.4	21.2	23.6	24.1	25.1	21.2	22.5

Note: Means calculated from Bankscope samples of 797 commercial banks, 1716 cooperative banks and 70 state banks in 15 states of the European Union, and 6784 commercial banks in North America. Information on sample and measurement, see below.

Source: Bankscope database, Bureau van Dijk.

Table 2.4 Asset quality of cooperative, commercial and state banks in North America and EU-15, 2006–12

		2006	2007	2008	2009	2010	2011	2012	Mean
Impaired loans/equity									
EU-15	Cooperative	37.2	35.6	41.8	49.0	57.3	62.5	52.2	48.0
	Commercial	27.2	30.4	39.1	51.9	59.4	69.2	71.1	49.7
	State	24.2	25.2	38.1	56.7	67.8	56.4	64.3	47.5
N. America	Commercial	4.2	7.3	19.1	32.7	27.7	23.2	18.3	18.9
Impaired loans/gross loans									
EU-15	Cooperative	6.7	6.3	6.8	7.5	8.1	8.0	7.0	7.2
	Commercial	3.2	3.3	4.2	6.5	6.5	7.9	9.5	5.9
	State	3.1	3.4	4.0	4.8	5.9	5.9	6.2	4.8
N. America	Commercial	0.6	1.0	2.4	4.6	4.3	3.9	3.2	2.9
Unreserved impaired loans/equity									
EU-15	Cooperative	24.1	22.9	26.9	30.7	37.5	40.4	33.2	30.8
	Commercial	13.2	16.5	19.6	27.6	29.7	37.0	41.4	26.4
	State	14.3	13.7	14.4	28.8	47.1	29.1	32.7	25.7
N. America	Commercial	5.9	11.0	18.9	25.4	21.6	17.3	14.1	16.3

Note: Means calculated from bankscope samples of 797 commercial banks, 1716 cooperative banks and 70 state banks in 15 states of the European Union, and 6784 commercial banks in North America.

Source: Bankscope database, Bureau van Dijk. Information on sample and measurement, see below.

time period and in the three business cycle phases within this period: in 2006 before crisis; from 2007 to 2008 amidst crisis; and during recovery from 2009 to 2012. These findings confirm aggregate cross-national comparisons (Andrianova, 2012) and bank-level comparisons (Ayadi et al., 2009, 2010) to suggest that institutional foundations of competitive advantage such as the insertion of alternative banks in society, politics, and public policy missions *improves* banking. This is true even as measured by indicators taken from banking studies that often presume the superiority of private banking and impatient capital.

CONCLUSION

Allen and Gale (2000) and Hall and Soskice (2001) feared that liberalization would cause longstanding financial institutions to unravel. Liberal market economies have, in fact, marginalized alternative banking groups. In the United States, local mutual savings banks peaked in the 1940s only to decline thereafter, especially after liberalization and deregulation caused crisis in the industry during the late 1980s. In the United Kingdom, local and regional cooperatives and trust savings banks were consolidated into a single group and demutualized in the 1980s, requiring £5.5 billion to avert failure after crisis in 2007–08. In contrast, liberalization (without draconian deregulation) in coordinated market economies has produced a different outcome, that of reinforcing two alternative, non-private banking pillars alongside private and foreign banks (ignoring special purpose banks as a fourth 'pillar'). The consequences appear severe. Transition to a single-pillar of private banking in liberal market economies seems to have magnified Minsky cycles of financial instability,[14] marginalized alternative banking groups, and worsened inequality, capital drain, credit rationing, and other downsides of financialization. In comparison, the two additional pillars of savings banks and cooperative banks with patient capital strategies and social missions have provided comparative advantages to coordinated market economies in terms of better financial stability, lower cost of banking crises, lower levels of capital drain and credit rationing, and institutional capacities to mobilize funds and forces against inequality and social exclusion.

Our time of liberal predominance (1980–2016) has lasted nearly as long as the period examined by Polanyi (1834–73). Although he did not mention them, savings banks, cooperative banks, and development banks emerged

---

[14] See special issue of *Accounting, Economics, and Law: A Convivium* entitled 'Banking, Finance, and Minsky's Financial Instability Hypothesis' (2013, Volume 3).

as social reactions of self-defense, both in his time and in ours. Instead of convergence toward private, market-centered banking, the patient capital practices of alternative banks have provided institutional foundations of competitive advantage over private banks.

Another of Polanyi's core arguments may also apply. In his view, interpreting the industrial revolution as caused by free markets rather than new techniques of mass production was among the worst mistakes of liberal theory (1944, p. 33). As new technologies of information and communication transform banking and finance in our time, contemporary banking theory and neoliberal policy designs risk repeating the same mistake with similarly stark consequences. New technologies have reduced the cost of many banking transactions *over 100 times*. However, instead of convergence toward private, money center banking, this chapter reports evidence and theory to suggest that the production frontiers of banking are being shaped not only by freer, more efficient markets, but also by hybrid reforms, complex path dependent trajectories, and institutional foundations of competitive advantage at alternative banks based on patient capital, stakeholder governance, long-term profit sustainability orientations, and relationship banking embedded in politics, society and public policymaking.

A longer-term, historical-institutional approach reveals transformative effects of the gradual accumulation of patient capital at alternative banks (Streeck and Thelen, 2005). Concepts and theories from banking studies and heterodox theories of the firm (Biondi et al., 2007; Hall and Soskice, 2001) help clarify the causal logic of patient capital at alternative banks and overcome the biases in financial economics and banking studies that arise from defining banks as profit-maximizing financial firms. Theories about banks as institutions designed to ameliorate market failures; theories of the institutional foundations of competitive advantage; and the large market shares of alternative banks that run on patient capital sum to suggest important differences between these institutions and private banks on the micro (bank) level of analysis. These approaches also make it possible to trace the consequences of alternative banking and patient capital up through the meso and macro levels of analysis (Deeg and Jackson, 2007). Further research on alternative banking promises to help clarify differences both within (Konzelmann and Fovargue-Davies, 2012) and across varieties of capitalism (Deeg, 2010). The destruction of alternative banking institutions in liberal market economies occurred largely as Allen and Gale (2000) feared. This has increased financial exclusion and weakened both social control and policy coordination. However, contrary to expectations about convergence toward private, market-based banking and the fears of Allen and Gale, large and often longstanding alternative banking groups in coordinated market economies (and many developing and emerging countries) have modernized to help counter financial exclusion, sustain solidarity, and improve public policy coordination.

The marginalization of alternative banking groups in liberal market economies has magnified Minsky cycles of financial instability, despite domestic downturns being partially offset by the advantages the United States and the United Kingdom enjoy as global finance centers with reserve currencies (Andrews, 2006). However, bank change in coordinated market economies appears to differ not only from the paradigmatic experiences of the United States and United Kingdom, but also from other domains across advanced economies where weakened labor unions, the reduction of employment protection and public pensions, and the dismantling of welfare state policies and institutions have prevailed. Further study of similarities and differences in bank change across advanced, developing, emerging, and transition economies will be required. However, substantial evidence supports our claim that cooperative banks and savings banks have used patient capital practices to reinforce cooperation across firms, households, and governments toward social missions or public policies such as human development, social services, culture, and support for small and medium enterprise. Alternative banks matter. They also provide an analytic window of opportunity to recover a rich legacy of largely lost theories, concepts, and practices of social banking and patient capital from the past to reassess change in the present.

REFERENCES

Aghion, B.A. (1999), 'Development banking', *Journal of Development Economics*, **58**(1), 83–100.

Aglietta, M. (2009), 'Towards a new model of long-term finance', in E. Paulet (ed.), *Financial Markets and the Banking Sector*, London: Routledge, pp. 9–38.

Allen, F. and D. Gale (2000), *Comparing Financial Systems*, Cambridge, MA: MIT Press.

Andrews, D.M. (ed.) (2006), *International Monetary Power*, Ithaca, NY: Cornell University Press.

Andrianova, S. (2012), 'Public banks and financial stability', *Economic Letters*, **116**(1), 86–8.

Ayadi, R., R. Schmidt, D.T. Llewellyn et al. (2010), 'Investigating diversity in the banking sector in Europe. Key developments, performance and role of cooperative banks', Brussels: Center for European Policy Studies.

Ayadi, R., R. Schmidt and S.C. Valerde (2009), 'Investigating diversity in the banking sector in Europe: The performance and role of savings banks', Brussels: Center for European Policy Studies.

Bank of England (2014), *Procyclicality and Structural Trends in Investment Allocation by Insurance Companies and Pension Funds*, London: Bank of England.

Berger, A.N., P. Molyneux and J.O.S. Wilson (eds) (2010), *The Oxford Handbook of Banking*, Oxford: Oxford University Press.

Bergier, J.-F. (1979), 'From the fifteenth century in Italy to the sixteenth century in Germany: A new banking concept', in R. Lopez (ed.), *The Dawn of Modern Banking*, Los Angeles, CA: UCLA Press, pp. 105–29.

Bhattacharya, S., A.W.A. Boot and A.V. Thakor (eds) (2004), *Credit, Intermediation and the Macroeconomy: Models and Perspectives*, Oxford: Oxford University Press.

Biondi, Y., A. Canziani and T. Kirat (eds) (2007), *The Firm as an Entity: Implications for Economics, Accounting and the Law*, London: Routledge.

Bogaert, R. (1966), *Les Origines Antiques de la Banque de Depot*, Leyden: Sijthoff.

Bresler, N., I. Grössl and A. Turner (2007), 'The role of German savings banks in preventing financial exclusion', *New Frontiers in Banking Services*, Berlin: Springer, pp. 247–69.

Bundesbank (2017), 'The performance of German credit institutions, April 2017', accessed 11 July 2017 at http://www.bundesbank.de/Redaktion/EN/Downloads/Statistics/Banks_Financial_Institutions/Banks/Statistics_of_the_banks_profit_and_loss_accounts/guv_tab4_en.pdf?_blob=publicationFile.

Büschgen, H.E. (1983), *Zeitgeschichtliche Problemfelder des Bankwesens der Bundesrepublik Deutschland* [Problems of the History of Banking in the Federal Republic of Germany], Frankfurt: M. Knapp.

Butzbach, O. and K. Mettenheim (eds) (2014), *Alternative Banking and Financial Crisis*, London: Routledge.

Cameron, E. (1953), 'The Credit Mobilier and the economic development of Europe', *Journal of Political Economy*, **61**(6), 461–88.

Carnevali, F. (2005), *Europe's Advantage: Banks and Small Firms in Britain, France, Germany and Italy since 1918*, Oxford: Oxford University Press.

Culpepper, P. (2005), 'Institutional change in contemporary capitalism: Coordinated financial systems since 1990', *World Politics*, **57**(2), 173–99.

Deeg, R. (2010), 'Institutional change in financial systems,' in G. Morgan, J. Campbell and C. Crouch et al. (eds), *The Oxford Handbook of Comparative Institutional Analysis*, Oxford: Oxford University Press, pp. 309–34.

Deeg, R. and G. Jackson (2007), 'Towards a more dynamic theory of capitalist variety', *Socio-Economic Review*, **5**(1), 149–80.

Deutsche Bundesbank (1976), *Deutsches Geld- und Bankwesen in Zahlen, 1876–1975*, Frankfurt: Fritz Knapp.

Erturk, I., J. Froud and S. Johal et al. (2007), 'The democratization of finance? Promises, outcomes and conditions', *Review of International Political Economy*, **14**(4), 553–75.

European Association of Public Banks (EAPB), *Annual Report 2012–2013*.

European Association of Savings Banks (EASB), 'Facts and figures', 2014.

G30 (2013), *Long-term Finance and Economic Growth*, accessed 3 July 2017 at http://www.group30.org/images/PDF/Long-term_Finance_hi-res.pdf.

Gide, C. (1906), *Principles of Political Economy*, London: George G. Harrap.

Grössl, I., R. von Lüde and J. Fleck (2013), 'Genesis and persistence of trust in banks', *DEP (Socioeconomics) Discussion Papers: Macroeconomic and Finance Series No. 7/2013*, University of Hamburg.

Guinnane, T. (2002), 'Delegated monitors, large and small: Germany's banking system, 1800–1914', *Journal of Economic Literature*, **40**(1), 73–124.

Hall, P.A. and D. Soskice (eds) (2001), *Varieties of Capitalism: The Institutional*

Foundations of Comparative Advantage, Cambridge, UK: Cambridge University Press.

Hardie, I. and D. Howarth (eds) (2013), *Market-based Banking and the International Financial Crisis*, Oxford: Oxford University Press.

Hoffrogge, R. (2011), 'Vom Sozialismus zur Wirtschaftsdemokratie? Ein kurzer Abriss über Ideen ökonomischer Demokratie in der deutschen Arbeiterbewegung' [From socialism to economic democracy? A brief outline of the ideas of economic democracy in the German workers' movement], in M. Bois and B. Hüttner (eds), *Geschichte einer pluralen Linken*, Berlin: Rosa Luxemburg Stiftung, pp. 93–101.

Jackson, G. and S. Vitols (2001), 'Between financial commitment, market liquidity and corporate governance: Occupational pensions in Britain, Germany, Japan and the USA', in B. Ebbinghaus and P. Manow (eds), *Comparing Welfare Capitalism*, London: Routledge, pp. 171–89.

Jones, B. and P. Nisbet (2011), 'Shareholder value versus stakeholder values: CSR and financialization in global food firms', *Socio-Economic Review*, **9**(2), 287–314.

Kay, J. (1991). 'The economics of mutuality', *Annals of Public and Cooperative Economics*, **62**(3), 309–18.

Konzelmann, S.J. and M. Fovargue-Davies (eds) (2012), *Banking Systems in the Crisis: The Faces of Liberal Capitalism*, London: Routledge.

Lall, R. (2012), 'From failure to failure: The politics of international banking regulation', *Review of International Political Economy*, **19**(4), 609–38.

Lowi, T. (1964), 'Review: American business, public policy, case-studies, and political theory', *World Politics*, **16**(4), 677–715.

Mettenheim, K. and O. Butzbach (2014a), 'Alternative banking history', in O. Butzbach and K. Mettenheim (eds) (2014), *Alternative Banking and Financial Crisis*, London: Routledge, pp. 11–28.

Mettenheim, K. and O. Butzbach (2014b), 'Alternative banking and recovery from crisis', paper presented at the Progressive Economy Forum, 5–7 March 2014, Brussels, accessed 3 July 2017 at http://www.progressiveeconomy.eu/sites/default/files/papers/Kurt%20Von%20Mettenheim%20Alternative%20Banking%20and%20Recovery%20from%20Crisis.pdf.

Mura, J. (ed.) (1996), *History of European Savings Banks*, Stuttgart: Steiner Verlag.

Peabody, F. (1908), 'Introduction', in J. Ford (ed.), *Co-operation in New England*, New York: Russell Sage Foundation, pp. v–xiv.

Polanyi, K. (1944), *The Great Transformation: The Political and Economic Origins of Our Time*, New York: Rinehart.

Ramanna, K. (2013), 'The international politics of IFRS harmonization', *Accounting, Economics and Law*, **3**(2), 1–46.

Schclarek, A.C. (2014), 'The countercyclical behavior of public and private banks: A review of the literature', in O. Butzbach and K. Mettenheim (eds), *Alternative Banking and Financial Crisis*, London: Routledge, pp. 43–50.

Schmidt, R., D. Bülbül and U. Schüwer (2014), 'The persistence of the three pillar system in Germany', in O. Butzbach and K. Mettenheim (eds), *Alternative Banking and Financial Crisis*, London: Routledge, pp. 101–22.

Schmidt, R., A. Hackethal and M. Tyrell (2002), 'The convergence of financial systems in Europe', *Schmalenbach Business Review*, **1**(2), 7–53.

Seidel, H. (1908), 'The German savings banks', *Zeitschrift für die gesamte Staatswissenschaft*, pp. 58–107, reprinted in National Monetary Commission (1910), *Miscellaneous Articles on German Banking*, Washington, DC: Government Printing Office, pp. 341–403.

Stiglitz, J. and A. Weiss (1981), 'Credit rationing in markets with imperfect information', *American Economic Review*, **71**(3), 353–76.

Streeck, W. and K. Thelen (eds), (2005), *Beyond Continuity: Explorations in the Dynamics of Advanced Political Economies*, Oxford: Oxford University Press.

US Census Bureau (1949), *Historical Statistics of the United States, 1789–1945*, Washington, DC: US Census Bureau.

Van der Zwan, N. (2014), 'Making sense of financialization', *Socio-Economic Review*, **12**(1), 99–129.

Vogler, B. (ed.) (1989–98), *L'histoire des Caisses d'Epargne Européenes* (5 vols), Paris: Les Editions de l'Epargne.

Zysman, J. (1983), *Governments, Markets, and Growth: Financial Systems and Politics of Industrial Change*, Ithaca, NY: Cornell University Press.

PART II

Public banks as stability anchors: Case studies

3. Facing the 2008 crisis: Brazilian Central Bank and public banking system as Minskyan 'big banks'[*]

Simone Deos and Ana Rosa Ribeiro de Mendonça

The financial crisis started in the US mortgage market, took broader proportions and became international and systemic by the end of 2008. As the crisis deepened and spread out, the Brazilian economy was hit hard when the country was otherwise experiencing the strongest economic growth since the 1970s. This expansionary cycle was characterized by a significant credit expansion.

In the last quarter of 2008, there was an important rise in uncertainty all over the world, including Brazil, which led to a sudden disruption of private credit market in the country. Among other determinants, the credit crunch caused a significant drop in GDP early in 2009. Policymakers responded with a broad set of policies to face the crisis. Two main pillars of those policies were: (1) the central bank taking actions in order to provide liquidity to the banking system, and (2) public banks[1] increasing credit supply.

The aim of this chapter is to discuss the policies adopted by the Brazilian government to face the crisis in 2008 and 2009. The focus will be on the role played by both the central bank and the system of public banks from a Minskyan perspective. The hypothesis is that the role of the Brazilian Central Bank and public banks, acting together, can be broadly interpreted

---

[*] This chapter was originally written in 2012. The idea was to focus on the policies adopted in 2008–09, just after the contagion in Brazil, mainly on the actions taken by the Brazilian Central Bank and public banks. A formal revision was made in 2016, but the original perspective and hypothesis were kept. It is worth pointing out that after we wrote the original version in 2012, many papers (for instance, Barbosa, 2014; Ferrari et al., 2014) were written and published in a similar perspective, shining more light on the broad debate surrounding the Brazilian response to crisis. The authors are grateful to Brunno Henrique Sibin for help with this chapter.

[1] Public banks are those that are fully owned or controlled by the government. The second section will provide additional details.

as that of a Minskyan 'big bank', performed in the context of the financial crisis in order to avoid a deep depression (Minsky, 1986 [2008]).

To this end, the chapter is organized as follows. The first section offers a discussion of the idea of a big bank, with Minsky's original proposition as the entry point. In the second section, the main features of the crisis in Brazil are presented, focusing on the 2008–09 set of events. In order to do that, some important characteristics of the Brazilian banking system are considered; afterwards, the aim is to present the channels through which the international crisis was transmitted to the Brazilian economy, as well as to assess its most immediate impact. In the third section, the policies that the government adopted to face the crisis in 2008 and 2009, especially those performed by the central bank and public banks, are presented and analysed with the perspective of big banks. We conclude by evaluating the interplay of the various factors that help to explain why the crisis was contained in the first couple of years after its outbreak.

THE ROLE OF BIG BANKS

According to Minsky (1986 [2008]), the banking system is crucial because banks are able to create money endogenously, allowing the economy to grow and portfolios of assets and liabilities to increase. In order to accomplish this, banking activity is quite innovative. In their constant search for higher earnings, banks often accept higher risks and more leverage. Thus, it can be inferred that, along the boom cycle, the economic system tends to become increasingly fragile and, in this sense, prone to financial instability and even crisis. Consequently, the financial regulatory regime should be built from the perception that markets do not tend to equilibrium when individual agents search for their best results. Fragility and instability are regular market results rather than market failures. But how must this endogenous process be faced?

This issue has to be analysed by combining the role of authorities as lenders of last resort – meaning the ultimate source of liquidity needed to supply, as widely as possible, key agents in financial markets who are short of such liquidity in critical moments – as well as their role as prudential regulators. However, Minsky (1986 [2008]) demonstrates the difficulties in regulating, as well as the necessarily transitory success of any regulation. Further, highlighting the dynamics of the ongoing process of undermining regulation, the author states: 'The history of money, banking, and financial legislation can be interpreted as a search for a structure that would eliminate instability. Experience shows that this search failed and theory indicates that the search for a permanent solution is fruitless' (Minsky,

1986 [2008], p. 349). However, while pointing out the inherent difficulties of regulating, the author states that regulators must take initiatives to prevent the development of practices that instigate financial instability. Assessing the role played by the Federal Reserve central bank in the United States in the mid-1980s, Minsky concluded:

> Federal Reserve must broaden its scope and take initiatives to prevent the development of practices conducive to financial instability [and] . . . has to be concerned with the effect upon stability of the changing structure of financial relations. This definition of responsibility stands in sharp contrast to the hands-off policy with respect to financial usages and institutions. (Ibid.)

For Minsky, the role of central banks as lenders of last resort is a key aspect of their role as big banks. For him, two main institutions are responsible for the fact that 'modern' economies can have significant recessions and long periods of stagnation, but not serious depressions: big government and big bank. The first is responsible for stabilizing output, employment and profits via deficits – operating on aggregate demand. The big bank, in turn, operates on the value of the inherited assets and on refinancing portfolios (Minsky, 1986 [2008], p. 43). The big bank is a key institution. For the author, the function of lender of last resort, the 'classic function', is crucial to avoid debt deflations and deep, long-lasting depressions. In this sense, one can say that the Minskyan central bank is a lender of last resort.

From the Keynesian perspective, the central bank's characterization as lender of last resort is tied to the vision of capitalist economy as monetary and financial. Routed in the tradition originating in the works of Keynes, and enlarging and updating this perspective, the Minskyan economy is one in which the future is unknown and financial crises feature high uncertainty and liquidity shortage. The central bank is, in such a situation, the only institution that can steer the market in order to avoid catastrophe (Minsky, 1986 [2008]).

Minsky has built the idea of big bank upon this theoretical perspective, as well as the historical and institutional background – for example, the actual role that many important central banks have been performing in capitalist economies mainly since the 1930s' Great Depression. The US economy is always present in the background of Minsky's analysis, and, in this framework, the combination of the big bank and big government was able to guarantee that the country could avoid another severe depression.

The idea of a big bank has to be understood taking into consideration the historical evolution and the institutional differences among countries. Providing liquidity for the financial system, in order to avoid a financial and systemic crisis, and supplying credit directly to the non-banking agents, in order to refinance positions and avoid a credit contraction with harmful effects all over the economy, are functions that can be performed by a group of public banks, in coordination with the central bank. In this sense, they can jointly play the role of big banks.

Effectively, the shortage of liquidity has to be avoided not only in the interbank market, but also in the non-bank market and non-financial sectors. To face crises, it is crucial to avoid sharp decreases in credit supply. Otherwise, credit crunches and debt deflations may spawn harmful effects that spread throughout the economy.

THE CRISIS IN BRAZIL

The current state of the financial system in Brazil stems from deep-rooted structural transformations that have taken place since the early 1990s. Among them one should consider: (1) a financial liberalization process, which allowed the entrance of foreign capital into the system; (2) a wide-spread trend of mergers and takeovers, interventions and liquidations of private banks, and the extinction or privatization of regional state public banks. The Brazilian banking system is complex, sophisticated and con-centrated, where universal banks and specialized institutions, such as credit cooperatives and investment banks, operate under strict regulation of the Brazilian Central Bank. And despite the relevant increase of capital markets in the last decade, the banking system is still the spinal column of the financial system. One important feature of the system is the presence of large domestic banks, private and public. And, despite the entry of foreign capital through mergers and acquisitions of private banks, as well as of the privatizations of public banks, these domestic banks still play a major role in the financial system.

Regarding public banks, the broad privatization programme that took place in the 1990s led to an important decrease in the state's government banks within the system. However, regarding federal public banks, the government took a different path. Against the trend of 1990s' liber-alization, the government retained ownership of Banco do Brasil[2] (BB), Caixa Econômica Federal (CEF), Banco Nacional de Desenvolvimento Econômico e Social (BNDES), Banco da Amazônia (BASA) and Banco do Nordeste do Brasil (BNB).

BASA and BNB are regional banks and BNDES is a development bank (see Nunes Ferreira and Rosa, Chapter 6 in this volume). Banco do Brasil

---

[2] Banco do Brasil is an open joint stock company with the federal government standing as its controlling stockholder.

and Caixa Econômica Federal are both universal banks (see Deos et al., Chapter 4 in this volume) and despite focusing on the financing of specific sectors and/or activities with special sources of funding, they operate as 'financial supermarkets', featuring a large variety of financial products and services including demand deposits.

It is important to note that, except for BNDES, all federal banks were capitalized by the federal government at the end of the 1990s and beginning of the 2000s, and fell under the same regulation framework as privately owned banks. This means that they have to face a complex range of goals: to reach their social mission as well as to obtain adequate individual results, measured by efficiency and profitability ratios. From 2003 to 2011, an important expansion of credit operations has developed in Brazil. This can be seen in the evolution of the credit operations/GDP ratio, which rose from 21.9 per cent in January 2003 to approximately 49.0 per cent in December 2011 (BCB, 2010).

The Contagion of the International Financial Crisis

The financial liberalization process throughout the 1990s and 2000s, and the broader integration into the international financial system, created two contagion channels spreading the financial crisis into the Brazilian system after Lehman Brothers bankruptcy in September 2008. The first channel regards Brazilian borrowers, banks as well as non-financial corporations, which faced great difficulty raising funds in international financial markets – of loans and/or bonds. Even though the main source of funding of Brazilian banks and corporations is domestic, and though only some credit lines are, to a certain extent, dependent on international funding as foreign trade financing, part of the contagion movement can be understood by the difficulties of raising external funds given the turmoil within international financial markets. Thus, dollar liquidity constraints were felt in different ways, especially by a decline in the rollover of long-term debts, a significant decrease in short-term loans to Brazilian banks and a reduction in the domestic borrowing from foreign funding (BCB, 2009a). Note that these restrictions ultimately led to a redirection of the market, turning to domestic credit.

The second channel is related to foreign investors. The losses in other markets prompted a call for movement and selling of positions in Brazilian capital markets, leading to a huge decrease in asset prices. At the same time, as cause and consequence of the fragile environment, a broad depreciation of the Brazilian currency took place, for two reasons: the effects of the initial and intense drop in commodity prices, given their impact on Brazilian exports; and, more importantly, the increased risk aversion that led to a flight to security found in central economies (Prates, 2010).

Besides all the fragilities that a quick and sharp depreciation of the currency can create, the portfolio exposure of some Brazilian corporations, especially exporters, in derivative markets, was substantial. Some were betting on the maintenance of the Brazilian currency appreciation, which had taken place over the previous couple of years, causing huge losses when the Brazilian currency depreciated. According to the Brazilian Central Bank (BCB, 2010), the exposure of these corporations to foreign currency derivatives was around US$37 billion (August 2008). The widespread perception of corporate vulnerability, connected to problems for banks that were counterparty in derivative operations, created an environment of fear in which some banks faced bankruptcy. Both contagion channels were mainly based on expectations.

Liquidity Crisis

The combination of circumstances depicted above with the highly uncertain international environment created a significant liquidity crisis in Brazil by the end of 2008. A standstill in the interbank market led to a 'liquidity puddle' around the biggest banks. The key issue was that liquidity became concentrated within the largest banks at the top of the banking system's hierarchy. The interest rate market and the exchange rate market both experienced high volatility, which made the move toward more liquid positions even more serious. Liquidity became increasingly necessary to handle daily adjustments or margin calls due to the involvement of banks in derivatives transactions (BCB, 2009a; Prates, 2010).

In this context, private banks, both domestic and foreign, imposed a credit shortage. In doing so, a relatively long period of sharp increase in credit supply – which had been taking place since 2003 – came to an end, which, in turn, led to a drastic decrease in the level of economic activity in Brazil during the last quarter of 2008. The total credit granted by domestic and foreign private banks came to a negative change in early 2009. Subsequently, the liquidity crisis turned into a credit crisis and spread from the financial system to the whole economy (BCB, 2009b, 2010).

During this period, some banks, especially small and medium-sized, faced liquidity problems. These institutions experienced a significant tightening of liquidity in both foreign and domestic currency markets, which was particularly complex as it occurred while they, as well as the rest of the system, were dealing with a strong balance sheet expansion with the increase in credit supply. The process of 'flight to safety' was also observed in the Brazilian domestic market, from privately issued bonds to other assets issued with federal government guarantees. This trend was widespread, but was led primarily by large investors, significantly impacting small and mid-sized banks, given their dependency on those investors (De Almeida, 2010; Mendonça and Deos, 2010).

The medium and small banks also suffered from withdrawals of demand deposits, which migrated to large private and public banks. The banks most affected experienced substantial deposits losses in the second half of 2008. If one considers deposit amounts greater than US$ 25 000,[3] not protected by the domestic deposit insurance system, the losses reached 31 per cent. What can be concluded from the situation depicted above is that, following the outbreak of the financial crisis, there was an intense increase in liquidity preference of agents, particularly banks, which led to a disruption within both the interbank market and credit market. The deterioration of credit markets adversely affected the level of activity, especially in economic sectors more dependent on credit (BCB, 2009a, 2009b).

FACING THE CRISIS: LIQUIDITY AND CREDIT POLICIES

In order to address increased instability, policymakers in Brazil – notably the National Monetary Council and the Central Bank, but also the Ministry of Finance, through federal public banks – set a broad range of policies to face the liquidity and credit shortage.

This set of policies relied on some specific features of the Brazilian monetary and financial system, notably: (1) the reserve requirement system; (2) specific legal restrictions on the role of the Brazilian Central Bank in providing liquidity; and last, but not least (3) the federal system of public financing, characterized by the presence of large and relevant public banks (De Almeida, 2010).

Effectively, the whole set of policies focused on two different issues: one aimed to deal with liquidity problems in the banking system in order to maintain its stability, and the other focused on sustaining credit to non-financial entities, aiming to minimize the detrimental credit crunch effects on the real economy (Mendonça and Deos, 2010).

Besides these more specific measures, the macroeconomic policy was also relaxed. Specifically, a sequence of cuts in the short-term interest rate was targeted and implemented by the Monetary Policy Committee, which meant a sharp decrease of five percentage points along nine months – from 13.75 per cent in October 2008, to 8.75 per cent in July 2009 (BCB, 2010).

---

[3] In December 2008 values.

Liquidity Measures

Facing the restrictions in foreign currency liquidity, the Brazilian Central Bank, accepting the possibility of overshooting the exchange rate, intervened on the foreign exchange market, providing liquidity through the use of a high volume of international reserves (US$205 billion, in August 2008). For this purpose, the BCB sold US$14.5 billion on the spot market, which at the time accounted for 7 per cent of the total amount of the country's international reserves, and additionally negotiated US$11.8 billion through repurchase agreements. BCB was also active in the derivatives markets, offering swaps which assumed liability positions in dollars, with the aim of ensuring hedge operations (BCB, 2009a, 2010).

In order to increase and redistribute banking reserves and federal public securities liquidity, BCB adopted measures regarding reserve requirements and the discount window. Furthermore, some changes were implemented in the Credit Guarantor Fund (FGC),[4] which meant a broader acting capacity, especially regarding the medium and small banks' liquidity problems.

With respect to reserve requirements, ratios were decreased (including that of demand deposits, time deposits, and savings deposits), aiming to increase liquidity within the whole banking system. Big banks were also prompted to use part of their reserve requirements to purchase credit portfolios from smaller banks. The purpose of this measure was to increase the liquidity of small and medium-sized institutions (BCB, 2009a, 2009b).

The reduction of reserve requirements involved an injection of about US$116 billion into the system, approximately 50 per cent of the volume of required reserves in the period immediately before the crisis, equivalent to 4 per cent of GDP (2009). Changes in reserve requirements was also needed to mitigate the weakening of smaller banks since a significant portion of the funds released, around 40 per cent, was used to purchase assets from smaller institutions in order to spread liquidity (ibid.).

The rules surrounding the discount window – for operations in domestic currency or guarantees for loans in foreign currency[5] – were relaxed: loans became longer, a more diversified set of banking assets, including loans and private bonds, was accepted in discount operations, and a broader range of financial institutions gained access. Moreover, the power of BCB

---

[4] The Credit Guarantor Fund (Fundo Garantidor de Crédito – FGC) is a deposit guarantee system and was established in 1995 as a private non-profit organization to protect the bank customers against problems in financial institutions. During the 2008–09 crises, its function was enlarged (BCB, 2009b).

[5] In order to cope with the shortage of resources in foreign currency loans, the range of assets accepted as collateral was widened, including Brazilian sovereign debt and credit operations to finance exports and imports, denominated or referenced in foreign currency.

to impose restrictive measures on the banks using this type of loan was strengthened (ibid.).

At the end of 2008, the National Monetary Council (CMN) changed the status of Credit Guarantor Fund (FGC), hoping to raise application limits for loan portfolios of financial institutions, time deposits, and other asset-backed receivables. The Brazilian Central Bank also allowed the removal of the assets acquired by the FGC from the calculated base of reserve requirements. Additionally, in 2009, CMN allowed the creation of time deposits with special and broader guarantees from FGC (BCB, 2009b, 2010).

All these mechanisms contributed to the strengthening of smaller banks, the most harmed by the liquidity crisis. Furthermore, after the establishment of time deposits with the special guarantee of the FGC, funds raised by these small institutions, heavily dependent on large lenders, increased by 24 per cent (BCB, 2010).

The range of measures discussed above has demonstrated the significant role of the Brazilian policymakers in coping with the liquidity crisis, within the boundaries of the institutional framework. This set of policies has contributed significantly to the re-establishment of liquidity conditions for the system.

Credit Market Measures

In line with measures adopted in order to restore liquidity in the financial system, some actions were taken to normalize conditions for non-financial actors, both households and corporations. These can be organized into two groups: policies created with the goal of re-establishing credit for specific sectors and the broader role played by public banks.

A set of initiatives were implemented to address and mitigate the stagnation of credit and both the Monetary Council and BCB changed the rules for credit channels and the reserve requirements. The mandatory application of funds raised through demand deposits was temporarily released and the mandatory application of funds raised through saving deposits to real estate loans was extended to real estate development companies.[6] Additionally, reductions for reserve requirements were allowed to banks that have increased rural credit. Furthermore, in order to supply credit for foreign trade, the BCB provided liquidity in US dollars to banks, conditioned upon the extension of credit to non-financial corporations.

---

[6] The Brazilian financial system includes mandatory channelling of funds raised through certain types of instruments for credit operations to specific segments: 65 per cent of the funds raised by savings deposits to real estate; 20 per cent of demand deposits to rural credit, and 2 per cent of demand deposits to microcredit.

Similar to the role played by the Central Bank and the Monetary Council, federal public banks – including Banco do Brasil (BB), Caixa Econômica Federal (CEF), Banco Nacional de Desenvolvimento Econômico e Social (BNDES), Banco do Nordeste (BNB) and Banco da Amazonia (BASA) – had an extremely important role in confronting the stagnation of credit and its deleterious effects on economic activity. They have: (1) increased the amount of credit operations; (2) decreased interest rates; and (3) acquired credit portfolios from fragile institutions (small and medium-sized banks). These initiatives resulted in an increase of public bank participation in the credit system, rising from 33.73 per cent in June 2008 (just before the crisis) to 42.74 per cent in September 2009. This reflected a growth of 61.41 per cent in the amount of credit they granted within the same period, compared with an increase of 14.25 per cent in credit granted by the three biggest private banks. It is important to mention that, despite the broad expansion of credit operations, public banks have maintained considerable profitability and efficiency ratios, including a low default rate – 3 per cent in December 2009 (BCB, 2010). It is also worth noting that these institutions have had an important role in addressing the liquidity crisis in the Brazilian financial system and, even more so, on the maintenance of credit levels within the economy as a whole.

In order to better understand the role played by BB, CEF and BNDES, their performance during the crisis will be briefly presented. Here, it is important to highlight their relevance within the Brazilian banking system at the end of 2009: regarding assets, BB was the first, BNDES the fourth and CEF the fifth largest bank.

The action of Banco do Brasil in addressing the crisis can be seen on different fronts. First, it promoted growth in credit granted to consumers and corporations, particularly to foreign trade and agriculture. Second, BB ramped up acquisition of credit portfolios of small banking institutions, following the policy proposed by the Brazilian Central Bank. Third, BB cut interest rates charged for a broad range of loans. One should also mention the acquisition of three public banks owned by state governments (Nossa Caixa Nosso Banco, Banco Estadual de Santa Catarina and Banco Estadual do Piauí) and the partial acquisition of a private bank (Banco Votorantim). These acquisitions resulted in an increasing of BB's market share within the credit system, from 17.8 per cent in September 2008 to 21.2 per cent in December 2009, and higher rates of credit portfolio growth: 50.03 per cent in the same period (BCB, 2010).

Historically, CEF has played a fundamental role in the financing of housing, basic sanitation, infrastructure and urban services. In 2008, it was responsible for more than 70 per cent of housing finance. It would be almost 100 per cent if only low-income borrowers were considered.[7] In order to face the crisis in Brazil, this institution acted mainly by: (1) expanding credit operations, especially, but not exclusively, to housing; and (2) cutting interest rates charged in credit operations. These actions led to increased participation in the credit of the system, rising from 6.6 per cent in September 2008 to 9.5 per cent in December 2009, representing a credit portfolio growth of 76.09 per cent (for BB and CEF, see also Deos et al., Chapter 4 in this volume).

Likewise, BNDES has historically been a key institution in the Brazilian financial system, especially in regards to long-term financing. Before the crisis, BNDES drastically increased its credit operations, focusing on huge investment projects. After the crisis, the bank has maintained this pace in terms of financing investments that otherwise might not have been funded given the contraction of domestic and foreign credit markets as well as shrinking capital markets (De Almeida, 2010).

Thus, BNDES played a very important role in addressing the crisis in Brazil. One should note that the disbursement of BNDES grew in 2009 (49 per cent higher than in 2008) and that, at the same time, the interest rates charged by the bank were reduced. As BNDES had a key position in long-term financing and foreign trade financing, policies implemented by this bank during the crisis were crucial for the maintenance of aggregate demand, particularly for investment decisions and external sector performance. Its participation in total credit grew from 8.62 per cent in September 2008 to 11.57 per cent in September 2009. This performance was only made possible in 2009 due to the National Treasury's injection of capital into the bank, allowing for such extraordinary growth.

CONCLUSION

If one considers what happened in Brazil during the period under analysis (2008–09) juxtaposed to the concurrent international scenario, one realizes that the crisis did not spread as widely and did not last quite as long in Brazil with respect to the fragility of the financial system as well as the negative effects upon the real economy.

This does not mean that the crisis was not important. The liquidity shortage, marked by a rise in liquidity preference, the stagnation of private sector credit operations, and a decline in economic activity growth, which

---

[7] For more details on the historical role of public banks in Brazil, see Chapter 4: 'Federal public banks in Brazil: Historical overview and role in the recent crisis', by Deos et al.

even turned negative in the last quarter of 2008 and first quarter of 2009, all illustrate the impact of crisis upon Brazil's economy.

This chapter sought to discuss some elements and policy actions that, combined, help to explain why the crisis did not take on wider proportions during the first couple of years.[8] These are: (1) institutional aspects of the financial system, particularly banks; (2) solid regulatory framework; (3) policy actions; and (4) macroeconomic policy, especially cuts in short-term interest rates.

It is possible to highlight a few peculiarities that could otherwise be understood as weaknesses within the system, but somehow contributed to softening the blow. Historically, the Brazilian banking system has not been prone to lending when compared to other systems, despite recent credit growth. One indication of this is seen in high capital ratios, which proved to be systematically above the 11 per cent minimum set by regulation (Basel). It is also crucial to stress the role of securities in banks' assets portfolios, particularly federal government bonds. This feature implies a high level of liquidity within the banking system. Furthermore, the abundance of government bonds, being liquid, safe and profitable in an environment of high domestic interest rates, somehow discouraged the excessive proliferation of more profitable but risky financial operations, as witnessed in other systems. One can add to this an incipient process of securitization of loans. Moreover, the high reserve requirements, a legacy from past periods of high inflation and an important monetary policy instrument, allowed for better management of the liquidity shortage during the most serious moments, and also contributed to the attenuation of small bank vulnerability, as discussed above.

It is worth noting another specificity of the Brazilian system, which adds to the importance of reserve requirements and the role of FGC in addressing the crisis: legislation sets limits to the BCB's role as lender of last resort, since it can provide liquidity only to solvent banks. This limitation does not apply to the discount window, widely used while the system was weakening, since the law does not prohibit the central bank from providing loans with maturity of less than 360 days (Chianamea, 2010).

Last, but not least, one should highlight the role that public banks can assume not only in the financial system, but also in the economy broadly understood, as long as they have a significant presence, as was the case in Brazil, and if there is an adequate institutional framework, including regulation and governance principles.

---

[8]   It is very important to mention that until 2011, and in spite of the international turmoil caused by the unfolding of the financial crisis, Brazil was positively affected by inflation in commodity prices and by the high economic growth in China, and that suffered with changes in this scenario from then on.

Banks controlled by governments can and should be used in order to reduce inequalities generated and reinforced by market players, via credit allocation to low-income borrowers, small and medium-sized corporations, more fragile economic sectors and regions, and by providing long-term financing. However, we believe that the role of these banks can go further still. They can and should be used to reduce the inherently cyclical behaviour of financial markets, to smooth movements both of contraction and expansion, as demonstrated by Brazilian federal public banks.

The discussion presented above highlights that not only the institutional characteristics of the Brazilian system have determined how the crisis was addressed, but also, and especially, that policymakers used those institutional specificities to react promptly to the crisis. The combined performance of the Brazilian Central Bank and Monetary Council, acting not only, but mainly, to guarantee systemic liquidity for the financial system, with the role of the public banks, which alternatively ensured liquidity for non-financial agents through the supply of credit, denotes a broad renewal of the big bank as theorized by Minsky.

BIBLIOGRAPHY

Banco Central do Brasil (BCB) (2009a), *Relatório de Estabilidade Financeira* [Financial Stability Report], May, accessed 3 July 2017 at http://www.bcb.gov.br/?RELESTAB.

Banco Central do Brasil (2009b), *Relatório de Estabilidade Financeira* [Financial Stability Report], April, accessed 3 July 2017 at http://www.bcb.gov.br/?RELESTAB.

Banco Central do Brasil (BCB) (2010), *Relatório de Estabilidade Financeira* [Financial Stability Report], April, accessed 3 July 2017 at http://www.bcb.gov.br/?RELESTAB.

Barbosa, N. (2014), 'Financial regulation and the Brazilian response to the 2008–2009 financial crisis', in L.C. Bresser-Pereira, J. Kregel and L. Burlamaqui (eds), *Financial Stability and Growth: Perspectives on Financial Regulation and New Developmentalism*, London: Routledge, pp. 171–5.

Chianamea, D. (2010), *Empréstimos em última instância: Conceitos e evolução* [Loans of Last Resort: Concepts and Evolution], Campinas: IE-Unicamp.

De Almeida, J.G. (2011), 'Como o Brasil superou a crise' [How Brazil overcame the crisis], *Revista de Economia Política*, **35**(3), accessed 3 July 2017 at http://www.scielo.br/scielo.php?script=sci_arttext&pid=S0101-31572015000300444.

Ferrari Filho, F. (2011), 'Brazil's response: How did financial regulation and monetary policy influence recovery?', *Brazilian Journal of Political Economy*, **31**(5), 880–88.

Ferrari Filho, F., A.M. Cunha and J.S. Bichara (2014), 'Brazilian countercyclical economic policies as a response to the Great Recession: A critical analysis and an alternative proposal to ensure macroeconomic stability', *Journal of Post Keynesian Economics*, **36**(3), 513–40.

Mendonça, A.R.R. and S. Deos (2010), 'O papel dos bancos públicos e a experiência brasileira recente' [The role of public banks and the recent Brazilian experience], *Dossiê da Crise II*, August, Porto Alegre: Associação Keynesiana Brasileira, pp. 63–6.

Minsky, H. (1986 [2008]), *Stabilizing an Unstable Economy*, New York: McGraw-Hill.

Prates, D.M. (2010), 'O efeito-contágio da crise global sobre os países emergentes' [The contagion effect of the global crisis on emerging countries], *Dossiê da Crise II*, Porto Alegre: Associação Keynesiana Brasileira.

4. Federal public banks in Brazil: Historical overview and role in the recent crisis[*]

Simone Deos, Camilla Ruocco and Everton Sotto Tibiriçá Rosa

Far from being characterized by balanced growth paths, capitalist economies, interrupted by exogenous shocks, are marked by endogenous dynamics of expansion, contraction and crises. However, in each historical moment and specific concrete experience, the characteristics of cycles are different. In a crisis context, in which there is no defined time horizon for re-establishing growth, the government's role is crucial, either in changing expectations, injecting demand into the system, or even by financing demand.

Indeed, crises affect central as well as peripheral economies, but with different frequencies, characteristics and social costs. The most recent international financial crisis, which has unfolded since 2007–08, has a notably Minskyan origin in the sense that it is associated with the endogenous development of a highly fragile financial environment in central economies, especially the United States. This crisis, arguably the most significant since the 1930s, has strongly affected the global economy and raised crucial questions concerning the regulation of financial systems, as well as the articulation of finance and development.

We can learn several lessons from the few years that have followed the eruption of crisis in the United States during 2007–08. One such lesson is that countries featuring less open financial systems, more direct presence

[*] This chapter was originally written in 2012, focusing on anticyclical action during 2008–11. The present version was revised in 2016. Unfortunately, specific data about credit are only available until 2011–12. The Brazilian Central Bank (BCB) changed the methodology of the statistical series in 2012, and the update of this data would not be possible without a loss of information prior to 2007. Regardless, the broad analysis in this updated version and the hypothesis we adopt take in consideration, in a more comprehensive way, what happened up to 2013, when there was a clear reversion of anticyclical macro policy in monetary policy in Brazil. The authors are grateful to Brunno Henrique Sibin for his help with this chapter.

of government and more room for intervention, including the implementation of anticyclical policies, proved to be relatively less sensitive to contagion. Brazil's case is a good example. In 2008–09, the country was hit hard by crisis, but it was able to mitigate the worst of the blow and has rebounded with growth rates greater than those observed internationally in the aftermath of the crisis: a growth of 7.5 percent in 2010, compared to a retraction of 0.1 percent in 2009. In 2011, the country's economy grew by 3.9 percent.

Despite international turmoil caused by the unfolding of the financial crisis, Brazil experienced inflation in commodity prices until 2011. However, with low rates of growth in China and price deflation of the main agricultural and mineral commodities, Brazilian exports – and growth – began to suffer progressively (MDIC, 2016). Brazil was also increasingly affected as the crisis deepened and spread throughout Europe in 2011. Nonetheless, in 2012, economic growth was pegged at 1.9 percent, and in 2013, it rose to 3 percent.

Our hypothesis is that historical-institutional characteristics of the Brazilian economy allowed for resilience in the face of crisis and offered conditions for more effective and agile policy responses, especially when juxtaposed with many economies in the center as well as in the periphery (among the exceptions are India and China). The anticyclical credit action taken by Brazilian public banks during the period 2008–13, implemented along with a corresponding broad macro policy, was particularly key for the relatively high economic performance.

However, after 2013, the anticyclical policies began to be undermined by the world economy's progressively deteriorating conditions. In this context, Brazil had its currency devaluated and experienced rising inflation. The country's macro policy tightened, first on the monetary side in 2013, followed by fiscal austerity in 2015 and 2016. Anticyclical policies were offset by the austerity's negative effects upon expectations and domestic demand. Increasing unemployment and the relevant slowdown in economic growth (0.1 percent in 2014) eroded confidence and, together with domestic political problems, paved the way for a prolonged period of austerity.

This chapter is organized in three sections. The first presents the historical role of public banks in the Brazilian economy. The second highlights the performance of Banco do Brasil (BB) and Caixa Econômica Federal (CEF) in the credit market, splitting the assessment into two periods: before and after international crises contagion, which took place in the last quarter of 2008. The third section evaluates the evolution of bank credit portfolios during the credit cycle that took place before macroeconomic policy reversion.

THE PUBLIC FINANCIAL SYSTEM IN BRAZIL

Despite attempts at building a long-term private financing system, industry, infrastructure, and other economic sectors such as real estate have historically been funded via (1) internal resources accumulated by the companies; (2) foreign capital; and (3) public credit. The private financial system was unable to finance investments involving greater volume, longer periods and higher risks, all characteristics of investments necessary for industrialization projects, which intensified in Brazil between the 1950s and 1970s (Carneiro and Carvalho, 2009; Hermann, 2010). Rather, private banks tended to operate in the short-term and with commercial credit.

In this scenario, the public banking system, and more specifically, federal banks – BB, CEF and the development bank Banco Nacional de Desenvolvimento Econômico e Social (BNDES; see Nunes Ferreira and Rosa, Chapter 6 in this volume) – had to shoulder the burden of financing long-term projects and accepted the increased risk needed to transform the country's economic structure. In turn, these banks began to strengthen their long-term financing through funds derived from compulsory savings. Such funds are still an important part of federal bank resources, serving as a stable and secure source of capital used for development operations.

BB and CEF: A Brief Historical Perspective

Founded in different historical moments and under distinct institutional arrangements, Banco do Brasil (BB) and Caixa Econômica Federal (CEF) are the main active federal public universal banks. Though differing in their performance models and areas of expertise, both prove quite strategic for the government.

BB was founded in 1905, when a banking crisis took its predecessor, Banco da República do Brasil, to the brink of bankruptcy. Due to the position Banco da República do Brasil occupied within the financial system as the primary holder of the country's deposits, and to its 'semi-official' role as the government's banker, the Treasury intervened to bail it out. The new bank, emerging in the bailout's aftermath, was named Banco do Brasil and was placed under the Federal Government's direct control (Andrade and Deos, 2009).

The Treasury became BB's majority shareholder in 1923 with the objective of using it to stabilize exchange rates. Furthermore, BB became the government's only agent for transactions in foreign currency. In March of 1942, BB enhanced joint action as a monetary authority – the bank guaranteed liquidity to the banking system and played an important role in the execution of monetary policy – while also serving as a commercial bank (ibid.).

In 1964, the Banking Reform Law created the Brazilian Central Bank (BCB), which assumed functions previously exercised only by BB, such as issuing currency and controlling rediscounts and mandatory reserves. However, an institutional model was defined for BB that preserved its hybrid nature, allowing it to continue to take action as a monetary authority while simultaneously operating as a bank for development and commercial purposes (ibid.).

In 1986, in the context of reform that accompanied the monetary stabilization plan, BB's relationship with the BCB and the Treasury was fundamentally changed. This was effectively the moment when the bank stopped exercising its role as a monetary authority.

CEF was created in 1861, and has operated entirely with government capital up to the present. CEF became Brazil's main bank for real estate financing, with its function defined in terms of sectors and types of operation. The absorption of Banco Nacional da Habitação (BNH)[1] functions and assets in 1986 consolidated this position, making CEF the biggest national source of real estate and urban development financing. CEF's current profile describes its performance in three interconnected dimensions: financing of infrastructure and urban sanitation projects; credit provision for housing real estate activity; and typical commercial banking operations (Vidotto, 2002).

In the wake of the 1980s' fiscal and foreign debt crises, Brazil entered a period of low growth rates and high inflation, after having just overcome the major challenges of industrialization. This period was also characterized by significant difficulties for public banks. BB and CEF assets were affected by the crises and faced changes in their liability structure, requiring them to solicit increased market funding (Hermann, 2010). However, in the meantime, they managed to maintain their operations in public programs.

The 1990s were marked by liberalizing reforms and the success of the 1994 monetary stabilization 'Real Plan', which was able to reduce inflation rates. Since banks had progressively and profitably adjusted to a system of high inflation, this newfound stability seriously affected the banking system.[2] Major transformations took place in the banking system,

---

[1] National Housing Bank, a former public bank.

[2] The financial float, also known as 'inflation profits' (*lucros inflacionários*), contributed up to a third to a bank's income, and was thus an important source of profitability. This income was obtained from allocating resources that were sitting in banks at zero cost (such as cash deposits and fee payments) to assets with high nominal interest rates (Salviano Jr, 2004).

featuring bailouts and a restructuring of large private banks, privatization of regional state public banks, a restructuring of federal public financial institutions and a broad internationalization of the system.

The restructuring of public banks occurred under the Program of Incentives for the Reduction of the State Public Sector in Banking Activity (PROES) and the Program for Restructuring Federal Banks (PROEF). In 1996, PROES was launched with the aim of privatizing regional state banks and reducing their share in the system. The program sought fiscal adjustment of regional states, since the state bank crisis reflected the fiscal crisis of their controllers. This set of banks – generally created between 1920 and 1970 – was a paramount component of the banking system. In 1996, immediately after the beginning of PROES, there were 25 regional state banks (plus some specialized banks), holding 17.6 percent of the total bank assets. However, by the end of 2001, following the most significant privatization operations, this share had fallen to less than 5 percent (Salviano Jr, 2004).

The measures adopted regarding federal banks led to their increased capitalization with strengthened positions within the credit market. If not for this capitalization in 1996, BB would have gone bankrupt. The injection of R$8 billion (about US$17.5 billion in 2012 values) adjusted the bank's capital to meet regulation requirements. Additionally, CEF went through a series of adjustments, including an injection of R$9.3 billion (US$10.4 billion in 2012 values) for capitalization in 2001 (Ruocco, 2011).

In response to the new conditions, the Brazilian government, while justifying the strategic nature of these banks, increasingly directed them towards the logic of private banks, to the detriment of public action (Andrade and Deos, 2009). This path was trodden more clearly in 1995, due to the adjustment of federal public banks to Basel I standards. In 2001, the process progressed further yet with changes in capital requirements, swaps of credit for Treasury bonds and the Treasury risk taking in official credit lines (Vidotto, 2005). Besides asset restructuring measures, rules were also established to avoid new portfolio imbalances in order to ensure greater operational efficiency as well as to strengthen corporate governance and improve internal controls.

Starting in 2001, after much of the reform had taken place, BB and CEF significantly increased their credit flows to several sectors. On one side, the reform program drove the reorientation of banks away from their public function, while on the other it allowed anticyclical operations to be implemented in the wake of the crisis of 2007–08. As defended by Vidotto (2010), the success of actions taken by public banks is due to three main factors: the size of these institutions within the system, the diversity of their operations, and overall management quality.

By the end of 2011, the public bank system comprised 13 institutions, representing 42.1 percent of the country's banking system assets. Among them, BNDES, BB and CEF stood out, with 11.8 percent, 18.2 percent and 10 percent shares in assets in 2011 respectively. This system also includes federal financial institutions with regional operations – Banco da Amazônia (BASA) and Banco do Nordeste do Brasil (BNB) – with a smaller share of total bank assets (about 0.2 percent and 0.5 percent respectively). Indeed, there is still a restricted set of regional state banks that are part of the public bank structure, which held a 1 percent share in total system assets in 2011 (BCB, 2012).

The Treasury holds 100 percent of the capital of CEF and BNDES. BB, BASA and BNB are publicly traded, with the Treasury as their main shareholder. Only BB has a significant share of capital actually traded on the stock market – in December 2011, the Federal Government held 59.1 percent of the company's shares. With the exception of BNDES, subordinated to the Ministry of Development, Industry and Foreign Trade (MDIC), federal banks fall within the jurisdiction of the Ministry of Finance (Vidotto, 2005).

Compulsory Savings Funds

Compulsory saving funds of fiscal or 'parafiscal' origins are integral elements of the public banking system in Brazil. Funds of fiscal origin are those whose resources stem from previously established taxes, which are later directed to the constitution and operation of certain funds. Funds of 'parafiscal' origin are those whose resources stem from specially created contributions to constitute a specific fund. The main funds founded upon compulsory savings are: (1) Fundo de Garantia do Tempo de Serviço (FGTS); (2) Fundo de Amparo ao Trabalhador (FAT); and (3) Fundo Constitucional de Financiamento do Norte (FNO), Fundo Constitucional de Financiamento do Nordeste (FNE) and Fundo Constitucional de Financiamento do Centro-Oeste (FCO).[3]

FGTS was created in 1966, after the establishment of compulsory monthly contributions by employers to the individual accounts of employees, at a rate of 8 percent of the wages. FGTS is a 'parafiscal' fund made up of a set of tied and individual accounts opened by employers on behalf of their employees. The latter may only use these resources in specific situations, such as dismissal without just cause, purchase of their own home, death, and so on (Cintra, 2007).

---

[3] The Employees' Severance Guarantee Fund (FGTS), the Worker Support Fund (FAT), the Constitutional Funds for the Financing the North (FNO), Northeast (FNE) and Midwest (FCO) respectively.

FGTS resources can both fulfill their long-term social security or emergency function, and finance real estate projects, especially low-income housing or urban development. FGTS earn 3 percent annual interest plus the Taxa Referencial (TR).[4] CEF is the fund operator, centralizing and managing the gathered funds, and then passing them on to the banks that act as intermediaries. Moreover, CEF is the biggest financial agent for this fund's resources (Mendonça, 2007).

Brazil's Constitution (1988) consolidated the resources from two already existing programs into the FAT, which is used for funding the unemployment insurance program. At least 40 percent of the resources collected by the fund are directed towards financing the Economic Development Programs that are in charge of BNDES. FAT represented 50 percent of BNDES liabilities in 2008, when it lost shares to Treasury capitalization.

FCO, FNO and FNE are fiscal funds created by the Federal Constitution (1988), which use 3 percent of the collection of Income Tax (IR) and Industrialized Products Tax (IPI) for financing programs for productive sectors in the north, northeast and midwest of Brazil. The aim was to provide resources for less developed regions in the country that might otherwise be left without support due to the state's limited intervention capacity in the 1980s. In 2011, 9.7 percent of the financing for rural credit came from Constitutional Funds (BCB, 2012).

Federal regional banks – BASA and BNB – and BB manage Constitutional Funds. The distribution of resources gathered from IPI and IR are as follows: 0.6 percent of the resources to FNO, 1.8 percent to FNE and 0.6 percent to FCO (Deos, 2007).

BB AND CEF's PERFORMANCE BEFORE AND AFTER THE CRISIS[5]

Credit in Brazil had uninterrupted growth from 2003 to 2011. Between March 2003 and December 2008, credit rose from 25.3 percent to 40.5 percent of GDP, reaching the record level of 49 percent of GDP in December 2011. Credit to households climbed from 6 percent in January 2003 to 15 percent of GDP in November 2011.

This path was conditioned by a series of changes that influenced the strategy of financial institutions. After a period of intense uncertainty regarding the Lula government, inaugurated in 2003, the prospect of less

---

[4] The TR, Reference Rate, is calculated by the BCB considering 30-day average rates used by commercial banks in their funding operations.

[5] Data are from BCB (2012), except when another source is explicitly stated.

external volatility and the expectation of an interest rate cut led banks to prioritize credit expansion (Prates and Freitas, 2009). The creation of a specific modality of credit – consigned credit (described further in the following section) – stands out, increasing loan volumes by virtue of lower default risk.

The Credit Cycle: 2003–08

Private banks drove the 2003–08 credit expansion (66 percent of all growth), peaking in 2007 when such banks were responsible for 75 percent of the growth in credit operations. With growth rates higher than those of their public competitors, private banks, both national and foreign, increased their share in credit markets consistently up to September 2008, the moment when the US financial crisis turned both systemic and international, adversely affecting Brazil's economy.

Throughout this growth cycle, household credit featured the most dynamism (Prates and Freitas, 2009). For borrowers, demand for loans was heightened by favorable expectations regarding the economy as well as the need for purchasing new durable goods. Thus, this segment of credit enjoyed much higher growth, until 2007. In March 2003, credit for legal entities (corporate credit) was approximately 68 percent higher than for individuals. This figure fell to just 6 percent higher by March 2007.

The consigned loan for which a deduction of monthly payments is made directly either on the payslip or pension payments (Law No. 10.820/2003) has mutual advantages for both lenders and borrowers. Payment is largely guaranteed and timely for the former. Given the low risk of default, this modality offers comparatively lower interest rates for the latter. Consigned credit's share in total personal credit jumped from 35.5 percent to 57.7 percent (2003–07).

Consigned credit was fundamental for maintaining the sustainability of the analyzed credit cycle. BCB (2010) pointed out that, despite the increase in household indebtedness in 2003–08, default and the degree of income commitment remained contained since most operations focused on modalities with lower risk. Payment of interest and principal rose from 15 percent of income in January 2005, stabilizing at around 18 percent between September 2005 and December 2008. Default remained at 3–4 percent, expanding again with the impact of international crisis in September 2008, especially for private bank operations. Households' indebtedness saw linear growth, from 18 percent in January 2005 to 30 percent in September 2008.

Corporate credit strengthened throughout the cycle, recording growth rates higher than those of loans to individuals in 2008. This is explained by the coupling of business credit expansion with overall Brazilian economic growth, starting in 2006. In July 2007, credit to individuals began to weaken in favor of credit to legal entities, coinciding with a new investment cycle in the country that lasted until September 2008.

Private banks led the 2003–08 credit cycle. Public banks, despite presenting lower growth rates as compared to the private sector, played a fundamental role in sustaining the cycle via industrial, rural and housing sector financing, according to Araújo and Cintra (2011). In relation to industrial investments, notwithstanding the crisis, BNDES was the main source of external financing for companies (see Nunes Ferreira and Rosa, Chapter 6 in this volume), and the same can be said about BB and CEF in rural and real estate financing respectively.

This path is further illuminated by the evolution of channeled credit,[6] granted especially by BNDES, BB and CEF, and representing more than 30 percent of Brazilian credit.[7] Since these banks also serve as development institutions, their operations are conditioned, in part, on mandatory loans with fiscal and 'parafiscal' funding (FAT, FGTS and the Constitutional Funds), as well as on bank deposit requirements. Regarding requirements, financial institutions should provide 25 percent of the cash deposits to the rural sector and 40 percent of rural savings at interest rates below market levels. Furthermore, 65 percent of savings account deposits should be allocated to financing housing and at least 2 percent of cash deposits are directed to microcredit programs (Araújo and Cintra, 2011).

Credit with channeled resources grew from 2003 to 2008, albeit at a much slower pace than credit with non-earmarked resources. This pattern only changed at the end of 2008, when public banks began to operate in an anticyclical manner.

It is worth highlighting BB's performance with respect to the rural sector. Given farm activities' high level of risk (due to issues ranging from climate change to international price swings), BB's channeled resources play a particularly crucial role. Credit to the rural sector expanded during the cycle. The public financial sector's high share of rural credit, more than 55 percent throughout the analyzed period, further demonstrates the fundamental nature of channeled resources for sustaining rural sector activities.

With regard to the housing sector, CEF's performance stands out. Throughout 2010, it was responsible for more than 75 percent of the real

---

[6] Mandatory application loans with interest rates set by the government. The purpose is to guarantee financing of sectors that are key for economic development, but not very attractive to private creditors due to high risk or lengthy maturity periods.

[7] BCB (2010).

estate credit. In 2011, this mark was maintained, with the real estate sector representing nearly 35 percent of the bank's granted credit volume. Indeed, there has been a heavy concentration of public finance within this segment since 2003, indicating a dependence of housing investments upon public resources.

Private banks entered the housing credit expansion relatively late, only operating more actively in 2008, making CEF the anchor for this modality in the initial phase. When the housing sector entered the cycle in late 2005, CEF operations expanded vigorously (IPEA, 2011).

The industrial sector experienced credit expansion only after 2005, when Brazil's economy began to experience renewed growth. Besides direct loans, BNDES operates through the transfer of resources to other financial institutions, such as commercial banks, both private and public. BB also plays an important role in industrial financing. BB's operations in this sector started to expand in 2005, confirming its continued importance for industrial financing throughout the credit cycle, but especially from 2006 to 2008.

The expansion of BB's loans to the industrial sector was facilitated by the transfer of resources from BNDES and by an increase of credit for the firms' working capital. The large expansion of public credit to industry, in addition to its already substantial share of this segment, was crucial for sustaining Brazil's industrial activity throughout the period in question.

The Anticyclical Operation after 2008

At the end of 2008, private banks pulled back credit operations, assuming a procyclical position. Conversely, public bank loans grew at a much faster pace than seen previously, and were thus largely responsible for credit's rising trajectory. This accounts for why the credit/GDP ratio continued to increase, reaching 45.2 percent by the end of 2010, and 49 percent in December 2011.

In 2009, the public financial sector was responsible for 76 percent of credit operation growth. In contrast, the private financial sector's share decreased from 63 percent in September 2008 to 58 percent in December 2010, dropping even further to 56 percent in January 2012. During the peak of risk aversion, private financial institutions adopted a conservative strategy. Public banks compensated the retraction of private banks, with the impact of softening the contagion effect of the international crisis and sustaining overall credit levels.

The funding stability of channeled credit was one of the central elements that enabled anticyclical operation on the part of public banks. With resources from compulsory savings, Constitutional Funds and requirements on current and savings accounts, channeled credit typically features more stable behavior in periods of expansion and retraction, guaranteeing a minimum level of loans at any given moment.

Throughout this period, channeled resources assumed a leading role in credit expansion. In 2009, a year of high uncertainty regarding crisis effects, public banks increased their share in all segments to which they provided channeled resources. In 2010, they also included the industrial and housing sectors. However, in the rural sector, public banks lost a portion of their share due to a new private bank strategy, exploiting the opportune moment in agribusiness (IPEA, 2011). In 2011 there was an expansion in credit, non-earmarked and channeled, although at a more modest pace as compared to the first quarter of 2008. The expansion of real estate credit was more consequential; it reached almost 5 percent of GDP at the end of 2011, constituting the most dynamic segment – and one in which CEF is the market leader.

The high growth of credit in the channeled resources segment resulted largely from the government's adoption of anticyclical policies designed to provide housing and infrastructure, and to promote working capital in the productive sector. It is important to highlight the Minha Casa, Minha Vida (My Home, My Life) program, which became one of the pillars for housing finance.

Regarding the industrial sector credit, public banks continued to expand in 2009, guaranteeing an annual growth rate of 4.6 percent, while private banks reined in loan activity. In 2010, when private banks seemed like they were going to react by increasing loans to industry by 5.6 percent, it was still the public sector that was primarily responsible for the increase, with a growth rate of 9.2 percent. In 2011, the growth of BNDES transfers was striking, along with the renewed expansion of bank direct loans.

BB and CEF expanded credit operations quarterly from September 2008 to December 2009. In the last quarter of 2008, the peak of the crisis, CEF and BB increased operations by 15.8 percent and 10.8 percent respectively, relative to the previous quarter. In March 2009, the private sector suddenly reduced credit operations, sliding into negative growth (–0.7 percent).

The anticyclical operations were not restricted to sectors that receive channeled resources. CEF expanded its housing credit operations, with a peak in annual growth of 54.59 percent in December 2009. This expansion was not limited to housing credit but rather took place throughout the portfolio: its share of loans to both individuals and legal entities increased. In December 2011, CEF accounted for 12.4 percent of all credit operations in the country, compared to 6 percent in September 2008.

With high annual growth rates, especially for household credit, BB's operations sustained not only the rural sector, but also consumption and industrial activity following the last quarter of 2008. In 2009, loans to individuals experienced the largest expansion, reaching an annual increase of 97 percent in September 2009 when compared to September 2008. In 2010, in the context of economic recovery and the resumption of private bank activities, BB's operations continued to expand. In December, loans to households and legal entities grew by 23 percent and 20 percent respectively. In 2011, loans to households represented one-third of BB's entire credit portfolio, with an expansion of 15.4 percent, most of which entailed consigned credit. In regard to the financing of legal entities, accounting for 42 percent of all credit, expansion was limited to 14.8 percent overall, with a growth of 19.5 percent for the small and medium enterprise segment. The agribusiness portfolio, which represented 20 percent of the bank's credit, expanded by 18 percent in 2011.

Finally, public banks reduced their spreads in 2009 and 2010. This ensured cheaper loans during a period of high liquidity preference among private banks. During this period, the average interest rate practiced by public institutions fell from 44.1 percent to 34.1 percent, despite the increase of more than 3 percent in the funding rate for cash deposits, term deposits and savings (BCB, 2010). This implied a reduction of 13 percent in the average spread of public banks, dropping from 34.2 percent to 21.1 percent. Since October 2008, spreads began to follow this trajectory until it was interrupted in November 2010, mainly for household credit. Starting in the first quarter of 2011, defaults increased again for the private financial sector.

In 2009, CEF promoted a systematic reduction in credit costs. Throughout the year, the bank reduced interest rates on commercial credit lines to individuals and legal entities seven times. At BB, the lower rates charged was exhibited in the annual spread: in 2008, the average overall spread at BB was 7 percent. In 2009 and 2010, this figure fell to 6.7 percent and 6.3 percent respectively.

EFFECTS ON BB's AND CEF's QUALITY OF CREDIT AFTER 2008

Public banks expanded their credit operations in a scenario of high uncertainty and increased liquidity preference, while the private credit circuit stagnated. Given this context, a relevant question arises: did the anticyclical strategy adopted by BB and CEF after 2008 have a negative effect on the quality of its portfolios or default levels?

Financial institutions in Brazil classify loans in an ascending order of risk (from AA to H),[8] according to debtor payment capacity, and weighing the nature, guarantee and magnitude of a given operation. The loan quality is reviewed periodically, and the corresponding classification should be altered as new information about the debtor indicates a new level of risk and/or when payments are late.

From 2008 until 2011, BB expanded its credit operations without presenting any significant deterioration in its portfolio. After September 2008, the best-quality credit (AA, A and B) expanded, with growth of 94 percent, 117 percent and 131 percent respectively. The three best credit levels represented nearly 80 percent of BB's credit portfolio at the beginning of the period in question. There was also an expansion in lower-quality loans, although at a more moderate pace: 18.4 percent for the aggregate of categories C to H, with the lowest category of credit growing 34 percent but remaining under 3 percent of total credit.

More significant changes in the BB portfolio occurred among high-quality loans, especially levels A and B. There are indications that BB promoted several refinancing actions between 2009 and 2010. After the second semester of 2010, BB's portfolio worsened slightly, with an increase in levels B and D. However, this was not reflected in loans of higher risk. BB's portfolio was of better quality in 2009 and 2010, compared to the second semester of 2010, due to the presence of level A loans.

CEF's strategy was based upon high-quality credit expansion (AA, A and B), especially level A credit (361 percent) throughout the period 2008–11, and after the second quarter of 2010, in AA loans (428 percent). CEF's loans are more concentrated around levels A, B and C, accounting for 83 percent of the portfolio. The lowest-quality loans (D to H) did not make up a significant portion of the portfolio, with their share dropping further during the period.

So, during the 2008–11 cycle, neither CEF nor BB suffered an overall worsening of portfolio quality. CEF increased their level of higher-quality loans, AA and A, with their 2011 portfolio featuring the highest quality within the period. Thus, the lower level of required provisions permitted further credit expansion by CEF, as well as by BB.

The lower default rate in public banks has resulted from the expansion of quality loans, better financing conditions (interest, installments and terms) and from the anticyclical position of their client refinancing. Private banks restricted their credit operations, maintaining defensive conditions and avoiding broader-based client refinancing. This tendency has resulted in higher default rates since 2011 (BCB, 2012). The defensive position

---

[8] Following BCB's determination.

of private institutions has both increased the risk of their portfolios and weakened their clients, with wide-ranging negative effects for the economy.

CONCLUSION

The Brazilian financial system features large public institutions equipped with broad and diversified scopes of action. During the expansion cycle, early 2003 to August 2008, BB and CEF stood out in their sectorial operations, confirming their role as development banks. These public financial institutions have had an important share of their operations tied to obligatory application loans, funded by fiscal and 'parafiscal' resources and deposits requirements. While private banks led the credit cycle until mid-2008, public banks were fundamental for sustaining key economic activities.

When the international financial crisis erupted and private agents assumed a procyclical position, resulting in interrupted credit expansion, raised spreads and liquidity prioritization, it was up to public banks to soften the blow. These public banks largely succeeded in preventing a sudden retraction of economic activity at the peak of uncertainty and liquidity contraction, and went on to provide the conditions for gains in production, income and employment. It is worth noting that although the stability of directed loan funding was important for guaranteeing loan levels, the bank anticyclical operations were not restricted to this single modality, since the expansion of credit operations occurred at every level of their portfolios. Moreover, BB and CEF were able to maintain the quality of their portfolios at levels even higher than those of private institutions, despite expanding their loans during a period of uncertainty and reversed expectations.

Beginning in 2013, macroeconomic policies increasingly tightened – first monetary, followed by fiscal – in order to fight rising inflation and contain capital flight and currency devaluation. Macroeconomic austerity has since redefined the landscape. The ongoing expansion of public credit, which was important until 2014, was offset by the negatives effects of tight monetary and fiscal policy, and by the worsening of private sector expectations and demand. The emergence of fiscal imbalances and a contraction of GDP (–3.8 percent in 2015) suggest that the anticyclical credit tools, in order to be effective, have to be coordinated better alongside the overall macro policy, including the policy mitigation of external vulnerability. This is the important lesson one should draw from the Brazilian case.

REFERENCES

Andrade, R. and S. Deos (2009), 'A trajetória do Banco do Brasil no período recente, 2001–2006: Banco público ou banco estatal "privado"?' [The trajectory of Banco do Brasil in the recent period, 2001–2006: Public bank or state-owned 'private bank'?], *Revista de Economia Contemporânea*, **13**(1), 47–79.

Araújo, V.L. and M.A. Cintra (2011), 'O papel dos bancos públicos federais na economia Brasileira' [The rise of federal public banks in the Brazilian economy], *Texto para Discussão No. 1604*, Brasília: IPEA.

Banco Central do Brasil (BCB) (2010), *Relatório de Economia Bancária e Crédito 2010* [Report on Banking and Economics and Credit 2010], accessed 4 July 2017 at www.bcb.gov.br/Pec/Depep/Spread/REBC2010.pdf.

Banco Central do Brasil (BCB) (2012), *Sistema Gerador de Time Series* [Time Series Generator System], last accessed 4 July 2017 at www4.bcb.gov.br/pec/series/port/aviso.asp.

Carneiro, R.M. and F.C. Carvalho (2009), *Relatório Síntese: Perspectivas da Indústria Financeira Brasileira e o Papel dos Bancos Públicos* [Summary Report: Perspectives of the Brazilian Financial Industry and the Role of Public Banks], Projeto de Pesquisa BNDES-Fecamp – 2008/09, IE/UNICAMP-IE/UFRJ.

Cintra, M.A. (2007), 'Análise das restrições ao uso dos fundos públicos – FGTS, FAT e fundos constitucionais de financiamento – e propostas de aperfeiçoamento' [Analysis of restrictions on the use of public funds – FGTS, FAT and Consitutional Funds – and proposals for improvement], Campinas: IE-Unicamp.

Deos, S. (2007), 'Fundos constitucionais de financiamento (FCO, FNO e FNE): Análise crítica, avaliação da situação e diretrizes' [Constitutional funds (FCO, FNO and FNE): Critical analysis, situation assessment and guidelines], Campinas: IE-Unicamp.

Hermann, J. (2010), 'O papel dos bancos públicos no financiamento do desenvolvimento Brasileiro' [The role of public banks in the financing of Brazilian development], in S. Vianna and M. Bruno and A. Modenesi (eds), *Macroeconomia para o Desenvolvimento: Crescimento, Estabilidade e Emprego, Vol. 4*, Brasília: IPEA, pp. 276–308.

Instituto de Pesquisa Econômica Aplicada (IPEA) (2011), 'BB, BNDES e Caixa Econômica Federal: A atuação dos bancos públicos federais no período 2003–2010' [BB, BNDES and Caixa Econômica Federal: The performance of the federal public banks in the period 2003–2010], *Comunicados do IPEA*, Brasília: IPEA.

Mendonça, A.R.R. (2007), *Fundo de Garantia do Tempo de Serviço: Avaliação da Estrutura Institucional e Gestão de Recursos (Relatório Final de Atividades)* [Service Assurance Fund: Assessment of Institutional Structure and Resource Management (Final Activity Report)], Campinas: IE-Unicamp

Ministério do Desenvolvimento, da Indústria e do Comércio Exterior (MDIC) (2016), 'Estatísticas de comércio exterior' [Foreign trade statistics].

Prates, D. and M. Freitas (2009), 'O mercado de crédito no Brasil: Tendências recentes' [The credit market in Brazil: Recent trends], in G. Biasoto Junior, L.F. Novais and M.C. Freitas (eds), *Panorama das Economias Internacional e Brasileira: Dinâmica e Impactos da Crise Global*, São Paulo: FUNDAP, pp. 215–34.

Ruocco, C. (2011), 'O papel dos bancos públicos na crise: Uma análise da atuação do BB e da CEF no período 2007–2010' [The role of public banks in the crisis: An analysis of the performance of BB and CEF in the period 2007–2010], course conclusion monograph, Campinas: IE-Unicamp.

Salviano Jr, C. (2004), *Bancos Estaduais: Dos Problemas Crônicos ao PROES* [State Banks: From Chronic Problems to PROES], Brasília: BCB.

Vidotto, C.A. (2002), 'O sistema financeiro brasileiro nos anos noventa: Um balanço das reformas estruturais' [The Brazilian finance system in the nineties: A balance of structural reforms], doctoral thesis, Campinas: IE-Unicamp.

Vidotto, C.A. (2005), 'Reforma dos bancos federais brasileiros: Programa, base doutrinária e afinidades teóricas' [Reform of Brazilian banks: Program, doctrinal basis and theoretical affinities], *Economia e Sociedade*, **14**(1), 57–84.

Vidotto, C.A. (2010), 'O caráter estratégico dos bancos federais: A experiência brasileira recente' [The strategic character of federal banks: The recent Brazilian experience], in F.G. Jayme Jr and M. Crocco (eds), *Bancos Públicos e Desenvolvimento*, IPEA, pp. 73–104.

5. Public banks and recent anticyclical policies: A comparison of the experiences of Brazil and Chile[*]

Ana Rosa Ribeiro de Mendonça and Brunno Henrique Sibin

Banks serve as integral actors within capitalist economies, mainly through their capacity to create money and to affect asset prices. The discussion surrounding resource allocation in credit markets is central, especially when considering the relevance of financing spending decisions. Such decisions prove fundamental to income and employment creation and therefore to the promotion of economic and social development. However, decisions about credit allocation do not always lead to development. Thus, it is necessary to rely on institutions and policies that present alternatives to the typical behaviour of the private agents.

The most widespread debate concerning public banks rests on the understanding that the role to be played by these institutions relates directly to immaturity or incompleteness in the development of systems and banking markets. In this regard, public financial institutions are justified to face the gaps left by the private sector concerning the attendance to the credit demands of certain economic segments, geographical areas and even related to the provision of certain financial services.

According to Nunes et al. (2014), the role to be played by public banks should go beyond addressing the deficiencies in the private credit allocation: they can contribute significantly to counter and mitigate the uncertainty and inherent instability found within capitalist economies. Following this line of arguments, this chapter departs from a broader view depicting the role to be played by these institutions, as: (1) pivots of specialized credit subsystems, including earmarked credit to housing sectors, agriculture and microcredit; (2) instruments of economic and social policies; (3) regulators of competition in the financial system; (4)

---

[*] This chapter was originally written in 2015, with data available up to the third quarter of 2014.

countercyclical actors; and (5) coordinators of investment decisions, in the case of development banks.

With these various roles to be played by public banks as a starting point, the present chapter aims to evaluate the experiences of Caixa and BancoEstado as active institutions and analyse their impact upon the Brazilian and Chilean economic systems, respectively. The central question is whether the performance of Caixa and BancoEstado following the international financial crisis can be understood as anticyclical. Our hypothesis is that BancoEstado acted mainly as part of the Chilean government's anticyclical policies, while the performance of Caixa was much more complex, being anticyclical directly following the crisis, but procyclical before and afterwards. To better analyse this issue, our chapter is organized as follows. After this introduction, the first section discusses privatization and the deregulation process of both banking systems, and also evaluates their composition. In the second section, after a brief description of the Chilean system, BancoEstado is analysed, with particular attention to its performance in 2008/09. Also in that section, the performance of Caixa in the credit market and the importance of its role on public policies in Brazil are discussed, after a short presentation of the Brazilian system, especially its public financing system. Last, final considerations are provided by way of conclusion.

LIBERALIZATION AND DEREGULATION OF THE CHILEAN AND BRAZILIAN BANKING SYSTEMS

Until the 1970s, financial systems in capitalist economies were highly regulated. This regulatory and supervisory system was intended to prevent the occurrence of systemic crises. Since then, in many countries, there have been active processes of liberalization and deregulation of the financial services industry. Gradually, restrictions on financial transactions were eliminated. The emergence and dissemination of technological and financial innovations were important elements of this movement. Regarding developing countries, pressures intensified towards the privatization of public banks and the entry of foreign banks, based on arguments stating the need to strengthen domestic financial systems and to improve their operational efficiency.

In Latin America, the liberalization process was deeper, due to the entry of foreign banks as well as the financial crises in the 1980s and 1990s. Thus, the governments of countries like Brazil and Chile actively participated in the bank consolidation process, which, during the second half of the 1990s, was driven primarily by market forces.

After the military coup of 1973, within a broader movement towards a liberalization of the Chilean economy, the Pinochet government privatized banks with the purpose of reversing the nationalization efforts under the Allende government. Unlike other banks, BancoEstado was preserved as a public institution.[1] The Chilean system has since become more concentrated and foreign participation has grown considerably.

A second wave of privatization took place from the mid-1980s, a move that started with Chile, but which subsequently occurred in many Latin American countries.[2] This process was marked not only by the sale and even liquidation of government-owned banks, but also by capitalization of those privatized. Improvements in regulation and supervision were withdrawn (Beltran, 2005).[3]

In the 1990s, the Brazilian government followed with a programme of financial liberalization. It encouraged the entrance of foreign financial institutions, mergers and acquisitions, liquidation of private banks and the privatization or closing of public banks. In the years following the inflation stabilization plan (Plano Real, 1994) and amid a drastic weakening of private banks, policymakers concentrated their efforts on restructuring the private banking sector and privatizing that of the public sector.

BANKING IN BRAZIL AND CHILE: A COMPARISON

An analysis of Brazilian and Chilean bank indicators as well as the market share of the institutions under review, contributes to the present discussion. First, in the Brazilian financial system, banks take on a central role. In Chile, besides banks, other financial institutions prove significant. Regarding the role played by non-bank institutions, their importance is connected to the deeper capital markets in Chile that are themselves directly associated with private pension funds.

In regard to amounts, the Brazilian system is not surprisingly much larger and has a more robust system of public financing. What draws attention in the case of Brazil, is the high tendency of Caixa and Banco do Brasil (BB) to lend, expressed in the share of loans within their portfolios. In Chile, one can easily observe the importance of BancoEstado and the small systemic participation of the development bank Corfo, especially in relation to the Brazilian development bank BNDES (Table 5.1).

---

[1] At the end of 1976, 13 public banks were privatized (Fischer et al., 2003).

[2] Note that the privatization of banks occurred within a broader process in which large public companies in different sectors were sold.

[3] The two biggest banks were sold, as well as a significant part of the major pension funds.

Table 5.1   Assets, loans and market share of public banks: Brazil and Chile, 2014

Assets and Loans of the Banking System (US$ thousands)

	Assets	Loans
	Assets	Loans
Brazil	2 809 770	1 174 675
Chile	303 098	218 032
Market Share (%)	Assets	Loans
BNDES	11.6%	10.0%
BB	19.0%	21.2%
Caixa	13.1%	17.7%
BancoEstado	15.1%	13.0%
Corfo	2.9%	2.3%

Source: Brazilian Central Bank and Chilean Central Bank.

Chile

Until 1973, the Chilean financial system was marked by the presence of a robust regulatory framework, with interest rate controls, quantitative restriction mechanisms and targeting of credit, in addition to the presence of large public banks. From 1974 onwards, with the change of political regime and within a broader economic opening, these mechanisms to control interest rates were abolished, the credit controls eliminated and many of the public banks privatized.

Still, in the times of crisis experienced by Chile in the late 1970s, pension reform (1981) took place, which constituted a landmark for the financial system structure, as it allowed for the development of the bond market, including those of a longer term. In 1986, the liberalization process again gained momentum: international investment capital funds were authorized and a new banking law and a new law on bankruptcy were institutionalized with the declared aim of improving the regulatory framework.

In the 1990s, additional changes in banking law were introduced, allowing for a greater internationalization of the financial system, the deregulation of investment funds and the insurance industry and the adoption of international supervisory standards. The resulting system is both diverse and deep, featuring a significant presence of large financial conglomerates, and characterized by the centrality of pension funds and a complex interconnection between banks and asset managers (Mendonça, 2015; OECD, 2011).

Chile's funding instruments help to further explain key characteristics of the country's economy. Banks play a central role, acting by means of different instruments in various segments. Santander-Chile (a foreign bank), Chile Bank (a domestic bank) and BancoEstado make up the three largest institutions, accounting for nearly 50 per cent of loans and total deposits (Mendonça, 2015). Non-financial companies are also funded through the placement of direct debt instruments. The development of this system was marked by instruments involving longer maturities available in the fixed income market, made possible by the mandatory private pension system (OECD, 2011, p. 10). The existence of protection mechanisms against inflation in contracts – *unidade de fomento* (UF) – also contributed to the development of long-term instruments (Mendonça, 2015).

The integration of the Chilean system with international markets is clearly illustrated by the considerable share of funds raised in such markets. The foreign ownership of financial institutions also remains relevant.

BancoEstado: The role played in the system

As mentioned above, BancoEstado, Chile's only public bank, ranks among the three largest Chilean banks. Created in 1953 by the merging of different savings banks, it became the largest in the country. Originally, it was meant to ensure credit to productive sectors and to those people not served by the private sector. In 1973, in the midst of liberalization, and thus constraints to the state intervention policies, BancoEstado's role was weakened and underwent major changes: the reduction of its social role and the strengthening of its private character. In the late 1980s, these restrictions were tightened further. In the 1990s, when the country transitioned back to democracy, it resumed its social and business functions. Subsequently, the maintenance of public enterprises was decided and a series of internal changes was implemented to recover and to stabilize the bank. BancoEstado also underwent an extensive process of comprehensive modernization, repositioning it within the financial system, and reaffirming its status as a public bank with a social role (BancoEstado, 2008, 2009).

In the 2000s, BancoEstado was kept as a public institution ruled by organic law and subject to the same regulation and supervision as private banks.[4] Its objectives dictate that it should pay attention to all of the country's territories, and prioritizes those sectors and segments least served by private institutions – particularly small businesses. It seems that its role is more attached to the idea of social inclusion than the promotion of

---

[4] An organic law has an intermediate status between that of an ordinary law and of the constitution itself. Organic law Banco del Estado of Chile DL 2079 of 1977 assures exclusive rights, but prohibits providing loans to the state or public companies.

economic and social development. Of course, it has to combine its social role with management efficiency (Mendonça, 2015).

Regarding the composition of its loan portfolio, BancoEstado is in charge of a significant share of housing loans,[5] as it is the largest Chilean bank in the segments of residential mortgage loans, educational loans and loans to microenterprises. Its share of housing financing to the low-income population is substantial: 99.9 per cent of lower debt.[6]

BancoEstado's anticyclical actions

In the last years of the 2000s, the Chilean economy and society suffered two major shocks: the international financial crisis (2008) and a severe earthquake (2010). Even with a sound financial system, far from the US case that led to the crisis, the Chilean economy suffered from the international crisis in late 2008 and early 2009. The economy felt the 'classic effects' of the crisis, facing a considerable rise in uncertainty and worsening international financing conditions. In the domestic market, it led to an increase in liquidity preference and a corresponding rise in interest rates, a shortening of maturities and restricted access to private credit. Regarding the foreign market, an intense capital outflow led to exchange rate depreciation (BancoEstado, 2009; Mendonça, 2015).

Two groups of strategies were used to address the most deleterious effects of the crisis within the Chilean economy: lack of liquidity and limited access to credit. Concerning the re-establishment of liquidity conditions, particularly in foreign currency, measures were taken by the BCC to ensure external liquidity to domestic actors. The retraction in the private banks' lending pace was confronted by increased activity on the part of BancoEstado (Mendonça, 2015).

Regarding the effects on credit, the restriction of access to foreign markets resulted in heightened demand for short-term funds in the domestic market. At the same time, bank liquidity preference was growing significantly. This combination led to important restrictions on access to credit and resulted, in 2009, in the stagnation of commercial and foreign trade lending, in contrast to what can be observed in previous and subsequent periods. However, BancoEstado's expansion compensated for this stagnation (Figure 5.1).

Chilean government itself took action to strengthen BancoEstado per-

---

[5] In mid-2014, housing loans accounted for 37.7 per cent of the bank's loan portfolio (Standard & Poor's Ratings Services, 2014).

[6] The portfolio is composed of residential loans in UFs, at fixed interest rates. The bank lends up to 80 per cent of the property value for periods of up to 30 years (Standard & Poor's Ratings Services, 2014).

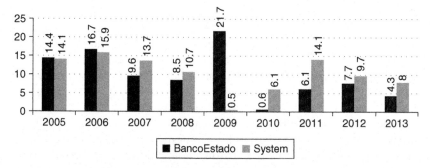

Source: Own elaboration based on BancoEstado Financial Reports, several years.

*Figure 5.1   Credit evolution: BancoEstado and banking system, 2005–13
             (rate of change %)*

formance: in 2008, a capitalization of 95 per cent of the profits from 2007 (US$100 million) was authorized and supplemented by the bank's own capitalization (US$500 million). Moreover, the capacity of the Guarantee Fund for Small Businesses (FOGAPE) was extended to US$130 million. BancoEstado, meanwhile, signed an agreement with 260 real estate companies, suggesting a reduction in mortgage interest rates (first 36 months) to support low- and middle-income sectors of the construction industry. The government also used the BancoEstado network for the payment of two '*bonos de apoyo a la familia*' (family support bonuses) (Mendonça, 2015).[7]

Up to 2008, BancoEstado loans evolved in line with the system, growing at sustained rates every year. In 2009, given the constraints and the increased costs for credit, BancoEstado started to act in the opposite direction from private banks, extending loans for businesses, lowering interest rates and creating new lines of credit, including the extended guarantees provided by FOGAPE (BancoEstado, 2009). Credit growth rates and the shift in market shares are instructive of such behaviour. BancoEstado lent at a faster pace than other institutions across all segments of borrowers, avoiding a credit crunch. The strongest contraction of private lending was in loans to companies, a segment in which BancoEstado action was more prevalent (Figure 5.1).

---

[7] A bonus of $40 000, as a payment to low- and middle-income families in winter, was awarded by the Chilean government in August 2009.

Brazil

The Brazilian financial system is complex, sophisticated and concentrated, marked by the presence of universal banks and specialized institutions, which operate under strict regulations imposed by the Brazilian Central Bank (BCB). Despite the growth of capital markets in the last decade, banks are still the backbone of the financial system.

A peculiarity of the Brazilian banking system is the presence of large domestic banks, private and public. Domestic banks continue to play a crucial role within the system, notwithstanding the entry of foreign capital through mergers and acquisitions of private institutions and the privatization of many public banks.

Regarding the state's public banks, a broad privatization programme implemented in the 1990s led to a significant decrease in both their number and importance. Nevertheless, a different path was designed for the federal public banks. Almost all were capitalized by the federal government and were subsequently put under the same regulatory framework and principles of governance as private banks. These institutions feature a complex range of objectives: to achieve their social mission while also maintaining efficiency and profitability.

In addition to these public banks, the Brazilian public financial system comprises compulsory savings funds, which are not the only source of federal bank funding, but are essential to guarantee stable institutional resources, fundamental to long-term operations: FAT (Fund for Workers), FGTS (Warranty Fund for Employees) and Constitutional Funds (FNE, FNO and FCO).

The Brazilian credit market – due to liquidity preference – is characterized by short-termism, a historically low relation of credit to GDP and extremely high interest rates. Among the explanations for this trend is the high macroeconomic instability, as seen in the high inflation rates for decades. Besides inflation, bank decisions on portfolio composition tended to favour the safety of government bonds, which partly explains the low proportion of credit to GDP. Price stabilization and changes in the regulatory framework were not enough to reverse the problem.

However, a new approach began to be designed in 2003, with an unprecedented increase in credit. This increase was supported by the combination of institutional and macroeconomic elements: the regulation of payroll loans, the lowering of interest rates and an increase in family income. The significant growth in credit extended to households can be explained by the historically restrained demand for credit, the greater capacity for indebtedness, comparatively low interest rates and, above all, greater access to credit.

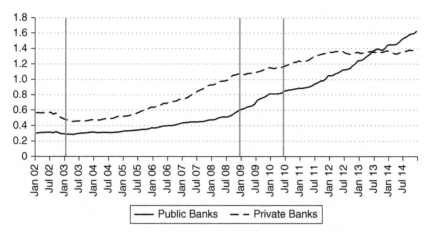

Source: Banco Central do Brasil.

Figure 5.2 Loans: Public vs private banks, Brazil, 2002–14 (R$ 2014)

A closer look enables the evaluation of the recent credit cycle in three distinct phases. The first (2003–08) was marked by the expansion of private and public bank credit portfolios. The second started at the very end of 2008 with the international financial crisis spillover effects. At this point, while private banks drastically reduced their supply of credit, public banks picked up the pace of credit extension. The third, which began just before the end of 2010, features a resumption of private bank action in credit markets and an even larger and intense movement on the part of public banks, which led public bank credit to exceed that of private banks (Figure 5.2). In order to understand the performance of public banks in each period, a closer examination of Caixa is needed.

Caixa: Role played within the Brazilian system
Caixa is a 100 per cent public financial institution and the third biggest institution in the Brazilian banking system (by assets, in 2014), established in 1861 to encourage savings and pledged loans. Historically, it has occupied a central role in housing finance. In the 1970s and 1980s, it accounted for 80 per cent of total housing funds through savings deposits, a fundamental funding instrument for real estate loans.

In the 1980s, Caixa absorbed the Government Severance Indemnity Fund (Fundo de Garantia por Tempo de Serviço – FGTS), a major source of low-cost resources for longer terms. This fund has the ability to contribute to the financing of social policies, especially through the provision of credit to sectors not served by the private financial system (Mendonça, 2009).

Beginning in the mid-1990s, the Brazilian Central Bank (BCB) carried out a major project to restructure banking regulation, adhering to Basel II and enlarging loan risk classification and provisioning. Caixa adjusted to the new regulatory framework after 2001, when the federal government launched a programme to strengthen federal banks, which involved a swap of assets, capitalization and the transfer of credit risk to the National Treasury and to the asset management company[8] (Swedish model) (Camargo, 2009).

Phase 1: Caixa and the resumption of credit provision (2003–07) In 2003, a new and more progressive government was established. A number of measures were implemented with the aim of developing and setting favourable conditions for the expansion of credit availability, such as the regulation of the liens regime, the establishment of a special tax regime for asset allocation and the creation of securitized debt instruments. Regarding households, payroll loans were created and regulated by the BCB, with Caixa serving as a pioneer among big banks. In the field of housing, the bank prepared for higher competition with private banks by making some internal improvements: reviewing processes, adapting risk analysis, reducing interest rates and raising financing loan maturities.

In 2004, Caixa expanded its credit operations, mainly through the extension of credit lines to small businesses and the self-employed and through the allocation of housing credit for the middle class. In order to increase its share within the payroll loan market, Caixa also acquired the portfolio of a private bank.

Many new Caixa housing credit lines were funded by the FGTS, with the adoption of special subsidies. They had the purpose of increasing family purchasing power for those with monthly incomes up to R$1500, a clear movement towards the inclusion of low-income families. Further, new measures were enacted in order to reduce the cost of credit to borrowers.

In 2007, the Brazilian government offered credit from the National Treasury to Caixa (R$5.2 billion), to enable the financing of urban sanitation and housing (within the Growth Acceleration Programme). Regarding housing credit, Caixa also increased housing loan maturities from 20 to 30 years (FGTS funds) (Mendonça, 2009).

The share of loans in the Caixa asset portfolio illuminates the bank's

---

[8] In different countries, asset management companies (AMCs) have been employed to address the overhang of bad debt in the banking system. The Swedish experience is the most widely known example. In early 1990s, when Sweden's economy suffered from a banking sector swollen with bad loans, the Swedish government organized publicly capitalized asset managers to be put in charge of managing poorly performing banking assets.

strategy and performance in the recent credit cycle. One can easily observe that housing loans have a major position within the loan portfolio. Despite some fluctuations over the period, the value of housing loans has always been above 50 per cent of the total portfolio. Moreover, there was a clear credit expansion during the period in question.

Phase 2: Caixa's anticyclical response to the crises (2008–10) In 2008, the Brazilian economy was hit by the financial crisis, at the height of a robust credit cycle and sustained economic growth. The rise in uncertainty led to increases in liquidity preference, especially that of private banks, which drastically reduced the loans. Small and medium-sized banks were also weakened by funding problems (Mendonça, 2015).

In order to mitigate the crisis, the government adopted a coordinated countercyclical policy, aiming to tackle the liquidity problem of the banking system and to maintain credit for companies. The role of public banks as part of a countercyclical policy was established through a political decision, in the search for ways to lessen losses resulting from the international economic crisis.

The public banks owned by the federal government (Caixa, Banco do Brasil and BNDES) initiated an intensive process of credit extension in order to offset the diminished private bank credit, preventing a credit crunch. They acted decisively by raising the pace of credit provision, mainly, but not exclusively, to those sectors most affected by the crisis: agriculture, construction industry, petrochemicals and the sale of durable goods. Moreover, Banco do Brasil and Caixa acquired small and medium-sized bank credit portfolios[9] and cut loan interest rates (IPEA, 2011).

In 2009, the Brazilian government launched the Program Minha Casa, Minha Vida (My Home, My Life) as part of the countercyclical policy, aiming to stimulate the generation of jobs and income and to mitigate the housing deficit affecting low-income families (Nunes et al., 2014).

One can easily ascertain that the federal government broadly supported Caixa, employing the bank as a central component of anticyclical policy. It is important to note that the capitalization programme was attached to the regulatory capital-level necessities rather than to funding. Caixa not only consolidated its prominent position in housing credit markets, but also affected the credit market's orientation towards households.

Phase 3: Caixa's growth acceleration A juxtaposition of the performance of public bank credit against the banking system as a whole helps

---

[9] Caixa acquired 35 per cent of medium-sized private bank Banco Pan, enlarging its positions within payroll credit and vehicle financing.

illuminate their role during the last period under analysis. The growth of public bank credit operations is a powerful indicator of their performance, much more than simply stimulating the economy, but rather actively offsetting movements made by private banks.

Regarding Caixa, from 2011 to 2014, a significant expansion of credit granted was largely enabled by its diversification of funding and was supported via capitalization from government treasuries and shares of state-owned companies. The main accounts of Caixa's portfolio, assets and liabilities (except for deposit accounts), indicate some clear movements. On the asset side, one can note the growing significance of housing loans (214 per cent), as well as the high growth of commercial loans (239 per cent) and credit to infrastructure (394 per cent), signalling a complementarity between these two types of operations. Concerning liabilities, there was a relevant increase of funding through bonds (real estate credit notes, mortgage notes) and the importance of FGTS was confirmed (Caixa Econômica Federal, Financial Statements; own elaboration).

In 2011 and 2012, Caixa announced the sale of R$2 billion in real estate credit contracts to FGTS, involving 40 000 household contracts – Certificates of Real Estate Receivables (CRIs).[10] Furthermore, the National Treasury announced new resources for public banks. Receiving part of these resources, Caixa allocated R$3 billion to finance construction materials and consumer goods and R$3.8 billion to infrastructure projects. At the time, Caixa capital increased by R$5.4 billion from Petrobras shares.

In the following two years, the National Treasury was authorized to issue R$8 billion in public debt securities to Caixa in order to enable the creation of the 'Minha Casa Melhor' (My Best Home) programme.[11] The R$8 billion credit was considered a hybrid instrument of capital and debt. As never seen before, Caixa also raised R$500 million in the international market through the issuance of subordinated debt. These bonds were eligible to comprise Caixa's Tier 2 capital under Basel 3 regulations, enabling the expansion of the real estate credit portfolio from R$10 billion to R$30 billion.

During this period, Caixa was broadly capitalized by its only shareholder, the National Treasury. One should note that the capitalization was related to capital needs, given the regulatory framework, more so than to funding needs, as was the case of other Brazilian public banks. At the end of the period, credit portfolio sales to Brazil's asset management company

---

[10] Securities backed by housing credit notes, representing sales of residential properties, commercial or urban lots.

[11] This programme was intended to furnish and equip houses acquired by borrowers under the Programa Minha Casa, Minha Vida.

(Empresa Gestora de Ativos, EMGEA) and specialized companies, particularly of non-performing loans, began to take place as a result of the fast pace of loans and the further deterioration of the Brazilian economy. However, these sales also allowed for renewed action in credit operations (Vidotto, 2010).

FINAL REMARKS

This chapter aimed to discuss the role played by public banks as anticyclical actors, considering the Chilean and Brazilian experiences (BancoEstado and Caixa respectively) following the international financial crisis. Our hypotheses was that BancoEstado acted mainly as part of the Chilean government's anticyclical policies, but that the performance of Caixa was far more complex, acting anticyclically just after the crisis, but procyclically before and subsequently.

Our starting point was the assumption that the performance of public banks should go beyond filling gaps left by private financial institutions. In both countries, the creation of public institutions aimed to stimulate economic and social development. The introduction of non-democratic regimes in both countries led to a change in the importance of these institutions: while in Brazil the public financing system was enlarged, in Chile, marked by a rigid political regime and liberal economic regime, the significance of public financial institutions lessened.

Both systems have undergone an intense process of economic liberalization, especially in the 1980s and 1990s. However, in both systems public institutions were maintained, albeit under different rules and increasingly subsumed by the logic of efficiency and profitability. It is undeniable that the Brazilian public financing system is larger and much more complex than that of Chile, as the former is marked not only by a diversity of banks, assuming different roles, but also by funding mechanisms that enable performance in specific segments, such as the Government Severance Indemnity Fund (FGTS) for low-income housing finance. Alternatively, BancoEstado relies solely on market funding.

After evaluating the role of these institutions in lending during the past two decades, it is possible to detect some peculiarities. In the years immediately preceding the international financial crisis, public banks in Brazil and Chile acted procyclically. In facing the spread of the crisis, their performance took on countercyclical orientation: public bank action was essential in order to avoid a credit shortage in the market and its deleterious consequences for the economy as a whole.

During the years following the crisis, one can distinguish the different ways these institutions performed within their respective systems: while BancoEstado decreased its activity in credit provision, Caixa continued to lend at a faster pace than private banks, contributing to further economic growth. Thus, the action of Caixa has been much more growth oriented. Encouraged by the Brazilian government, it carried out a broader mandate than the label of anticyclical actor would suggest.

BIBLIOGRAPHY

BancoEstado (2008), *Memoria Anual: Estados Financieros* [Annual Report: Financial Statements], accessed 9 March 2016 at http://www.corporativo.banco estado.cl/transparencia/memorias.

BancoEstado (2009), *Memoria Anual: Estados Financieros* [Annual Report: Financial Statements], accessed 9 March 2016 at http://www.corporativo.bancoestado.cl/transparencia/memorias.

BancoEstado (2013), *Memoria Anual: Estados Financieros* [Annual Report: Financial Statements], accessed 9 March 2016 at http://www.corporativo.bancoestado.cl/transparencia/memorias.

Banco Central de Chile (BCC) (2008), *Informe de Estabilidad Financiera* [Financial Stability Report], accessed 9 March 2016 at http://www.bcentral.cl.

Banco Central de Chile (BCC) (2009), *Informe de Estabilidad Financiera* [Financial Stability Report], accessed 9 March 2016 at http://www.bcentral.cl.

Banco Central do Brasil (BCB) (2016), *Sistema Financeiro Nacional, Informações Para Análise Econômico-Financeira, Balancetes, Vários Anos* [National Financial System, Information for Economic-Financial Analysis, Balance Sheets, Various Years], accessed 9 March 2016 at http://www4.bcb.gov.br/fis/cosif/balancetes. asp.

Beltran, A.R. (2005), 'História de la concentración y privatizacion de la banca Chilena' [History of the concentration and privatization of Chilean banks], paper to the Confederacion de Sindicatos Bancarios y Afines, accessed 4 July 2017 at https://www.sbif.cl/sbifweb/servlet/ArchivoCB?ID_IMAGEN=12500000000004326.

Caixa Econômica Federal (2009), *Balanços e Demonstrativos Financeiros, Vários Anos* [Balance Sheets and Financial Statements, Various Years], accessed 9 March 2016 at http://www.caixa.gov.br/site/paginas/downloads.aspx.

Caixa Econômica Federal (2014), *Balanços e Demonstrativos Financeiros, Vários Anos* [Balance Sheets and Financial Statements, Various Years], accessed 9 March 2016 at http://www.caixa.gov.br/site/paginas/downloads.aspx.

Caixa Econômica Federal (2015), *Balanços e Demonstrativos Financeiros, Vários Anos* [Balance Sheets and Financial Statements, Various Years], accessed 9 March 2016 at http://www.caixa.gov.br/site/paginas/downloads.aspx.

Camargo, P.O. (2009), *A Evolução Recente do Setor Bancário Brasileiro* [The Recent Evolution of the Brazilian Banking Sector], São Paulo: Editora Unesp and Cultura Acadêmica.

Corbo, V. and K. Schmidt-Hebbel (2003), 'Efectos macroeconómicos de la reforma de pensiones en Chile' [Macroeconomic effects of pension reform in Chile], in *Federación Internacional de Administradoras de Fondos de Pensiones: Resultados y Desafíos de las Reformas a las Pensiones*, Santiago de Chile: FIAP, pp. 259–351.

Fischer, R., S. Pablo and R. Gutiérrez (2003), 'The effects of privatization on firms and on social welfare: The Chilean case', *Latin American Research Network Working Paper No. R-456*, Washington, DC: Inter-American Development Bank, Research Department.

Hornbeck, J. (2009), 'Financial regulation and oversight: Latin American financial crises and reform lessons from Chile', *Congressional Research Service*, accessed 9 March 2016 at https://www.crs.gov.

Instituto de Pesquisa Econômica Aplicada (IPEA) (2011), 'Banco do Brasil, BNDES e Caixa Econômica Federal: A atuação dos bancos públicos federais no período 2003–2010' [Banco do Brasil, BNDES and Caixa Econômica Federal: The performance of federal public banks in the period 2003–2010], *Comunicados do IPEA No. 105*, accessed 4 July 2017 at http://www.ipea.gov.br/portal/images/stories/PDFs/comunicado/110810_comunicadoipea105.pdf.

International Monetary Fund (IMF) (2011), *Chile: Financial System Stability Assessment, IMF Country Report No. 11/261*, accessed 9 July 2016 at https://www.imf.org/external/pubs/ft/scr/2011/cr11261.pdf.

Mendonça, A.R.R. (2009), 'Fundo de garantia do tempo de serviço: Gestão de recursos e papel de financiador das políticas de habitação e saneamento', *Anais do II Encontro internacional da Associação Keynesiana Brasileira*, Porto Alegre, 2009.

Mendonça, A.R.R. (2013), 'Notes on development banks and the investment decision: Finance and coordination', paper at the 17th Conference of Research Network Macroeconomics and Macroeconomic Policy: The Jobs Crisis: Causes, Cures, Constraints, Berlin.

Mendonça, A.R.R. (2015), 'Bancos de desenvolvimento e políticas anticíclicas: Um estudo de experiências no Brasil e Chile' [Development banks and anticyclical policies: A study of experiences in Brazil and Chile], in *Brasil: Em Busca de um Novo Modelo de Desenvolvimento*, CGGE.

Nunes, A., A.R.R. Mendonça and S. Deos (2014), 'The role of Brazilian public banks facing inequality: Some reflections on the case of Brazilian Development Bank, Caixa and the federal regional banks', paper to the IX Global Labour University Conference, Berlin.

Organisation for Economic Co-operation and Development (OECD) (2011), *Chile: Review of the Financial System*, accessed 9 March 2016 at http://www.oecd.org/finance/financial-markets/49497488.pdf.

Standard & Poor's Ratings Services (2014), 'Banco del Estado de Chile', *RatingsDirect*.

Superintendencia de Bancos y Instituiciones Financieros (SBIF) (2016), *Información Financiera, Estados Financieros* [Financial Information, Financial Statements], accessed 9 March 2016 at http://www.sbif.cl/sbifweb/servlet/InfoFinanciera?indice=4.0.

Vidotto, C.A. (2010), 'Caráter estratégico dos bancos públicos federais: A experiência brasileira recente' [Strategic character of federal public banks: The recent Brazilian experience], in F.G. Jayme Jr., F. Gonzaga and M. Crocco (eds), *Bancos Públicos e Desenvolvimento*, Rio de Janeiro: IPEA.

PART III

Public banks and development

6. The role of the Brazilian Development Bank (BNDES) in Brazilian development policy[*]

Adriana Nunes Ferreira and Everton Sotto Tibiriçá Rosa

The Brazilian Development Bank (BNDES) is a heavyweight among development banks worldwide. In 2010, its total disbursement amounted to US$96 billion, a bit more than China's development bank and three times as much as the World Bank (own calculation based on BNDES, 2010). BNDES has represented the development model followed by Brazil since its foundation in 1952. Sole provider of long-term financing for industrial investments of the country's economy, BNDES has been Brazil's main financial arm. Its role throughout the country's economic history has shifted along with the role of the state within the economy and is itself an expression of changes in what development means for the government.

BNDES is subject to criticism from both liberals who accuse it of causing market distortions through providing credit at lower interest rates than those found in the private system, and from various sectors of the left wing, who would like to see more credit provided to small firms and other sectors, notably more work-intensive ones. Yet, it cannot be denied that the history of Brazilian development, with its historical limitations, is intertwined with BNDES's history.

The purpose of this chapter is to build a periodization that makes it possible to follow BNDES's history as a key part of Brazil's development policy. The development vision that guided the bank's creation has its origin in the ideas of early authors of the Economic Commission for Latin America and the Caribbean (ECLAC). In the first phase of our periodization, from 1952 to 1980, BNDES acted as an investment coordinator and long-term credit provider for the various stages of import substitution that characterized Brazilian industrialization.

---

[*] The authors are grateful to Brunno Henrique Sibin for his help with this chapter.

The 1980s, known as the 'lost decade', marked the bank's first major identity crisis, when the industrialization model based on import substitution was exhausted, indicating the Brazilian economy's external financial vulnerability. The 1989 elections brought Fernando Collor to power, who asserted that the state should give way to the market, acting as the coordinator of private agents. Collor launched a neoliberal reform package recommended by the Washington Consensus: liberalization, deregulation and privatization. Thus, a new mission was set for BNDES – managing the National Programme of Destatization (PND, i.e., privatization; see BNDES, 1991). The 1980–2002 period is the subject of this chapter's third section, covering the crisis and the neoliberal response that followed.

In 2003, the first Lula administration followed the strategy lines of his predecessor. During this period, the bank turned to support exports. However, the second Lula administration, as well as Dilma Rousseff's first mandate, set a new mission for BNDES and the government in general, as a consequence of gains made by 'developmentalists'. While facing contagion effects stemming from the international financial and economic crisis of 2008–09, the bank proved to be a critical arm of the government's financial policy.

Before we proceed with the analysis of various stages of the bank's performance, we will briefly present the ECLAC development vision, which guided BNDES in its early years.

ECLAC's EARLY VISION: OVERCOMING UNDERDEVELOPMENT THROUGH INDUSTRIALIZATION

The ECLAC's prevalent 'structuralist' thinking resulted in a significant transformation in the theoretical apparatus surrounding the study of underdeveloped economies.[1] This perspective contended that dynamics between so-called 'peripheral' economies and the system's 'centre' should receive treatment differing from those based on classical and neoclassical theories. Further, this position observed an inevitable 'deterioration of the terms of trade' – the price reduction of exported products relatively to the imported ones – increasingly weakening peripheral economies.

So, thinkers from ECLAC – Raúl Prebisch, Aníbal Pinto, Celso Furtado, among others – formed a movement in the early 1930s within such economies: the implementation of import substitution and a prescribed set of

---

[1] For a good assessment of the developmentalist debate in Brazil, see Bielchovsky (2004).

policies aiming to introduce an industrialization process through import substitution. This new model would grant the state a primary role and led Latin American economies to grow at significant rates during the decades of the 1950s and 1960s.

In the early 1970s, growth rates were cooling, inflation increasing and the balance of payments turning negative due to 'dynamic failure' or 'structural heterogeneity'. These scenarios were characterized by low incorporation of the workforce in the economically most productive segments of the economy; weakness of the internal consumer market stemming from high income concentration; low capacity generation of endogenous technological progress; and by the generation of structural deficits in the current account in the balance of payments (Lessa, 1977).

Within this context, Latin American countries gave way to the emergence of neoliberal government during the 1980s. In Brazil, the neoliberal response came at the end of the 1980s and continued through the 1990s.

THE YEARS 1952–80: SUPPORT FOR HEAVY INDUSTRIALIZATION[2]

This section presents the most relevant aspects of BNDES operations in the context of industrialization during the period 1952–80. It was at this time of economic history that 'developmentalist state' intervention was consolidated in Brazil. Two developmental phases can be identified: the first, considered a democratic phase, encompasses Getúlio Vargas's second government (1951–54), Juscelino Kubitschek's government, in which the Target Plan was implemented (1956–60),[3] Joao Goulart's government ending in 1964, when the country was already in a moment of crisis and economic downturn; and a second phase under the military regime, which alternatively can be considered a non-democratic order, extending from 1964 until the early 1980s' Latin American debt crisis, when fiscal crisis and the country's external debt undermined the support of both the dictatorship and the Brazilian state in general.[4] The support for the state failed to return with the reinstatement of democratic rule.

Under a poorly developed financial system, with banking institutions operating primarily by providing working capital and commercial

---

[2] The following account is largely based on BNDES (2002b, 2002c).

[3] The Target Plan was a broad investment programme organized by the government in partnership with national and foreign private initiatives aiming to promote industrialization in the country.

[4] For interesting interpretations of the capitalist development in Brazil, see Belluzzo and Coutinho (1982).

credit, BNDES emerged as the main source of long-term resources in the economy.

In order to present this institution's features and historical relevance, this section is divided into two parts: the first briefly presents changes in BNDES funding throughout the various stages of Brazilian industrialization. The second proceeds with an analysis of the Bank's activities, identifying benefitting sectors and the various kinds of support offered to public and private investments.

BNDES Funding from 1952 to 1980

BNDES was founded in 1952 within the scope of the technical and financial cooperation of Brazil–United States Joint Committee (CMBEU). The group performed a complete diagnosis of the main deficiencies in the structure of Brazil's approach to industrialization. Under this Commission, the World Bank and Eximbank funded a portion of the projects designed by CMBEU, responsible for raising an equal amount in Brazilian national currency. BNDES was created to manage the resources of the so-called 'Re-equipment Plan', an infrastructure programme featuring investments in rail network projects and electric power generation. The sources of funding for BNDES changed over the years. According to Prochinik (1995), it is possible to characterize the BNDES sources of funding, between 1952 and 1980, in three distinct stages.

In the first stage, between 1952 and 1966, funding was made up of compulsory loans[5] and from specific sector fund creation and administration. It is worth mentioning a few such funds: the Federal Fund for Electrification, the National Railway Fund and the Paving Fund. BNDES also began to manage the resources of the Railways Renewal and Improvement Fund, the Merchant Navy Fund (FMM) and the National Port Fund.

Beginning in 1964, already an aspect of the military regime's institutionality, and amidst financial and tax system reform, BNDES received an influx of new resources, including 20 per cent of income tax revenue. Furthermore, in the context of linked funds, Financiamento de Máquinas e Equipamentos Industriais (Financing of Industrial Machinery and Equipment – FINAME) was created as a fund for the purchase of machinery and equipment.

The second stage, between 1967 and 1973, was marked by the instability of funding sources. During this period, BNDES capitalization was under-

---

[5] On top of income tax (1952–62), but also through transfers from the proceeds of income tax.

taken within the framework of Brazil's fiscal budget and the National Monetary Council's monetary budget.

In the third stage of funding, between 1974 and 1988, resources coming from social contributions to the Social Integration Programme and Public Servant Investment Fund (PIS-PASEP) were managed by BNDES, ensuring greater stability to funding and diminishing dependence on government budgets. Another point worth noting is that the return on funded projects became increasingly relevant throughout the analysed period.

Thus, evidence shows that during the heavy industrialization period (1952–80), Brazil had an important long-term lender financial agent. In this sense, the main modifications to funding correspond to major government programmes and strategies at each stage of the Brazilian economy's structural transformation process.

BNDES Activities from 1952 to 1980

BNDES actions during this period took place in three ways: (1) direct loans in the national currency; (2) concessions of external loans and concession endorsements on behalf of BNDES or the National Treasury; (3) capitalization of private companies, especially after 1966, with the creation of BNDESPAR (BNDES Participações SA). The first addressed the provision of repayable loans, shareholding in companies benefiting from such loans and the holding of direct investments.

One should note that BNDES's actions were not limited to disbursements of funds. In its first decade in operation, the bank was a key coordinator of the private sector's investment. Even without transferring funds, BNDES was significant in its endorsement of projects for external financing and in its organizing entrepreneurs to string together a sequence of private investment, with or without the participation of public investment. Its joint action with the monetary and fiscal authorities, which exceeds the typical nature of financial institutions, is one of the central features of BNDES's contribution to the transformation and continued support of ongoing economic development.

BNDES's priorities for disbursements changed over time (BNDES, 1992, 2002a). In the 1950s and early 1960s, investments in infrastructure areas were priorities. The Target Plan was dedicated to infrastructural projects – with an emphasis on the electricity sector – and basic industry.

In the following period, 1962–66, the country underwent a cyclical slowdown phase, once the multiplying effects from huge Target Plan investments ran out. Nevertheless, the BNDES's disbursements represented nearly double the amount available throughout the Target Plan. In this context, FINAME was created in order to finance the purchase of machinery and industrial equipment (1964), alongside the first initiatives to support small and medium-sized enterprises. In 1966, BNDESPAR was created with the aim of promoting capital market expansion and ensuring an alternative form of support to private companies via capitalization (Bernadino, 2005).

In 1967, the economy began to recover, starting its period of greatest economic growth. At this stage, companies' demand for resources intensified and rising disbursements were granted by BNDES. Beginning in 1974, after nearly a decade of accelerated growth, the internal capacity for supply in the fields of basic industrial inputs, fuels and particularly capital goods proved to be insufficient. The import coefficient of industry rose, reproducing Brazil's external dependency, a condition that worsened due to the impacts of the first international oil shock in 1973.

The government acted to counter the external vulnerability by launching PND II, a new block of investments oriented towards overcoming the external vulnerability of the Brazilian economy – that is, dependency on oil, capital goods and intermediate goods. This move was clearly linked to the state's long-term development strategy.

BNDES played a fundamental role in the coordination of activities and in the financing of PND II. Its disbursements, during the course of PND II, focused on the private sector, notably in machinery and equipment as well as in basic industry. This represented the greatest phase of disbursements by BNDES in this first analysed period (for data, see BNDES, 2002b).

With the second oil price shock and the US interest rates hike in 1979, Brazil initiated a process of voluntary macroeconomic adjustment, later enforced by IMF conditions and creditor demands. In the 1980s, macroeconomic policy conduct overlapped with economic stabilization objectives for the achievement of the development goals, including income generation and employment. During this period, Brazil began to intensify financial adjustment measures in the private sector. The Brazilian Central Bank took over much of the dollar-denominated debt of banks and private corporations in a process that was known as 'external debt statization'. However, contrary to expectations, private investment did not resume. BNDES was also affected and had to forego some of its traditional functions. The bank's first identity crisis had begun.

THE 1980s' CRISIS AND THE NEOLIBERAL RESPONSE 1980–2002

The 1980s began with a deep trade deficit stemming from the second oil price shock and the highly indebted public sector, which was also overwhelmed by Volcker's[6] interest rate hike. The recessive adjustment that followed was worsened in 1982, following the Mexican moratorium and the resulting limits to credit flows into Brazil, leading the country to seek aid from the IMF.

The exchange currency devaluation policy established in 1983 had a profound impact on agents who had debts in dollars and proved to be one of the most significant sources of inflationary pressure on the economy.

State-owned enterprises (especially in energy, fuel and public transport) reduced their prices to relieve private sector costs and aid economic recovery, but ended up with considerably greater financial strains. At the same time, large private companies increased their mark-ups, reduced their debts and underwent a significant financial reorganization. Private capital began to finance the increasingly indebted government through the purchase of government bonds, instead of focusing on production and investment. Thus, the private sector turned from debtor in relation to the external sector, into a public sector creditor.

The next section briefly discusses the main modifications of BNDES funding in the 1980s and 1990s, while the subsequent section describes the main lines of action to 2002.

BNDES Funding in the 1980s and 1990s

In the first half of the 1980s, no major changes regarding resource transfers to BNDES were observed, with the exception of a substantial increase in BNDES's accrued profits as a source of funding – largely as a result of the return of sound long-term credit offered through PND II (for data, see BNDES, 2002b; Banco Central Brasil data; and Ipeadata).

In the Constitution of 1988, the first after the long military regime, a significant change in BNDES funding was introduced: it established that at least 40 per cent of PIS/PASEP resources would be transferred to BNDES and destined for economic development programmes. The remaining 60 per cent would finance the unemployment insurance programme (*programa do seguro-desemprego*). The Workers' Support Fund (FAT) was created, made up of the PIS/PASEP collections committed to

---

[6] American economist and Chairman of the Federal Reserve, 1979–87.

the unemployment insurance programme (60 per cent) and interest paid by BNDES for the use of the remaining 40 per cent.

There was also a substantial increase in resources mobilized by BNDES following 1995, when disbursements associated with the new bank's mission of privatization support, here called 'destatization agent', begin to gain volume.

Main Lines of Action from 1980 to 2002

In the decade of 1980, BNDES acted mainly in three directions: first, it continued to support some long-term investments contracted under PND II; second, it acted by aiding the financial restructuring of struggling private sector companies; and third, it provided financial support to exports. In the face of evidence that the previous development model had been exhausted, BNDES's mission turned to favour the 'competitive integration'[7] of the Brazilian economy.

Additionally, two important institutional changes occurred in 1982: the bank, until then called BNDE, became known as BNDES (earning the 'S' for 'Social') when it began to manage the Social Investment Fund (FINSOCIAL) resources, deriving from a tax on income. The main purpose of this change was to channel bank support to food, housing, health, education, and small farmer programmes.

However, as shown in Curralero (1998), the resources directed to the social area, originally a sizable amount, decreased substantively over the course of the decade (for data, see BNDES, 1992, 2002a). The 1989 elections brought Fernando Collor to power, a representative of the national bourgeoisie, brandishing the flag of Brazilian neoliberalism. Trade and financial liberalization, deregulation, and a pervasive privatization process were the integral aspects of what was proposed to be the new development alternative.

BNDES was nominated as the organ in charge of managing the destatization programme and the National Fund for Privatization to finance the National Plan for Destatization. However, because of the economic and political crisis that followed structural reforms, it was only during the Fernando Henrique government that the privatization process was effectively implemented.

According to Franco (1998), the new neoliberal development model was supposed to overcome the import substitution legacy of a poorly

---

[7] This thesis was developed mainly by Julio Olimpio Mourão, who advocated the need for a 'pragmatic evolution toward a new development'. For his text on the strategic planning processes that prevailed in the BNDES system between 1983 and 1990, see Mourão (1994).

competitive industry and structural inflation. Both trade liberalization and foreign direct investment were thought to increase the competitiveness of Brazilian industry, which would then strengthen price stabilization via a nominal exchange rate anchor after imposing new forms of productive sector pricing.

BNDES's total disbursements fell continuously during the 1980s. When in 1993 BNDES took on the role of privatization financial agent, the trend reversed. At the height of privatization, the bank's disbursements in relation to the actual value in 1995 tripled (BNDES, 2002d).

Two notes about the comprehensive Brazilian privatization process, in which BNDES was the protagonist, are worth mentioning. First, when examining the sectors covered here, it is clear that electric energy and telecommunications were the major targets (BNDES, 2002c). This problematizes the government's thesis, according to which the entry of foreign investment, at first perhaps causing a trade balance worsening, would in the second stage restore positive trade balances, as supply imports would decrease and exports would increase. However, the privatization targets were not, in their majority, export sectors.

Second, a significant part of the privatization process was also a process of denationalization. In the period from 1995 to 2002, which includes the peak of the privatization process, the percentage of foreign investors was 53 per cent (own calculation, MDIC data).

In this regard, it is worth mentioning that there was, after 1994, an important flexibilization of BNDES's criteria and operational standards, which allowed for the expansion of sectors approved for funding, such as commercial and service sectors, infrastructure, and public service concessions. Furthermore, Constitutional Amendment No. 6 of 1995 eliminated the distinction between national and foreign capital companies and levelled their access conditions to official agency credit as well as to government incentives and grants.

Curralero (1998) as well as Carneiro et al. (2009) point out that the national companies' access to BNDES financing was hindered in relation to multinationals due to another factor: an intensification of private logic (instead of development logic) in the credit analysis within the assessment of BNDES funding applications, resulting from the creation of the Credit Committee in 1994. An analysis of BNDES disbursements by sector shows that the most significant leap in the period between 1997 and 1998, at the privatization process peak, occurred in the participation of trade and services sectors (Curralero, 1998).

At the end of this decade, the major devaluation that followed the exchange rate regime change caused exporting sectors to increase their demand for credit. Hence, by the end of the privatization process,

BNDES migrated from 'Bank of Destatization' to 'Bank of Export': the disbursements for exports doubled between 2001 and 2002, and explain both the elevation of total disbursements and the increased participation of the bank's disbursements to manufacturing industries (ibid.).

BNDES FROM 2003 TO 2014: A NEW MISSION?

The hypothesis guiding this section is that, in the recent period, a development policy for the country began to be designed, although, for some critics, too timidly. In the first phase of this last analysed period, Lula's government implemented his economic policy in a conservative way in order to appease fears created in the market by the rise to power of a politician originating from the union movement. It was seen, at that time, as an open conflict between the 'developmental' side, who believed that the bank should have a 'structuring role', and the side that favoured a vision of this institution as closer to an investment bank with a private profitability criteria.

It is at the second mandate, however, that the 'structuring' role for the bank began to be designed. The support for infrastructure, micro and small enterprises and innovation policies all headed in that direction. Moreover, the bank was set to have, along with other federal public banks, a decisive role as the government's financial policy arm in coping with the effects of the international crisis upon the Brazilian economy.

The Main Funding Sources from 2003 to 2014

Throughout the 2000s, the Workers' Support Fund (FAT) was a fundamental source of resources for the bank, rising to 43 per cent of total contribution in 2007 (Figure 6.1). In addition to the large contribution, its stability also made it critically important to BNDES.

According to Rosa (2013), opponents of earmarked credit in the economy argue that FAT's resources should not be exclusively allocated to BNDES, but instead should also fund private banks, which could then provide long-term credit. Others argue that a 'good and profitable' project should be able to find financing via retained earnings or through the capital market, without needing BNDES support. Moreover, opponents assert, the very existence of BNDES prevents the development of alternative financing channels.

The proponents of BNDES's earmarked credit, on the other hand, cite the 'fungibility' between BNDES credits and credits with free resources –

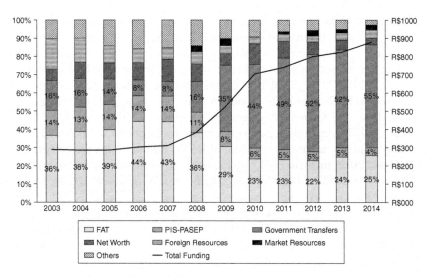

Source: Own elaboration on BNDES data.

Figure 6.1 Composition and evolution of contributions of BNDES funding, 2003 to 2014 (% and R$ billions of 2014)

that is, that there are no obstacles for companies to finance their investments at market conditions – does not apply (Carvalho, 2005; Hermann, 2010; Torres-Filho, 2005). Rather, many of those investment projects would be considered not profitable if long-term credit had as its reference the short-term basic rate – SELIC (Sistema Especial de Liquidação e Custodia) rate – and if investors took into account currency risks.

While coping with the effects of the international crisis of 2008 in Brazil, a new important fund source arose: National Treasury loans. One can observe in Figure 6.1 the large increase in participation of these resources, reaching almost 50 per cent of the contributed amount following 2010, during a phase of major expansion in the total amount of resources.

Lines of Action from 2003 to 2014

Despite being quite conservative, the conduct of Lula's first administration policy proposed an important initiative with regard to development. In March 2004, an industrial, technology and foreign trade policy package (Política Industrial, Tecnológica e de Comércio Exterior – PITCE) was released. However, during Lula's second term, the bank took on its structuring role more decisively. The new priorities announced included:

stimulus to infrastructure, innovation, support for micro and small enterprises and the internationalization of Brazilian companies. A series of industrial and technological policy actions were launched thereafter.

The first of such plans were the Productive Development Policy (PDP) – from 2008 to 2010 – and the Action Plan for Science, Technology and Innovation for National Development (PACTI) – from 2007 to 2010. Along with these, the Growth Acceleration Programme (PAC) was released in August 2007, constituting a broad programme of public and private investments in infrastructure, to the order of R$500 billion for the period between 2007 and 2010. In 2010, PAC 2 was announced – envisioning investments of R$1 trillion by 2014, two-thirds of which went to the energy sector.

BNDES has had a decisive role both in designing the plans and in providing support to private sector companies in every area. In July 2009, the bank implemented the BNDES Programme of Investment Support (PSI). Nearly half of the PSI resources, up until December 2011, were intended for micro, small and medium enterprises (MSMEs). This line of action fits the bank's discourse on the need to enhance access for this category of companies to long-term credit as a way to encourage a better income distribution and an overall increase in employment. The creation of the BNDES Card stands as another step towards the strengthening of micro and small enterprises.[8] All of these bank initiatives[9] resulted in a huge increase in disbursements, reaching R$187 billion in 2014 (BNDES data).

BNDES also increased lending for micro and small enterprises, especially from 2010 onward. In respect to the number of operations, the addition of micro and small companies to the category of natural persons[10] (individuals) led to their disproportional increase, up to 35 per cent of those approved by the bank in 2011.

Another important line of action, present up to today within the bank's discourse, was support for capital market development. The bank operated as a securities underwriter, including operations of internationalization, and the restructuring of companies, mergers and incorporations.

Finally, it is worth considering the importance of BNDES's counter-cyclical action in confronting the effects of the international crisis in the country. Between the last quarter of 2008 and the end of 2009, there was

---

[8] The BNDES Card is a preapproved credit line intended for the purchase of necessary items for micro, small and medium enterprises (MSMEs) with manufacturing facilities in the country and that are registered at the BNDES Card Operation Portal.

[9] It must also be taken into account that there was a significant amount of resources engaged in works related to the World Cup in Brazil, which did not fit properly into any strategic line of action, but rather responded solely to short-term needs.

[10] The individuals entitled to receive BNDES financing are microentrepreneurs, farmers and self-employed truck drivers.

a strong retraction of private bank credit. Other public banks (see Deos and Mendonça, Chapter 3 in this volume) as well as BNDES had a fundamental compensatory role, extending its direct funding and launching new lines of credit.

FINAL CONSIDERATIONS

BNDES mirrored, along its various phases, the vision of development held by the leaders of the Brazilian economy. For the ECLAC thinkers, who initially fed the development vision that gave rise to the bank, development could only be accomplished through industrialization based on the import substitution process. So, BNDES took a prominent position with regard to Brazil's industrialization process, with a significant role in the planning and coordination of agents, policies and sectors.

The 1980s witnessed the exhaustion of the import substitution process and featured a deep financial crisis within the Brazilian economy. In this context, BNDES played a fundamental role in the financial recomposition of heavily indebted private agents. The end of the decade was followed by the neoliberal response. The bank found its role shifted to privatization (destatization) agent and denationalization coordinator. This phase lasted until the end of the 1990s.

Beginning in the 2000s, the Brazilian economy began to find a new direction, marking a new phase for the bank. Its bureaucracy had a crucial role in the development of several key industrial policy initiatives.

Throughout these phases, BNDES has always been preserved as the Brazilian government's financial arm for development policies. Even when there was no development policy, when the bank went through its two identity crises, the bank and its bureaucracy remained on 'stand by' – without fulfilling its structuring role but still accounting for about 90 per cent of corporate earmarked credit in Brazil.

However, one may ask, to what type of development did the bank lend its competence? ECLAC's hope that industrialization would give rise to development with endogenous technical progress and social justice has not yet materialized.

REFERENCES

Belluzzo, L.G. and R. Coutinho (1982), *Desenvolvimento Capitalista no Brasil – Ensaios sobre a Crise* [Capitalist Development in Brazil – Essays on the Crisis], São Paulo: Brasiliense.

Bernardino, A.P. (2005), 'Fontes de recursos e atuação do BNDES sob uma perspectiva histórica' [Sources of BNDES resources and performance from a historical perspective], *Revista do BNDES*, **12**(23), 53–73.

Bielschowsky, R. (2004), *Pensamento Econômico Brasileiro – O Ciclo Ideológico do Desenvolvimentismo* [Brazilian Economic Thought – The Ideological Cycle of Developmentalism], Rio de Janeiro: Contraponto.

Brazilian Development Bank (BNDES) (1991), *Programa Nacional de Desestatização: Relatório de Atividades 1991* [National Programme of Privatization: Activities Report 1991], accessed 5 July 2017 at https://web.bndes.gov.br/bib/jspui/handle/140 8/3683.

Brazilian Development Bank (BNDES) (1992), *BNDES, 40 Anos: Un Agente de Mudanças* [BNDES, 40 Years: An Agent of Change], Rio de Janeiro: Gabinete da Presidência, Departamento de Relações Institucionais.

Brazilian Development Bank (BNDES) (2002a), *BNDES 50 Anos de Desenvolvimento* [BNDES, 50 Years of Development], accessed 5 July 2017 at www.bndes.gov.br/SiteBNDES/bndes/bndes_pt/Galerias/Convivencia/Publicacoes/Consulta_Expre ssa/Setor/BNDES/200209_17.html.

Brazilian Development Bank (BNDES) (2002b), *BNDES 50 Anos – Histórias Setoriais* [50 Years of BNDES –Sectoral Stories], accessed 5 July 2017 at http://www.bndes.gov.br/SiteBNDES/bndes/bndes_pt/Galerias/Convivencia/Publicaco es/Consulta_Expressa/Setor/BNDES/200212_3.html.

Brazilian Development Bank (BNDES) (2002c), 'Corporate presentation', Accounting Department, Financial Area, April.

Brazilian Development Bank (BNDES) (2002d), 'Privatização no Brasil 1990– 1994/1995–2002' [Privatization in Brazil 1990–1994/1995–2002], accessed 5 July 2017 at http://www.bndes.gov.br/SiteBNDES/bndes/bndes_pt/Galerias/Convivencia/Publicacoes/Consulta_Expressa/Tipo/Estudos_Especiais/200207_3.html.

Brazilian Development Bank (BNDES) (2010), *Annual Report 2010*, accessed 11 July 2017 at http://www.bndes.gov.br/SiteBNDES/bndes/bndes_en/Institucional/Investor_Relations/Annual_Report/annual_report2010.html.

Carneiro, R.M., D. Prates, M.C.P. Freitas and A.M. Biancareli (2009), *Mercado de Crédito Bancário: Relatório do Subprojeto II do Projeto de Estudos sobre as Perspectivas da Indústria Financeira Brasileira e o Papel dos Bancos Públicos* [Banking Credit Market: Report of Subproject II of the Study Project on the Prospects of the Brazilian Financial Industry and the Role of Public Banks], Instituto de Economia/Unicamp.

Carvalho, A. (2005), 'A política industrial e o BNDES' [Industrial policy and the BNDES], *Revista do BNDES*, **12**(23), 17–27.

Curralero, C.R.B. (1998), 'A atuação do sistema BNDES como instituição financeira de fomento no período 1952/1996' [The performance of the BNDES as the financial institution for development in the period 1952/1996], Master's dissertation, Campinas: IE/Unicamp.

Franco, G.H.B. (1998), 'A inserção externa e o desenvolvimento' [Internal insertion and development], *Revista da Economia Política*, **17**(3), 121–47.

Hermann, J. (2010), 'Papel e funcionalidade dos bancos públicos: Notas sobre a experiência Brasileira recente (1995–2009) [Role and functionality of public banks: Notes on the recent Brazilian experience (1995–2009)], *Annals of the AKB Conference*.

IPEA (n.d.), Várias séries históricas data [Various time series data], accessed 31 May 2016 at http://ipeadata.gov.br/.

Lessa, C. (1977), 'Visão Crítica do II PND' [Critical view of PND II], *Revista Tibiriçá*, **2**(6) 47–72.

Mourão, J.O. (1994), 'A integração competitiva e o planejamento estratégico no sistema BNDES' [Competitive integration and strategic planning in the BNDES], *Revista do BNDES*, **1**(2), 3–26.

Prochnik, M. (1995), 'Fontes de Recursos do BNDES' [BNDES resource sources], *Revista do BNDES*, **2**(4), 143–80.

Rosa, E.S.T. (2013), 'Transformação estrutural e ação anticíclica: Aspectos teóricos da intervenção estatal sobre o sistema financeiro, experiências históricas e o caso Brasileiro recente' [Structural transformation and anticyclic action: Theoretical aspects of state intervention on the financial system, historical experiences and the recent Brazilian case], *Discussion Paper No. 34*, Goiânia: UFG/FACE.

Torres-Filho, E.T. (2005), 'A reforma do sistema FAT-BNDES: Críticas à proposta Arida' [The reform of the FAT-BNDES: Criticism of the Arida proposal], *Revista do BNDES*, **12**(24), 31–42.

7. Public banks and financial intermediation in India: The phases of nationalization, liberalization and inclusion

Pallavi Chavan*

A major landmark in the history of Indian banking has been the creation of a vast public banking system. The most important outcome of public banking has been the significant growth in financial intermediation and financial development. As observed by a noted scholar on India's banking development, 'even the ardent critics of India's growth strategy would admit that what the country achieved in the area of financial sector development *before the present reform process began*, particularly *after bank nationalization*, was *unparalleled* in the financial history of any nation in the world' (Shetty, 1997, p. 253; emphasis added). This chapter provides a review of the development of public banks in India following bank nationalization in 1969 through the 2010s, and analyses the role played by these institutions in facilitating financial intermediation.

Prior to bank nationalization in 1969, private banks dominated the banking system in India (Goyal, 1967). With the nationalization of the Imperial Bank as the State Bank of India (SBI) in 1955, a public space was created within the otherwise private banking sector. However, the real boost to public banking came with the nationalization of 14 major commercial banks in 1969, which was followed by the nationalization of eight more banks in 1980. The rationale for bank nationalization on such a large scale was the redistribution of finance. It was argued that private banks, which dominated the banking space till then, were not guided by any 'positive social objectives' and were regarded as highly 'selective and exclusive' in their credit policies (Goyal, 1967, p. 20).

* The author thanks Christoph Scherrer, C.P. Chandrasekhar, R. Ramakumar and Himanshu Joshi for their useful comments along with Smita Kulkarni for help with data entry. The views expressed here are personal views of the author and not of the organization to which she is affiliated.

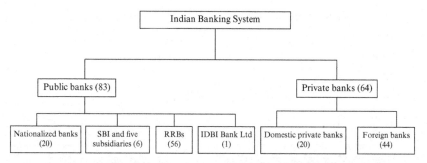

Note: Figures in brackets indicate the number of banks, as of March 2015.

Source: Compiled from *Statistical Tables Relating to Banks in India* – 2014–15, RBI, accessed 5 July 2017 at https://www.rbi.org.in/scripts/AnnualPublications. aspx?head=Statistical%20Tables%20Relating%20to%20Banks%20in%20India.

Figure 7.1 Structure of the Indian banking system, 2015

Public banks dominate the current financial system in India. Public banks refer to banks, including regional rural banks (RRBs), in which the government holds a major stake (Figure 7.1). In 2015, public banks held about 50 per cent of the assets of the entire financial system, which included insurance companies, non-banking financial companies and mutual funds (RBI, 2015a). Within the banking space, public banks formed the single largest group, controlling over 75 per cent of total bank branches and banking business in India (bank credit plus bank deposits) (Figure 7.2).

This chapter delves into the role played by these institutions in the process of financial intermediation in India. Financial intermediation typically is the process of mobilizing savings and channelling them towards investments in the real economy (Gorton and Winton, 2002). Here, it is captured through (1) trends in national savings and investments; (2) various regional and sectoral indicators such as the availability of banking services in rural areas and India's economically backward geographical regions; (3) trends in credit to two sectors of national priority: agriculture, the single largest employment generating sector with direct linkages to the spread of banking in rural areas; and infrastructure and other core industries, a sector of priority for India as a developing economy.

The chapter highlights the way banking policy in India has perceived public banks, and how changes in this policy have directly shaped the involvement of public banks in the process of financial intermediation. For this discussion, broadly three phases of banking policy are identified: bank nationalization, financial liberalization and financial inclusion. Following this is an analysis of broad trends in the growth of public banks

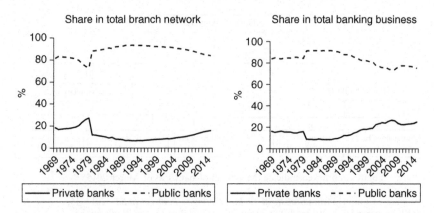

Note: Though RRBs came into existence in 1974, the aggregated data are available only from 1980 onwards. Hence, there is a jump in the series for that year in both graphs.

Source: Calculated from *Basic Statistical Returns of Scheduled Commercial Banks in India*, RBI, various issues.

Figure 7.2   Private and public banks in India, 1969–2015

in India since their establishment. The next section analyses the role of public banks in financial intermediation along the lines discussed above. The chapter ends with major concluding observations and suggests a way forward for public banks in India.

PUBLIC BANKS AND BANKING POLICY

The Bank Nationalization Phase – Between 1969 and 1991

While arguing in favour of bank nationalization, then Prime Minister Indira Gandhi described it as a necessary condition for the formation of economic policies in a 'socialist pattern' (RBI, 2005, p. 39). In the period following bank nationalization, public banks were perceived as a means of redistribution and planned economic development. Accordingly, the 1970s and 1980s saw a host of policy measures taken towards expanding public bank branches and business into rural and semi-urban areas with the objective of financing agriculture and small industries. Hence, this phase is often described in the literature as the phase of 'social and development banking' (Wiggins and Rajendran, 1987).

First, the branch licensing policy was strengthened in order to expand banking operations in rural areas. In 1977, the branch norm was changed to 1:4 from the earlier 1:2, such that banks (both public and domestic private) had to open at least four branches in unbanked rural areas for every one branch opened in metropolitan/port areas. Banks were asked to allot at least 25 per cent of their total branches to unbanked rural areas (Copestake, 1985).

Second, the lead bank scheme was implemented in 1969 to address credit gaps at regional and sectoral levels by providing 'integrated banking facilities' in every district in the country (Gadgil Study Group, cited in RBI, 2005, p.61). Given the importance of public banks in the Indian banking system, they were designated to act as lead banks for the identified districts.

Third, sectoral credit targeting in the form of priority sector lending was introduced. The scheme of priority sector lending was originally applicable only to public banks, but was later extended to private (domestic and foreign) banks as well. Priority sectors included agriculture, small-scale industries (SSIs), small transport operators, retail trade, housing and education (RBI, 1996). From 1985 onwards, at least 40 per cent had to be advanced to priority sectors. Even before nationalization, there was an effort to direct bank credit to agriculture and SSIs, but there were no targets specified for any of these sectors. With bank nationalization, this scheme was formalized and specific targets were laid down for the aggregate and sectoral levels (RBI, 2005).

Given the involvement of commercial banks alongside credit cooperatives in providing finance to agricultural production to support the Green Revolution in Indian agriculture, this phase is often described as the phase of multi-agency approach to rural/agricultural credit (Bansil, 1986). This was different from the policy approach taken after the nationalization of the SBI, in which the SBI was expected to indirectly support agricultural credit by aiding credit cooperatives (Ray, 2009).

Fourth, this phase also saw a considerable increase in statutory pre-emption (reserve requirements) applicable to the banking sector in the form of the statutory liquidity ratio (SLR). This pre-emption resulted in directing large amounts of bank deposits into government securities. Although SLR was introduced as a prudential tool, it became a means of financing the fiscal deficit by the banking sector over time (RBI, 2008).

Fifth, the differential rate of interest (DRI) scheme was introduced in 1972 to provide credit from public banks at a regulated interest rate to individuals below the poverty line. Sixth, to give focused attention to the rural poor, the public banking space was widened through the creation of RRBs in 1974.

The involvement of public banks in the provision of rural credit further increased after the introduction of various rural poverty alleviation programmes, the most important being the Integrated Rural Development Programme (IRDP) in 1979–80.

Thus, regulatory authorities chose to control not only the total volume of bank credit and interest rates at which it was advanced, but also decisions regarding who to lend to and for what purpose. This is what was described as the 'promotional aspect of monetary management' in India (Raj, 1974). Such management was made possible through the creation of public banks.

The Financial Liberalization Phase – Between 1991 and 2005

The 'promotional aspect of monetary management' came under criticism during the financial liberalization phase. Financial liberalization was an integral part of economic liberalization and structural 'reforms' espoused in India during this phase. The Committee on the Financial System (CFS), established by the central government in 1991, argued that redistribution objectives had to be pursued as part of fiscal rather than monetary policy. Accordingly, it called for dismantling various controls over the banking system introduced with the objective of redistribution, arguing that these controls eroded the financial health of banks. Among various concerns, the CFS highlighted the erosion in asset quality, low capital base/ provisioning and profitability, and weaknesses in management and internal controls (RBI, 1991).

Interestingly, the CFS did not advocate a complete dilution of the public ownership of banks. Instead, it stated that 'ensuring the integrity and autonomy of operations of banks. . .is by far the more relevant issue at present than the question of their ownership' (RBI, 1991, p. xxxi). However, it suggested a 'positive declaration' from the government ensuring no further nationalization of banks to pave the way for a more dynamic private banking sector (RBI, 1991, p. 73).

Incidentally, several official committees from the 1970s onwards also recognized the problems ailing public banks (Shetty, 1997). Given that nationalization was a 'revolutionary step', it was expected to face 'lethargy and roadblocks' over time and needed 'periodic evaluations' for 'mid-course corrections' (Shetty, 1997, p. 254). However, none of these committees questioned or rejected the redistributive or social banking objectives, as the CFS did in 1991 (ibid.).

Evidently, the financial liberalization phase marked a distinct change in the official thinking about public banks compared to the earlier phase. It was declared in official circles that social and development banking had 'outlived its purpose' and banks had to move towards 'more commercial modes of operation' (RBI, 2001).

Accordingly, the Indian banking policy witnessed a number of far-reaching changes that were aimed at partial or complete deregulation of public banks. First, though the government continued to be the major shareholder, it gradually reduced its stake in public banks while keeping it above the statutory floor of 51 per cent, which could be described as partial privatization (Sathye, 2003). The entry of institutional and retail shareholders in public banks was permitted. The shares of many public banks (excluding RRBs) were listed on stock exchanges to enable them to raise capital, thereby bringing in new standards of disclosure and corporate governance (Subbarao, 2011).

Second, in order to increase competition with public banks, new licences were granted to domestic private banks. There was also an increased presence of foreign banks during this period driven by India's commitment to the World Trade Organization (Leeladhar, 2007). In order to increase the scale of operations of public banks, there was a push for their consolidation by way of amalgamation, particularly in the case of RRBs (RBI, 2014).

Third, the priority sector lending policy was not dismantled, as recommended by the CFS, but major changes were made in the definition of priority sectors. The most noteworthy change was in the definition of agricultural credit, both in its 'direct' (given directly to agricultural producers or farmers) and 'indirect' (given to entities that supported agricultural production, such as input and storage dealers, and warehouse operators) categories.

The changes in the definition of priority sectors related to: (1) a sharp increase in credit limits assigned for various forms of indirect agricultural credit; and (2) including new forms of agricultural activities (such as soft drink production) and new kinds of agriculturists under direct agricultural credit (Ramakumar and Chavan, 2007). For example, loans given to corporations involved in agricultural (and allied) production were included as part of agriculture; this essentially equated large corporations with farmers in getting agricultural credit. As argued by Ramakumar and Chavan (2007), these changes were part of a conscious shift in public policy on agriculture to promote large-scale, commercial, capital-intensive forms of agricultural production and post-production activities.

Fourth, interest rate regulations on priority sector advances were gradually removed in order to provide greater autonomy to banks in pricing their products. Fifth, statutory pre-emptions in the form of both cash reserve ratio (CRR) and SLR were reduced in a phased manner in order to increase banks' control over loanable resources. Sixth, the branch licensing policy was changed in 1992 to give autonomy to (public and domestic private) banks to rationalize their branch networks. The 1:4 norm for opening branches was abolished (RBI, 2008).

Apart from the above-mentioned measures aimed at deregulation, there were also newer prudential regulatory and supervisory measures introduced to improve the financial soundness of the banking sector, including capital adequacy, non-performing loan (NPL) recognition, and on-site/off-site supervision (see Rajeev, Chapter 12 in this volume). Some of these measures were expected to, indirectly if not directly, influence the involvement of public banks in their pursuit of social banking objectives (Chandrasekhar and Ghosh, 2007a, 2007b).

The Financial Inclusion and Infrastructure Financing Phase – Post-2005

Though the period after 2005 was a continuation of the financial liberalization policy, there was a distinct change in the approach to banking in general, and public banking in particular, with an explicit commitment to 'financial inclusion'. This was also the period when the first United Progressive Alliance (UPA) government came to power with support from the Indian Left, opening up greater space for inclusive economic policies (Ramachandran and Rawal, 2010). Financial inclusion, a part of these policies, was defined as 'the process of ensuring *access to appropriate financial products and services* needed by all sections of the society in general, and *vulnerable groups* such as low income groups in particular, at an *affordable* cost in a *fair* and transparent manner by *regulated mainstream institutional players*' (Chakrabarty, 2011; emphasis added). Though the policy objective of 'financial inclusion' was similar to the one that had prompted bank nationalization, it was to be pursued in the broader context of financial liberalization, taking into account 'business considerations' to ensure the 'long-term sustainability of the process' (RBI, 2008, p. 304).

Consequently, this phase witnessed the return of some, if not all, redistributive mandates on the banking sector seen in the bank nationalization phase earlier. However, these mandates were to be pursued by banks in an environment of greater operational autonomy through interest rate deregulation, reduction in statutory pre-emptions and broadening of the definition of priority sectors.

The key policy changes during this phase for financial inclusion are outlined as follows. First, a branch authorization policy was introduced wherein banks were allowed to open branches through annual authorizations. They could open a branch at any centre without the prior permission from the Reserve Bank of India (RBI), provided that at least 25 per cent of the total branches opened during the year were located at unbanked rural centres (serving less than 10000 persons). This resembled the branch licensing policy after bank nationalization.

In addition, the Business Correspondents (BCs) scheme was introduced in 2006 to facilitate branchless banking. BCs were banking agents who used information and communication technology to deliver banking services to rural areas. The list of eligible BCs was widened over time to include both non-profit and for-profit entities (including telecom companies and non-banking financial companies [NBFCs]) to make financial inclusion a commercially viable process.

Second, public and domestic private banks were asked to prepare three-year board-approved financial inclusion plans (FIPs) starting in 2010; these were for the expansion of banking outreach through branch and non-branch means. The targets set under the FIPs were subsequently aligned with the Prime Minister's People's Money Scheme (Pradhan Mantri Jan-Dhan Yojana: PMJDY) announced in August 2015 with the aim of achieving universal financial inclusion. Under this programme, both public and domestic private banks were asked to open deposit accounts to bring all unbanked individuals into the banking fold by August 2016.

Third, as the commitment to inclusive finance was partly a result of the general decline in rural credit seen in the 1990s following financial liberalization as well as signs of agrarian distress, there was a distinct push to revive the flow of agricultural credit during this phase (Ramakumar and Chavan, 2007). Consequently (public and domestic private sector) banks were instructed to double the flow of agricultural credit starting in 2004 and spanning the next three years under a 'comprehensive credit policy' (ibid.). An interest subsidy scheme for agricultural credit was also introduced by the government for public banks in 2006–07, which was made applicable to domestic private banks in 2013–14.

Apart from financial inclusion, this phase also witnessed the increased involvement of public banks in infrastructure (power, roads/ports/civil aviation and telecommunications) and other core industrial financing (coal, cement, iron, steel and other metals). Originally, the major vehicles for infrastructure financing in India were development finance institutions (DFIs) created in the 1950s and 1960s, mainly in the public sector, along with budgetary allocations and the internal resources of public sector enterprises engaged in infrastructure (GoI, 2012a). However, most of the DFIs were converted into universal banks in the wake of financial liberalization to create larger banks to compete with global financial players (RBI, 1998). Furthermore, the pressure on public banks to finance infrastructure increased significantly since the mid-2000s as budgetary allocations proved to be inadequate to meet the increasing demand for infrastructure investment (GoI, 2012a).

During this phase, a number of policies were adopted to boost the flow of bank credit to infrastructure and to ensure that these loans did not create liquidity or credit stress for banks. These included: (1) facilitating partial/full takeout financing of infrastructural loans by banks; (2) issuance of long-term bonds by banks for facilitating infrastructure financing; and (3) facilitating periodic refinancing and restructuring of infrastructural loans (see www.rbi.org.in for details). While these measures applied to all banks, public banks were expected to be their major beneficiaries given greater involvement of these banks in infrastructure financing.

TRENDS IN PUBLIC BANKING

Given the dominance of public banks in the Indian banking system, the overall intensity of banking business in the country (defined as the ratio of total banking business [credit plus deposits] per capita to per capita income) closely corresponded with the intensity of business of public banks (Figure 7.3).

Moreover, changes in banking business intensity were closely associated with the three policy phases delineated in the section above. Between 1969 and 2015, intensity of public banks showed three structural breaks – in 1980, 1990 and 2005. The period from 1975 to 1980 was marked by a sharp increase in banking intensity against a lower base. The second period from

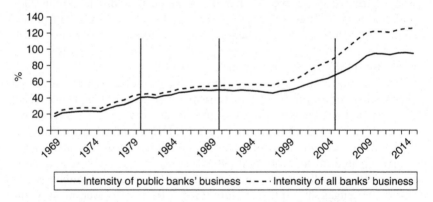

Note: Intensity refers to public banks' business (credit plus deposits) per capita as a percentage of per capita income. The lines represent the three structural breaks in the series using the Bai-Perron break point trend regression. The break point relates to the series on intensity of public banks' business. However, it is similar to the one observed in the case of intensity for all banks' business.

Source: Calculated based on *Basic Statistical Returns of Scheduled Commercial Banks in India*, RBI, various issues and *Socio-Economic Statistics: India*, Central Statistics Office (CSO), various issues.

Figure 7.3   Intensity of public banking business per capita, 1969–2015

1981 to 1990 showed a relatively slower increase/stagnation, while the third (1991 to 2005) showed a decline over the 1990s followed by recovery over the first half of the 2000s. The final phase (2006 to 2015) showed a much sharper increase. The outreach of bank branches (defined as population per bank branch) displayed broadly similar changes as banking intensity (author's calculations based on RBI data).

ROLE OF PUBLIC BANKS IN FINANCIAL INTERMEDIATION

Public Banks and National Savings/Investment

The rates of savings and investments are telling indicators of the extent of financial intermediation in any economy. As the key financial intermediary in the Indian context, public banks have played a pivotal role in financial intermediation by transforming deposits mobilized from the surplus sectors and channelling them as credit towards deficit sectors. The role of public banks in the process of financial intermediation can thus be discerned by juxtaposing the trends in the outreach/intensity of business of public banks with the rates of savings/investment (defined as the ratio of savings/investment per capita to per capita income).

The rates of per capita savings/investment showed three distinct structural breaks, dividing the entire period of analysis into four phases: the first phase from 1969 to 1974 showed a very rapid increase in these rates; the second phase from 1975 to 1980 was marked by a relatively slow increase in these rates; the third phase from 1981 to 1990 recorded a further slowdown in these rates. The fourth phase from 1991 through 2014 did not reflect a consistent trend; there was a rapid increase in these rates till 2008 followed by an equally sharp decline thereafter.

The financial savings rate could also be divided into four phases based on three break points in 1979, 1995 and 2008. The decline in financial savings rate after 2008 was even sharper than the overall savings rate, primarily due to high inflation during this period putting downward pressure on both personal disposable income and real rates of return on financial instruments (RBI, 2012).

While the break points for national savings/investment rates and financial savings rate are not exactly comparable, it is possible to draw two broad observations based on these series.

First, there was a significant increase in all three rates till 1980. This was also a period during which both outreach and intensity of business of public banks increased sharply. Juxtaposing these trends, the role of public banks in stimulating financial intermediation in the phase following bank nationalization was fairly evident. This observation about an increase in savings and investment behaviour following bank nationalization was also made by Joshi and Little (1994), who observed that, 'the *increasing degree of financial intermediation* was closely associated with the very rapid spread of commercial banking throughout the country after bank nationalization in 1969 ... *Financial repression was therefore mild* and any *deleterious effects on savings were offset by the rapid spread of banking*' (p. 255; emphasis added; see also Roland, 2005).

Second, during the financial liberalization and inclusion phases, the role of public banks in the process of financial intermediation has been less clear. This can be on account of the growing role of other kinds of financial intermediaries, including capital markets, in meeting savings and funding requirements; the economic slowdown that followed the global financial crisis and reflected in a slowdown in savings/investment rates after 2008 despite a rise in branch outreach during this period; and a steep rise in public banks' NPLs making them risk averse in lending to the credit-intensive industrial sector (see issues of *RBI Annual Report, Report on Trend and Progress of Banking in India* and *Financial Stability Report* after 2008 for a discussion on some of these developments). Although the period from 2005 to 2008 is often regarded as a high savings/investment phase for India, the slowdown in savings/investment rates after 2008 was even sharper, thus offsetting the increase achieved earlier. It is evident, therefore, that the increase in bank outreach and business intensity after 2005 has not translated into any credible and long-lasting gains in savings/investment rates so far.

Public Banks and Rural Banking

A major way in which public banks have aided financial intermediation in India has been through their contribution to rural banking. As the rural population has accounted for over two-thirds of India's population since 1971, the expansion in rural banking has meant access to banking services for a large section of the population.

The present-day rural banking network in India is almost entirely attributable to public banks. In 2015, public banks accounted for 87 per cent of the total bank branches serving rural areas. Importantly, public banks have been prominently active in small villages (with populations of less than 10 000) as compared to private banks.

There was a dramatic rise in rural bank outreach following bank nationalization. The rural population per bank branch decreased sharply within a span of 16 years between 1969 and 1985, from 76 100 to 14 400 persons.

However, there were distinct signs of decline in rural branch outreach after 1990, primarily attributable to the closure of rural bank branches during this period (Ramakumar and Chavan, 2011; Shetty, 2005; Subbarao, 2012). In 1990, the rural population per bank branch was 13700 persons, which rose to 16600 persons by 2005.[1] Thereafter, however, branch outreach in rural areas showed a revival once again (Ramakumar and Chavan, 2011), and by 2015, there were 10600 persons per bank branch in rural India. In 2015, the average branch outreach in urban areas was 8300 persons.

Along with branch outreach, the relative supply of bank credit to and mobilization of deposits from rural areas also expanded after bank nationalization. In 1975, per capita bank credit in rural areas was only about 8 per cent of that in urban areas, while per capita deposits made up about 14 per cent. From such low levels, the ratios increased moderately but steadily to reach about 15 per cent and 17 per cent, respectively, by 1990. However, as rural branch networks shrank thereafter, the relative availability of bank credit to and deposits from rural areas also declined. In 2005, the two ratios were at a lower level of 10 per cent and 15 per cent, respectively. Given the likely diversion of deposit resources from rural to urban areas, the decline during this phase was expectedly steeper for credit than deposits. In line with the increasing outreach of rural branches, however, the ratios of both credit and deposits for rural areas revived moderately after 2005. In 2015, the ratios were 11 per cent and 16 per cent, respectively.

Notwithstanding the rise, an average Indian in a rural area still receives only about 11 per cent of the credit received by an average Indian from an urban area. This underlines the vast distance that needs to be covered in ensuring an equitable distribution of banking services across rural and urban areas in the country.

Another telling indicator of the magnitude of financial exclusion is that only about 5 per cent of India's close to 6000 smaller villages (with population of less than 10000) are served by a bank branch (author's calculation based on RBI data). It can be argued that even though the spread of branches is limited, there is an effort to encourage non-branch means, including BCs, to extend banking services to rural areas in the phase of financial inclusion. And rightly so, the growth in BCs, although initially slow, has been impressive in recent years such that nearly all villages identified for financial inclusion reported the presence of BCs by 2015 (RBI, 2015b). However, notwithstanding such growth, it is also acknowledged by now that agent-based banking may not necessarily be a credible means

---

[1] A direct comparison of rural outreach is not possible on account of changes in the definition of rural centres over time. Even after accounting for these changes, a decline in rural outreach was still evident after 1990; see Ramakumar and Chavan (2011).

of accessing banking services, especially given the concerns about mobile/ telecom connectivity, safety and viability of this banking mode (Bansal and Srinivasan, 2009; Kishore, 2012). A reported coverage by BCs may, therefore, not translate into an effective coverage. BCs may act as complements but not exactly substitutes for branch banking. This thinking is also reflected in the recent push by the RBI to open more 'brick and mortar' branches for better banking coverage.[2]

Public Banks and Economically Backward Regions

In the bank nationalization phase, there was significant expansion in banking outreach to regions that can be classified as economically backward: the northeastern, eastern and central regions.

In 1975, branch outreach in the three backward regions ranged between 51 100 and 79 400 persons. By 1990, outreach in these regions ranged between 16 000 and 18 000 persons, significantly narrowing the gap between them and the three vanguard regions: northern, western and southern regions.

Following the initiation of the financial liberalization policy, however, there was a distinct decline in the branch outreach in the three backward regions (Chavan, 2005; Shetty, 2005). Among these, the most adversely affected region was the northeastern region, which is largely isolated from the mainland. In 2005, branch outreach in the northeastern region had risen to 23 000 persons, while in the central and eastern regions it was placed at 20 000 persons and 19 000 persons, respectively.

Signs of revival in branch outreach, however, were once again evident after 2005. The revival in this period was so significant that it compensated for the decline seen in the 1990s across all three regions. The population per bank branch in 2015 in the three backward regions ranged between 13 000 and 15 000 persons, which was much lower (implying better outreach) than the levels in 1990.

A similar trend could also be seen in the case of credit intensity (ratio of bank credit per capita to per capita income) in the three backward regions.[3] Between 1980 and 1990, there was a rise in credit intensity in these regions. In 1990, the bank credit received by an average person from the

---

[2] See RBI circular 'Roadmap for opening brick and mortar branches in villages with population more than 5000 without a bank branch of a scheduled commercial bank', 31 December 2015, accessed 5 July 2017 at https://www.rbi.org.in/scripts/NotificationUser.aspx? Id=10187&Mode=0.

[3] This ratio is worked out taking average bank credit per capita for the region divided by average per capita income/net domestic product (NDP). The regional per capita income is a weighted average at current prices (taking the share of each state in the regional population as the weight).

northeast was about 5 per cent of his or her contribution to the regional income. The ratio was 12 per cent and 19 per cent, respectively, for the central and eastern regions. By contrast, the ratio ranged between 23 and 30 per cent for the economically vanguard regions.

After a standstill or even a backsliding in the liberalization phase, credit intensity increased in all three backward regions once again after 2010. By 2014, which is the latest year for which data on regional income are available, the ratio ranged between 15 per cent and 27 per cent in these three regions. By contrast, in the economically vanguard regions, the ratio was on a steady increase in the 1990s through the 2010s, and ranged between 85 per cent and 119 per cent in 2014.

Public Banks and Agricultural Credit

Though there has been a fall in the share of agriculture in India's GDP over the years, it has continued to be the single largest source of employment (49 per cent in 2011). Evidently, financing agriculture implies financing the production credit needs of the majority of India's population.

As already discussed, commercial banks were required to provide credit to agriculture after nationalization by way of priority sector lending. Though both public and private banks were mandated to lend to agriculture, since the 1970s, public banks have accounted for 95 per cent of the total agricultural credit (author's calculations based on RBI data). Moreover, there has been a difference between public and private banks in the extent of meeting the agricultural credit targets. The difference has been relatively less for total agricultural credit (given the presence of indirect means of meeting this target at banks' disposal). However, it has been rather stark for direct agricultural credit, which included credit given directly to farmers (author's calculations based on RBI data).

The intensity of agricultural credit, defined as the ratio of agricultural credit from commercial banks to agricultural GDP, showed a rise from 2 per cent in 1971–72 to 44 per cent in 2013–14. However, like the other series considered so far, this increase was interrupted during the liberalization phase (author's calculations based on RBI data). Given the rise resumed after 2005, the gap between agricultural credit intensity and overall credit intensity narrowed to a considerable extent.

Though there was a revival in the intensity of bank credit to agriculture in the 2000s, this trend needs to be interpreted carefully on account of a significant widening of the definitions of both direct and indirect agricultural credit that started during the phase of financial liberalization (Ramakumar and Chavan, 2007, 2014). As a result, in several respects, the increase in agricultural credit in the 2000s was different in character from the one noted in the 1970s and 1980s. First, the growth in agricultural credit during this phase was mainly on account of indirect agricultural credit (ibid.). Second, even though there was also an increase in the growth of direct agricultural credit, this was driven by large-sized loans, owing largely to the inclusion of credit to corporates engaged in agricultural production. By contrast, there was a steep fall in the share of small borrowal accounts (SBAs) in agriculture, accounts with a credit limit of less than Rs0.2 million, which broadly represented the credit flow to small farmers (operating less than 2 hectares of land) (ibid.). Third, there was a shift in agricultural credit towards urban areas and away from rural areas, which are commonly associated with agricultural activities, during this period (ibid.).

It is pertinent to note that notwithstanding the emphasis on commercial farming, Indian agriculture is dominated by small farmers. In 2010–11, about 85 per cent of the total landholdings in India were small in size (less than 2 hectares) accounting for about 44 per cent of the total area operated (GoI, 2012b). Smallholdings also accounted for a major portion of the total leased-in area; this indicated the presence of tenant cultivators under the category of small cultivators (about 53 per cent of the total leased-in land in 2012; NSSO, 2015). These farmers neither reside in urban areas nor can they raise and service large-sized agricultural loans. Hence, even if there was a return of public banks to agriculture in the 2000s, the extent to which these banks reached out to marginalized sections within agriculture remained questionable (GoI, 2010; Ramakumar and Chavan, 2007, 2014).

Public Banks and Infrastructural Credit

The role of public banks in credit intermediation after 2005 cannot be appreciated fully without analysing their financing of infrastructure and other core industries. The share of banks in general, and public banks in particular, in financing infrastructure and core industries showed a rapid increase after 2009 from about 16 per cent to about 27 per cent in 2015 (author's calculations based on RBI data).

However, this increased financing of infrastructure turned out to be the main source of stress for public banks during this period. The NPL ratio for the banking sector in general, and public banks in particular, showed a moderate increase after 2008 with the outbreak of the global financial crisis and became stark after 2011 (Chavan and Gambacorta, 2016). Following the increase in NPLs, there have been policy initiatives to wean the infrastructure sector away from bank funding by developing the corporate bond market and take out financing. However, these measures have met with limited success and the dependence of infrastructure financing on banks has continued to rise over time (Chandrasekhar, 2015).

The poor loan quality has affected the overall performance of public banks, including their profitability (through higher provisioning) and financial soundness (through lower reserve accretion leading to weakening capital buffers) after 2011, the very two objectives of the policy of financial liberalization.[4]

CONCLUDING OBSERVATIONS AND THE WAY FORWARD FOR PUBLIC BANKS

In India, a large public banking system was created through bank nationalization in 1969. Not only were banks placed under public ownership, they were also regulated by a banking policy that aimed at achieving social and economic redistribution. There were a number of favourable changes in the growth and distribution of banking in India through the 1970s and 1980s, spearheaded by public banks. First, branch outreach across the country witnessed a rapid increase. The expansion in branches was particularly striking in rural areas and in underdeveloped geographical regions of the country, including the northeastern, eastern and central regions. Though the gap in banking development between the backward and vanguard regions remained wide, there was some progress towards bridging the gap. Second, there was increased penetration of bank credit in agriculture. Notably, there was a discernible relation between the growth of public banking and the growth of national savings and investment during this phase. In a way, this contradicted the oft-made claim that the Indian banking system was financially repressed after nationalization and needed to be liberalized to enhance financial intermediation.

During the financial liberalization phase that began in the early 1990s, however, there was a distinct decline in most banking development indicators. The proponents of financial liberalization justified this policy on the grounds that pursuing social objectives through banks during the earlier phase had eroded the profitability and soundness of the banking system. While public banks retained their public character, there was a deregulation or dilution of most policy measures introduced in the earlier phase with the objective of redistribution. Public banks remained the largest segment of the Indian banking system even in the face of rising competition from domestic and foreign private banks.

The period after 2005 marked the third phase in banking policy, which witnessed a return to the redistributive agenda within the broader contours

---

[4] For data on profitability and capital positions of public banks, see various issues of the *Financial Stability Report* from 2011 onwards at www.rbi.org.in.

of financial liberalization. Public banks were viewed as conduits for financial inclusion and enhancing the flow of agricultural credit to address concerns relating to agrarian distress. They were also viewed as conduits for financing infrastructure and core industrial sectors following the closure of DFIs. The phase after 2005 thus saw public banks taking on the dual task of extending banking services to the underserved sections as well as large industrial projects.

On the positive side, there was a revival in branch penetration in rural areas and underbanked geographical regions after 2005. There was also a striking recovery in the growth of agricultural credit. However, this recovery had to be examined in light of the broadening of the definition of agriculture as part of financial liberalization. Given these definitional changes, the benefit of this revival in agricultural credit to the farming community in general, and small farmers in particular, remained questionable.

On the negative side, there were signs of stress building up in these banks over time, mainly because of increased exposure to infrastructure and core industrial sectors. The attempt to fulfil the responsibilities of DFIs, without due regard to commercial viability and environmental/legal considerations, turned out to be a source of vulnerability for these banks (Chandrasekhar, 2011; Ghosh, 2014; also see Rajeev, Chapter 12 in this volume). Generally, commercial banks tend to mobilize resources through large numbers of small deposits on the liabilities side, and hence when they fund lumpy projects involving long gestation periods on the assets side they may be exposed to both credit and liquidity risks. The recent episode of NPLs of Indian public banks, therefore, cannot be regarded as a special case but needs to be seen as an inherent source of vulnerability given the way banking institutions operate (Ghosh, 2014).

Further, the sustained increase in national savings/investment, which was evident in the bank nationalization phase, could not be recreated in the financial inclusion period. In fact, the period after 2008 witnessed a severe decline in savings and investment rates, notwithstanding the increase in bank outreach.

To address the existing vulnerability, there have been suggestions to privatize public banks to provide them greater autonomy and enhance efficiency (RBI, 2013b, 2014). Interestingly, however, the weak financial health of public banks during this phase has itself been an outcome of the policy of financial liberalization (Chandrasekhar, 2014).[5] Private ownership, whether more efficient or not, is certainly not expected to be more

---

[5] Moreover, studies find that the operational efficiency of public banks has, in fact, been better than their private counterparts; see Das and Ghosh (2006); RBI (2008, 2013a); and Sathye (2001).

conducive to redistribution, as has been shown by the history of banking in India. India offers an excellent illustration of how public banks backed by public regulation have been able to reach out to rural areas, backward regions and underserved sectors. As shown in this chapter, the pursuit of a redistributive banking policy and the reversal of such a policy has brought about striking changes in the regional and functional outreach of banks, and consequently, the process of financial intermediation and development.

Given the staggering levels of financial exclusion, a redistributive banking policy is inevitable for India, with public banks as the key agency in this endeavour. However, an important lesson from history has also been the need for professional and transparent management of these banks. There is also a need for better regulatory and supervisory oversight of these banks to avoid a repeat of the recent episode of NPLs. The issue of recapitalization also requires a careful scrutiny to provide adequate capital support, in order to: (1) enable public banks to migrate to an advanced capital adequacy framework; (2) address their present concerns about NPLs; and (3) preserve public ownership. Finally, the policy of converting DFIs into universal banks too requires a rethink. India needs large financial institutions, as seen in the case of Brazil, to finance infrastructural projects. The lack of large-scale funding with a pressure on public banks to take on risky and illiquid project loans may only aggravate the shortage of medium/long-term capital for the industrial sector, while undermining the overall health of the banking system.

REFERENCES

Bansal, Y. and N. Srinivasan (2009), 'Business correspondents and facilitators: The story so far', *CAB Calling*, No. 33, April–June.

Bansil, P.C. (1986), *Economic Problems of Indian Agriculture*, New Delhi: Oxford University Press and IBH Publishing.

Central Statistics Office (various issues), *Socio-Economic Statistics: India*, New Delhi: CSO.

Chakrabarty, K.C. (2011), 'Financial inclusion and banks: Issues and perspectives', speech at the FICCI UNDP Seminar, New Delhi, 14 October.

Chandrasekhar, C.P. (2011), 'Development banks – Their role and importance for development', accessed 5 July 2017 at www.networkideas.org/alt/apr2011/Devel opment_Banks.pdf.

Chandrasekhar, C.P. (2014), 'The sources of bank vulnerability', *The Hindu*, 1 March, accessed 5 July 2017 at http://www.thehindu.com/opinion/columns/Chandrasekhar/ the-sources-of-bank-vulnerability/article5739374.ece.

Chandrasekhar, C.P. (2015), 'The future of public banking', *Macroscan*, 21 August, accessed 5 July 2017 at http://www.macroscan.org/cur/aug15/cur21082015Public_ Banking.htm.

Chandrasekhar, C.P. and J. Ghosh (2007a), 'Basel II and India's banking structure', *The Hindu Business Line*, accessed 5 July 2017 at http://www.thehindubusinessline.com/todays-paper/tp-opinion/basel-ii-and-indias-banking-structure/article1649968.ece.

Chandrasekhar, C.P. and J. Ghosh (2007b), 'The potential fall-out of Basel II', *The Hindu Business Line*, accessed 5 July 2017 at http://www.thehindubusinessline.com/todays-paper/tp-opinion/the-potential-fallout-of-basel-ii/article1651530.ece.

Chavan, P. (2005), 'Banking sector reforms and growth and distribution of rural banking in India', in V.K. Ramachandran and M. Swaminathan (eds), *Financial Liberalization and Rural Credit*, New Delhi: Tulika Books.

Chavan, P. and L. Gambacorta (2016), 'Bank lending and loan quality: The case of India', *BIS Working Paper No. 595*.

Copestake, J. (1985), 'The transition to social banking in India: Promises and pitfalls', *Development Policy Review*, **6**(2), 139–64.

Das, A. and S. Ghosh (2006), 'Financial deregulation and efficiency: An empirical analysis of Indian banks during the post-reform period', *Review of Financial Economics*, **15**(3), 193–221.

Ghosh, J. (2014), 'Public banks and the burden of private infrastructure investment', *Macroscan*, 14 February, accessed 5 July 2017 at www.macroscan.org/cur/feb14/pdf/Public_Banks.pdf.

Gorton, G.B. and A. Winton (2002), 'Financial intermediation', *NBER Working Paper No. 8928*, May.

Government of India (GoI) (2010), *Report of the Task Force on Credit Related Issues of Farmers*, New Delhi: GoI.

Government of India (GoI) (2012a), *Twelfth Five Year Plan (2012–2017) – Faster, More Inclusive and Sustainable Growth Volume I*, New Delhi: GoI.

Government of India (GoI) (2012b), *Agriculture Census – 2010–11*, New Delhi: GoI.

Goyal, S.K. (1967), 'Banking institutions and Indian economy', *ISID Working Paper No. 1*, New Delhi: Institute for Studies in Industrial Development.

Joshi, V. and I.M.D. Little (1994) (eds), *India: Macroeconomics and Political Economy – 1964–1991*, Washington, DC: World Bank.

Kishore, A. (2012), 'Business correspondent model boosts financial inclusion in India', *CommunityDividend*, 1 October, accessed 5 July 2017 at https://www.minneapolisfed.org/publications/community-dividend/business-correspondent-model-boosts-financial-inclusion-in-india.

Leeladhar, V. (2007), 'The evolution of banking regulation in India – A retrospect on some aspects', speech at the Bankers' Conference, 26 November, Mumbai.

National Sample Survey Office (NSSO) (2015), *Household Ownership and Operational Holdings in India, Report No. 571*.

Raj, K.N. (1974), 'Monetary management and nationalization of banking in India', in A. Mitra (ed.), *Economic Theory and Planning: Essays in Honour of A.K. Dasgupta*, Calcutta: Oxford University Press.

Ramachandran, V.K. and V. Rawal (2010), 'The impact of globalization and liberalization on India's agrarian economy', *Global Labour Journal*, **1**(1), 56–91.

Ramakumar, R. and P. Chavan (2007), 'Revival in agricultural credit in the 2000s: An explanation', *Economic and Political Weekly*, **42**(52), 57–64.

Ramakumar, R. and P. Chavan (2011), 'Changes in the number of rural bank branches in India, 1991 to 2008', *Review of Agrarian Studies*, **1**(1), 141–8.

Ramakumar, R. and P. Chavan (2014), 'Agricultural credit in the 2000s: Dissecting the revival', *Review of Agrarian Studies*, **4**(1), 50–79.

Ray, A. (2009), *The Evolution of the State Bank of India – The Era from 1955–1980*, New Delhi: Penguin Books.

Reserve Bank of India (RBI) (1991), *Report of the Committee on the Financial System*, Mumbai: RBI.

Reserve Bank of India (RBI) (1996), *Circulars on Credit Policy*, Mumbai: RBI.

Reserve Bank of India (RBI) (1998), *Report of the Working Group for Harmonising the Role and Operations of DFIs and Banks*, Mumbai: RBI.

Reserve Bank of India (RBI) (2001), 'Developmental issues in micro-credit', speech by Jagdish Capoor, *RBI Bulletin*, March.

Reserve Bank of India (RBI) (2005), *The Reserve Bank of India – History, Volume 3 – 1967–1981*, Mumbai: RBI.

Reserve Bank of India (RBI) (2008), *Report on Currency and Finance – 2006–08*, Mumbai: RBI.

Reserve Bank of India (RBI) (2012), *RBI Annual Report – 2011–12*, Mumbai: RBI.

Reserve Bank of India (RBI) (2013a), *Report on Trend and Progress of Banking in India – 2012–13*, Mumbai: RBI.

Reserve Bank of India (RBI) (2013b), *Banking Structure in India – The Way Forward*, Mumbai: RBI.

Reserve Bank of India (RBI) (2014), *RBI Annual Report – 2013–14*, Mumbai: RBI.

Reserve Bank of India (RBI) (various issues), *Basic Statistical Returns of Scheduled Commercial Banks in India*, Mumbai: RBI.

Roland, C. (2005), 'Banking sector liberalization in India', paper prepared for the Ninth Capital Markets Conference, Indian Institute of Capital Markets, accessed 5 July 2017 at unpan1.un.org/intradoc/groups/public/documents/apcity/unpan024227.pdf.

Sathye, M. (2001), 'Efficiency of banks in a developing economy: The case of India', accessed 5 July 2017 at https://crawford.anu.edu.au/acde/asarc/pdf/papers/conference/CONF2001_13.pdf.

Sathye, M. (2003), 'Privatization, performance and efficiency: A study of Indian banks', World Bank Conference on Bank Privatization, October, Washington, DC.

Shetty, S.L. (1997), 'Financial sector reforms in India: An evaluation', *Prajnan*, **25**(3–4), 253–87.

Shetty, S.L. (2005), 'Regional, sectoral and functional distribution of bank credit', in V.K. Ramachandran and M. Swaminathan (eds), *Financial Liberalization and Rural Credit*, New Delhi: Tulika Books.

Subbarao, D. (2011), 'Corporate governance of banks in India in pursuit of productivity excellence', speech at the Indian Chambers of Commerce & Industry – Indian Banks' Association Conference, Mumbai, 23 August.

Subbarao, D. (2012), 'Agricultural credit – Accomplishments and challenges', speech delivered at the Thirty Years Anniversary Celebration of NABARD, Mumbai, 12 July.

Wiggins, S. and S. Rajendran (1987), *Rural Banking in Southern Tamil Nadu: Performance and Management: Final Research Report No. 3*, University of Reading, UK.

8. Governance of development banks under uncertainty

Tamilla Tagieva

State-owned development banks have often been criticized for ineffectiveness. High levels of non-performing assets (NPAs) causing recapitalizations of government resources seriously undermine the position of these banks in many countries. Not only their financial standing, but also the ability of development banks to produce developmental impact has been questioned (La Porta et al., 2002, p. 290). These and other criticisms have led many to suggest the privatization of state-owned development banks (for example, Caprio et al., 2004, p. 1; Scott, 2007, p. 5). Hence, the survival of development banks has become a matter of concern, especially taking into account a high number of development bank closures and privatizations since the Latin American debt crisis of the 1980s (Bruck, 2005, p. 9; Caprio et al., 2004, p. 2).

Recognizing the important role that state development banks play in correcting market failures, this chapter proposes to shift attention from privatizing development banks towards searching for strategies on how to strengthen them and ensure their survival in the world of finance. To be able to do that, one has to understand what kind of problems and challenges development banks have to face in the course of their day-to-day activities.

Politicization of development banks is often said to be the reason for their poor performance and inefficiency (Dinc, 2005; La Porta et al., 2002; Micco and Panizza, 2006). It has been claimed that development banks are captured by politicians who use the banks to create jobs and give subsidies in order to receive 'votes, political contributions, and bribes' (La Porta et al., 2002, p. 266). These political influences over development banks slow down economic growth and the advancement of the financial sector, particularly in low-income countries (La Porta et al., 2002, p. 290).

Politicization, however, is not the only challenge faced by development banks. As Scherrer argues in Chapter 14 of this volume, political expectations were only one reason among others that led some German *Landesbanken* to pursue profit-maximizing strategies instead of maximizing social welfare (mission creep). Applying neoinstitutional theory, he states that in addition to politicization the desire to be like their competitors (represented by the private banks, for example, Deutsche Bank) and the influence of modern finance theory led *Landesbanken* management to stray from their original public mission.

Hence, development banks may be negatively influenced not only by politicians, but also by private banks and other actors in their environments. For example, borrowers that receive preferential treatment under government programmes and do not repay their loans also weaken development banks. Or rating agencies may give low credit ratings to some development banks, thereby hindering these banks from raising capital in bond markets at a lower price. The findings of the present research suggest that development banks are successful if they are able to respond to and overcome challenges and uncertainties stemming from their environments. As a result, a stronger pattern of self-control (understood as relative independence from various actors) exhibited by development banks may eventually increase their chances of survival.

The focus on the organizational survival of development banks is inspired by Thompson's *Organizations in Action* (1967). Although Thompson's book was written many decades ago, his theory has 'survived the test of time remarkably well' (Kamps and Polos, 1999, pp. 1779–80). It has also been substantiated by a more recent empirical investigation (Nutt, 2010).

This chapter begins by highlighting the different environments for development banks in economically highly developed (the so-called developed countries) and in economically less developed countries (developing countries). The more volatile, uncertain environment in developing countries features prominently throughout the chapter. The following sections discuss how development banks can fulfil their purpose in such an unstable environment. More specifically, they will focus on the relationships of development banks to their governments, (potential) suppliers of capital, their borrowers, credit rating agencies, private banks, international (European Union) institutions and the general public.

DIFFERING ENVIRONMENTS IN DEVELOPING AND DEVELOPED COUNTRIES

The term development bank indicates its purpose: facilitating development through providing loans. What development actually means is open to interpretation (Ziai, 2014). Currently, the United Nations Sustainable Development Goals (SDGs) express the consensus among governments on the ultimate goals of development such as eradication of extreme poverty, gender equality and the right to education. Obviously, achieving these goals on a sustainable basis requires substantial material resources. Therefore, the SDGs entail 'inclusive and sustainable' industrialization as a means to generate income that 'allows for rapid and sustained increases in living standards for all people' (UN, n.d.). These goals imply an international consensus on development banks' mission to support industrialization in pre-industrial societies. Since developed countries are already industrialized, their development banks are mainly charged with the task of maintaining the international competitiveness of their economies (Hatch, 1997, p. 25; Schmit et al., 2011, pp. 63–75).

It is not only the goals of development banks that vary between developing and developed countries; the way these banks operate differs as well. As the overall environment in developed countries is more stable and predictable (for instance, due to strong institutions and macroeconomic stability), the way development banks operate there tends to be standardized (the so-called mechanistic organization; Hatch, 1997, p. 76). Hence, rules and procedures in such organizations are likely to be duly followed. In contrast, the unpredictable and more fluid contexts in developing countries require more flexible (organic) organizations, where rules and procedures may not be duly implemented (Hatch, 1997, pp. 76–7). As Fry also notes, financial regulations 'generally [are] enforced much more consistently and effectively in the developed than in the developing countries. The same regulations on paper [in developing countries] may be quite different in practice' (Fry, 1995, cited in Collster, 2007, pp. 11–12).

DEVELOPMENT BANKS AS ADAPTIVE SYSTEMS

Thorne and Du Toit emphasize the importance of an 'enabling environment' for development banks (2009, pp. 681, 689). They claim that these banks are not able to succeed 'in a largely dysfunctional environment' (p. 689). To be successful, development banks need macroeconomic and political stability as well as 'micro-economic environment with proper regulation, acceptable infrastructure', among others (p. 681). Yet, most of these indicators exist in the more or less predictable environments of developed countries, whereas environments in developing countries are plagued with instabilities. Following this logic then, development banks should operate only in developed countries with enabling environments.

Meanwhile, the absence of the enabling environment does not discourage multinational private banks to open up their businesses in developing countries where they are able to survive by pursuing various strategies such as building alliances 'with an established local firm' (Deloitte, 2014, p. 14).

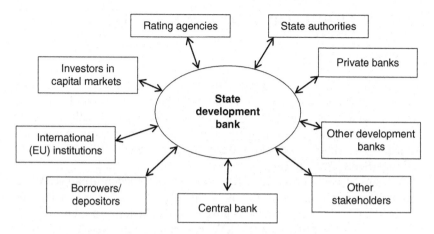

Figure 8.1   Task environment of state development banks

Also, governments in East Asian countries were able to successfully lead industrialization in unsteady environments thanks to 'their ability to learn' and 'the ability to respond to changes in the environment' (Stiglitz, 1996, p. 154).

Hence, survival requires development banks to be 'adaptive systems' (ibid.). Applying Thompson's *Organizations in Action*, these banks have to interact with various actors (Figure 8.1), which makes them dependent on these actors. From time to time, actors challenge development banks. Overcoming these challenges means that development banks are able to successfully manage (reduce) their dependency on others, which provides banks with some power in their environments (Thompson, 1967, pp. 27–32; Tosi, 2009, p. 83). More powerful organizations hence have better chances of surviving. Adapting strategies coupled with the enhancement of technological knowledge (understood as 'a system of cause/effect relationships which lead to a desired result') is what should help development banks to overcome challenges and manage (to reduce) their dependencies on others (Thompson, 1967, pp. 18, 30–36, 159–60).

Input sources that organizations need to acquire in their environments include raw materials, capital, labour, knowledge as well as social legitimacy (Hatch, 1997, pp. 85–6).

The next section provides an analysis of the task environment in which development banks operate, actors and resources on which these banks depend, and strategies that they (could) use to respond to challenges stemming from their environments. Three critical input sources of development banks (capital, knowledge and social legitimacy) will be reflected upon.

RAISING DEVELOPMENT BANK FUNDS

Government Transfers

Development banks may depend on their governments resource-wise, which politicians may use to exert undue influence over these banks (the problem of politicization). Thus, as a general rule, along with providing share (equity) capital, governments support development banks with direct transfers (subsidies) that reimburse costs associated with concessionary lending (Scott, 2007, p. 21).

In terms of capital resources, Kreditanstalt für Wiederaufbau (KfW), a 'good practice' German promotional bank (UN, 2015, p. 3), is less dependent on the German government as government transfers represent a rather insignificant source of capital for KfW compared to its alternative sources (see the next subsection). Moreover, the manner in which the German government transfers subsidies displays some elements of standardization. Thus, each year the German national budget allocates funds for KfW used for interest rate reductions for programmes initiated by the German government and implemented (funded) through KfW (Schroeder et al., 2011, pp. 32, 40). KfW is further distanced from the German government in a way that the bank is allowed to retain profits (but not to distribute them). The net profit of KfW is transferred to its statutory reserves (Article 10 of the Law Concerning Kreditanstalt für Wiederaufbau 1948; KfW, 1948). The rules that do not allow 'dividend payments to the public owners strengthen DBs' [development banks'] independence and increase their own equity and thus their promotional and risk-absorbing capacity' (UN, 2015, p. 24).

In contrast to KfW, the Vietnam Bank for Social Policies cannot exhibit the same strong pattern of self-control, because it is heavily dependent on government subsidies. The bank 'operates with a negative interest rate spread, making it unable to survive without government subsidies' (De Luna-Martinez and Vicente, 2012, p. 11). In a World Bank survey of development banks, 18 per cent of banks that obtained government subsidies confirmed that they cannot manage well their resource dependency on their governments, meaning that without government transfers they are not able to function sustainably (De Luna-Martinez and Vicente, 2012).

Not only do government subsidies give rise to resource dependency of banks on their governments, but also (unplanned) bank recapitalizations. For example, between 1993 and 1995 the Indian government provided new capital for Indian state-owned banks with the aim to 'repair the damage of the past' under a pre-designed recovery programme (Mathur, 2002, p. 2246). Later, it recapitalized the state banks on a 'case to case basis', meaning that this support was 'neither regular nor pre-designed' (Mathur, 2002). Such non-standardized, ad hoc support in times of no financial or economic crisis may undermine the incentives for prudent behaviour among managers of development banks (ibid.). This kind of support may also give rise to (or intensify already existing) informal contacts, between politicians and development banks, which in turn may lead to untenable levels of NPAs. Undue political interference led to the increase of indebtedness of Indonesian and Malaysian development banks (Stiglitz and Uy, 1996, p. 267).

It is not only resource dependency on governments that may lead to the politicization of development banks; development banks are also institutionally dependent on their governments. Thus, governments not only establish development banks, they can also close them. In between, governments can tightly control them (for instance, via participating in board decision-making) or allow them a high degree of organizational independence. This institutional dependence of development banks upon their governments frequently gives rise to undue political influence on loan allocation. Increasing institutional distance between development banks and governments via introducing a stakeholder governance model could be one way to depoliticize development banks (see Part V of this volume).

Capital Markets as an Alternative Source

According to Thompson, maintaining alternatives – that is, accessing different sources of funding – can reduce overbearing resource dependency of development banks on their governments (Thompson, 1967, pp. 32–3). Deposit-taking development banks diversify their capital sources by collecting deposits from the public. If development banks are exempted from paying taxes, deposits may serve as a substantial resource base for concessionary lending (Scott, 2007, p. 20). However, for a number of reasons, this source of capital is not very widespread among development banks (De Luna-Martinez and Vicente, 2012, p. 10; De Olloqui and Arancibia, 2013, pp. 9–10).

The most popular alternative source for development banks is capital markets (De Luna-Martinez and Vicente, 2012, p. 10). For example, KfW 'raises more than 90% of its funds' in capital markets (KfW, n.d.). KfW is able to raise capital rather inexpensively thanks to its high credit rating (AAA) that 'reflects that on the Federal Republic of Germany' (Standard and Poor's, 2013, p. 3). The guarantees of Germany, a country with strong economic (and political) fundamentals, provide an 'enabling environment' for KfW and a certain degree of independence from day-to-day politics.

Unlike KfW, development banks in a number of developing countries are less able to diversify their capital sources due to their immature domestic capital markets (Herr and Priewe, 2005, p. 135). Governments may even explicitly prohibit development banks from searching for and using alternative capital sources, as in the case of Mexican development bank Financiera Rural (De Luna-Martinez and Vicente, 2012, p. 10).

Credit ratings of those national development banks that are allowed to tap capital markets tend to reflect the country's sovereign credit rating (in the case that a rating agency believes that the government is more likely to provide adequate and well-timed support to the bank) (Standard and Poor's, 2015, p. 7). For instance, mirroring the 'BB' sovereign rating of Brazil (Fitch Ratings, 2016a), the BNDES also has relatively low ratings, with a long-term foreign and local currency issuer default rating of 'BB' in 2016 (Fitch Ratings, 2016b). Thus, development banks in developing countries may not be able to raise capital at the same favourable terms as KfW and to translate this capital into concessional loans. In such cases, these development banks have to turn to their governments to be able to lend at concessionary terms.

To sum up, rating agencies may pose constraints on development banks owned by developing countries. Cheaper capital in bond markets as an alternative source of capital has yet to be accessed by development banks in countries with weak fundamentals.

Adapting Strategies of Weaker Development Banks

Despite difficulties in accessing cheaper capital in bond markets, some weaker development banks do not 'wait' for the enabling environment in their countries and hence good ratings. Instead, they attempt to adapt to the given situation and diversify (and enlarge) their sources by 'contracting' (Thompson, 1967, pp. 34–5) with other (stronger) development banks that enjoy better ratings. For example, in 2014, Italian Cassa Depositi e Prestiti (Fitch rating BBB+ as of 21 August 2016) was able to attract KfW funds equal to 500 million euros (Fitch Ratings, 2016c; UN, 2015, pp. 23–4). This form of cooperation allows weaker banks not only to access alternative sources of capital, but also to 'acquire [more] prestige' in their environments (Thompson, 1967, pp. 33–4), because cofinancing with stronger banks may send positive signals to rating agencies and other actors (see, for example, the Black Sea Trade and Development Bank – Moody's, 2016, pp. 2–3).

Alternatively, weaker banks may choose a 'coalescing' strategy (Thompson, 1967, pp. 35–6), which involves inviting (stronger) entities such as governments or other development banks onto their boards in order to secure access to alternative sources of capital and benefit from higher ratings. For instance, the African Development Bank (AfDB), initially conceived as 'an all-African institution' in 1982, had to accept the membership of non-regional governments such as the United States, European countries and others (FAN, 2007, p. 6). Thanks to the new AAA-rated member states, the AfDB receives 'a ratings uplift of the issuer credit profile' by two marks to 'AAA' (Standard and Poor's, 2014, p. 17).

One should be aware, however, that cooperation with stronger development banks (often owned by donor countries) may expose weaker development banks to donor influence. The literature on aid effectiveness contains numerous examples in which, along with providing aid, donors promote their geopolitical and commercial interests as well as ideas (IBON International, 2009; Wan, 1995–96).

Development Central Banking

Development banks may diversify their capital sources by cooperating with national and foreign central banks. Central banks may fulfil the task of 'development central banking' – that is, participating in the process of development (Epstein, 2015, pp. 6–7). Herr and Priewe mention this developmental role of the central bank, seen as a 'circuit starter' capable of triggering economic growth (Herr and Priewe, 2005, p. 152). Brimmer also notes that development central banking entails 'providing [equity] capital to development institutions. . .; extending credit to development banks and purchasing their securities' (Brimmer, 1971, cited in Epstein, 2015, p. 7). To mention a few examples, KfW enjoys 'access to the European Central Bank's refinancing operations, and most of its securities are eligible as collateral' (Standard and Poor's, 2013, p. 10). In 2014, the People's Bank of China (China's central bank) cofinanced the Africa Growing Together Fund jointly with the AfDB (AfDB, 2014).

Reducing the resource dependence of development banks on their governments with the help of central banks can be more effective if central banks are relatively independent from governments. In addition to that, one should keep in mind that development central banking is sustainable as long as it does not hinder 'the maintenance of financial and macroeconomic stability' (Epstein, 2015, p. 7).

STRENGTHENING DEVELOPMENT BANKS' OPERATIONAL KNOWLEDGE

Making Borrower Behaviour More Predictable (Buffering)

The relative independence of development banks from their governments does not yet guarantee a strong pattern of self-control or the survival of development banks. NPAs originate not only from undue political influence, but also because development banks (in developing countries) find it difficult to manage (reduce) their dependency on borrowers once loans have been given. Imperfect knowledge of development banking technology may be held responsible for NPAs as well. Given the open-endedness (uncertainty) of knowledge (Thompson, 1967, pp. 1, 14), development banks are advised to constantly search 'for more effective procedures' (knowledge) (Thompson, 1967, p. 160) that can help them better manage their dependency on borrowers. This then allows for better self-control by organizations and increases the likelihood of their survival (ibid.).

While information asymmetry may lead private banks to ration credit (Stiglitz and Weiss, 1981), development banks do not always have this option and are supposed 'to allocate resources toward riskier projects' (De Olloqui and Arancibia, 2013, p. 9). In addition to that, in some developing countries banks are seriously challenged by borrowers' culture and discipline that are impaired as a result of loan waiver programmes (see Rajeev, Chapter 12 in this volume). To adapt to such an unpredictable environment, Thompson suggests that organizations 'buffer environmental influences', which prevents unwanted situations and hence 'minimize[s] surprise' (Thompson, 1967, p. 20).

To make borrower behaviour more predictable and prevent a loan from becoming an NPA (buffering), India has been both learning by doing and importing innovations from abroad. The Grameen Bank's methodology, for example, was imported and tested in India, but had limited success (Sriram, 2003, pp. 68, 70). A true Indian innovation, however, is the self-help group programme. This initiative allowed banks to hedge their risk and ensures better loan repayment (see Rajeev, Chapter 12 in this volume).

When lending to large borrowers, development banks may apply buffering strategies such as estimation of loan default probability and early remedial action. KfW, for instance, has a 'uniform master scale' in which four categories can be distinguished: investment grade, non-investment grade, watch list and default (KfW, 2014). The watch list, particularly, 'serves to identify potential problem loans early and, if necessary, to make preparations for handling these loans' (KfW, 2014, p. 27). NPAs and sometimes watch list loans are transferred to loan restructuring units of KfW, which allows 'the involvement of specialists from an early stage to ensure professional management of problematic loans' (ibid.).

To prevent loan defaults by borrowers and ensure their financial health, development banks have to turn to buffering strategies, but buffering requires additional resources to be spent (Thompson, 1967, p. 21). This is one of the reasons why maximum efficiency is hardly achievable in development banking. Therefore, it is argued in this chapter that development banks cannot be judged based on the criterion of efficiency maximization.

Developmental Impact

Knowledge creation may help not only in buffering, but also in elaborating strategies on how to make maximum use of available bank resources (intensive use of resources). One such strategy includes attaching maximum developmental impact to loans (Colby, 2012, p. 20; Schmit et al., 2011, p. 80) instead of merely 'recycling. . .capital' (Wan, 1995–96, p. 522).

Developmental impact can be both direct and indirect. Direct impact entails indicators such as number of companies served, loans issued, employment and exports (De Olloqui, 2013, pp. 34–5). Indirect impact (positive externality) includes, for instance, 'changes in. . .[the firm's] production chain that will augment its productivity, which could, in turn, affect other neighbouring firms, or those with which it is linked' (Maffioli and Rodriguez, 2013, p. 42).

'Signalling effects' are another example of indirect impact. Thus, in the case of East Asian development banks 'close ties to the government' ensured that their loans 'provided information to entrepreneurs and other banks on the areas that the government was promoting' (Stiglitz and Uy, 1996, p. 265). Also, loans from the Japan Development Bank 'preceded the increase in a firm's borrowing from private banks' (Stiglitz and Uy, 1996, p. 266).

Development bank practices may also produce 'demonstration effects' (International Finance Corporation, n.d.; Smallridge and De Olloqui, 2011, p. 7). Demonstration effects induce 'other market participants to change their behaviour' (International Finance Corporation, n.d., p. 1). Demonstration effects encourage so-called mimetic behaviour (DiMaggio and Powell, 1983, p. 150), which reflects 'a desire to be or look like' (Hatch, 1997, p. 84) a successful organization. An important feature of a demonstration effect 'is that the replication by other players must occur without direct involvement' by a development bank (Castalia Strategic Advisors, 2013, p. 7). What is more, demonstration effects 'increase. . .development impact at little or no additional cost' (Castalia Strategic Advisors, 2013). Patterns of changed behaviour include 'a bank deciding to start lending in a new sector, a new developer financing a project similar to the one implemented with. . .[the development bank's] support', and so on (International Finance Corporation, n.d., p. 1).

Development banks may maximize developmental impact by creating *meaningful* linkages between projects, people, institutions and processes. Creating meaningful linkages are especially important if coordination failures exist. Thus, 'developing a steel-manufacturing industry does not pay unless there is a steel-using industry; and developing a steel-using industry does not pay if there is no steel-manufacturing industry' (Stiglitz, 1996, p. 160). To give an example, Indian banks are strongly encouraged to take an integrated approach to agricultural value chain finance 'rather than a fragmented view of production' (Ashok et al., 2015, p. 130). It is also claimed that 'infrastructure in isolation can never address the entire gamut of issues that exist along the value chain, unless it is meaningfully linked to value chain' (Ashok et al., 2015, p. 129).

Development banks not only create meaningful linkages, they also attempt to maintain existing linkages in the economy by virtue of counter-cyclical lending during recession periods. Development banks are known to be stabilizers during crises when private banks experience credit crunch (see Mendonça and Deos, Chapter 1 in this volume).

The constant search by development banks for better knowledge of buffering strategies and for ways to maximize developmental impact affecting as many people and enterprises as possible may allow for better control over environments and eventually help development banks gain another important resource – social legitimacy.

IMPORTANCE OF SOCIAL LEGITIMACY

Private banks seriously challenge the existence of state development banks, especially if the latter directly compete with private banks. A telling example is the fate of the German *Landesbanken* at the hands of the European Competition Commission (see Seikel, Chapter 9 in this volume). The Commission's actions also impacted KfW, which 'agreed to spin off' the IPEX-Bank (KfW, 2007, p. 7); the latter can no longer benefit from the state guarantee (Standard and Poor's, 2013, p. 4). Hence, Thorne and Du Toit's enabling environment (2009) of developed countries may still be insufficient to ensure the strength and survival of development banks.

In order to adapt to this challenging environment and survive, development banks may choose not to compete with private banks, but rather to focus on complementing private sector banking (Rudolph, 2009, p. 7). Development banks may coalesce or build coalitions in order to collectively respond to challenges on the institutional level. With the help of coalitions such as the Association of German Public Banks and the European Association of Public Banks development banks can try to mobilize public opinion and action.

However, in non-democratic countries development banks may find it difficult to mobilize public opinion and action as these are political and intellectual elites (not the general public) that dominate decision-making (Andrews, 2007, p. 162). Therefore, for political and intellectual elites in non-democratic countries, output legitimacy earned by development banks based on their effective performance (Lieberherr, 2016, p. 457) may have more relevance.

In more or less democratic countries, social legitimacy may be crucial because decision-making in such countries is based on consensus rooted in civil society (Andrews, 2007, p. 162). Ability to mobilize social opinion and action may give development banks some power in the task environment. Consequently, not only may output legitimacy earned by development banks make a difference, but so may input and throughput legitimacy (Schmidt, 2010, p. 5). Thus, development banks may win social support not only by performing effectively, but also by providing conditions for (indirect) 'participation by and representativeness of the people' (through fair and unpoliticized election or appointment of bank management, for example) referred to as input legitimacy (Schmidt, 2010). People in democratic countries value throughput legitimacy that includes 'openness to pluralist consultation with the people' (ibid.). In this regard, the stakeholder governance model may be seen not only as an instrument with which to reduce institutional dependence of development banks on their governments and hence undue political influences, but also as a way 'to link political [and bank management] decisions with citizens' preferences' (Boedeltje and Cornips, n.d., p. 2).

CONCLUSION: TOWARDS A STRONGER PATTERN OF SELF-CONTROL

In this chapter, development banks were analysed utilizing the insights from the sociology of organizations, particularly Thompson's *Organization in Action* (1967). The exploration shows that development banks may be dependent not only on their governments, but also on investors in capital markets, rating agencies, borrowers, other (stronger) development banks, inter- and supranational institutions, private banks and central banks. This broader view helps to reveal a wide array of challenges that development banks have to face.

Dependence on governments goes beyond institutional channels (like the government representatives sitting on boards). Resource dependency especially in the form of non-standardized ad hoc requests for government funds might also lead to undue political influence. To strengthen development banks' independence, it is recommended that development banks diversify their board membership via stakeholder governance as well as search for alternative (non-government) capital sources.

The enabling environment in developed countries provides development banks with better credit ratings, which in turn leads to lower refinancing costs. In contrast, development banks in developing countries tend to refinance themselves in capital markets at less favourable conditions for obvious reasons. Nevertheless, some weaker development banks do not wait for the enabling environment and good ratings, but attempt to adapt to the given circumstances. They diversify and enlarge their capital sources by contracting or coalescing with other (stronger) development banks. This cooperation with stronger banks allows weaker development banks to acquire not only capital, but also better ratings. National and foreign central banks may also provide capital for development banks.

The unpredictable behaviour of borrowers may imperil development banks' financial position. Buffering against these environmental risks includes (along with keeping a capital reserve) improvements in the capacity to create and apply knowledge. For instance, the risks of NPAs can be reduced by enhancing risk assessment and monitoring techniques. Acquiring more knowledge about borrower behaviour can also be used for innovative strategies to incentivize borrower repayment morale or capacity. In general, searching for more knowledge and opportunities may advance strategies of development banks for maximizing the developmental impact.

Effective performance by development banks helps them secure social support as well as the support of political and intellectual elites. Democratic decision-making within development banks (stakeholder governance) as well as fair and transparent appointments of board members may find the support of the informed public. Mobilization of public opinion in more or less democratic countries may help to counter pressures coming from private banks. In non-democratic countries, political and intellectual elites decide on development banks' survival and output legitimacy earned by the latter may therefore be of more importance than input and/or throughput legitimacy.

REFERENCES

African Development Bank (AfDB) (2014), 'AfDB announces US 2 billion fund with China', *African Development Bank Group*, accessed 1 October 2016 at http://www.afdb.org/en/news-and-events/article/afdb-announces-us-2-billion-fund-with-ch ina-13165/.

Andrews, J.C. (2007), 'Rationality in policy decision making', in F. Fischer, G.J. Miller and M.S. Sidney (eds), *Handbook of Public Policy Analysis: Theory, Politics, and Methods*, Boca Raton, FL: CRC Press, pp. 161–71.

Ashok, M.V., G. Mani and D.K. Panwar (2015), 'Monograph. Financing agricultural value chains: Challenges and Opportunities', accessed 10 November 2016 at http://nabard.org/auth/writereaddata/tender/1409165859Monograph-Financing%20agr icultural%20value%20chain.pdf.

Boedeltje, M. and J. Cornips (n.d.), 'Input and output legitimacy in interactive governance', accessed 10 November 2016 at repub.eur.nl/pub/1750/NIG2-01.pdf.

Brimmer, A.F. (1971), 'Central banking and economic development: The record of innovation', *Journal of Money, Credit and Banking*, **3**(4), 780–92.

Bruck, N. (2005), 'Future role of national development banks in the twenty first century', Background Paper, UN Department of Economic and Social Affairs, December.

Caprio, G., J.L. Fiechter, R.E. Litan and M. Pomerleano (eds) (2004), *The Future of State-Owned Financial Institutions*, Washington, DC: Brookings Institution Press.

Castalia Strategic Advisors (2013), *IFC Demonstration Effect Study (Draft). Report to the International Finance Corporation*, accessed 10 November 2016 at http://www.ifc.org/wps/wcm/connect/f4c23b80433b40e48178ed384c61d9f7/Ifc+demo nstration+effect.pdf?MOD=AJPERE.

Colby, S. (2012), 'Explaining the BNDES: What it is, what it does and how it works', *Artigos*, **3**(7), accessed 6 July 2017 at rss.cebri.org/bndes.pdf.

Collster, R.K. (2007), 'A new approach to development banking in Jamaica', *Development Financing Series No. 193*, accessed 5 November 2016 at http://repositorio.cepal.org/bitstream/handle/11362/5173/1/S0700301_en.pdf.

De Luna-Martinez, J. and C.L. Vicente (2012), 'Global survey of development banks', *Working Paper No. 5969*, World Bank, February.

De Olloqui, F. (ed.) (2013), *Public Development Banks: Toward a New Paradigm?*, Washington, DC: Inter-American Development Bank.

De Olloqui, F. and P. Arancibia (2013), 'Overview and recent evolution of public development banks', in F. de Olloqui (ed.), *Public Development Banks. Toward a New Paradigm?*, Washington, DC: Inter-American Development Bank, pp. 1–18.

Deloitte (2014), 'Banking across borders. International expansion opportunities for emerging market-based banks', *Perspectives*, accessed 14 November 2016 at https://www2.deloitte.com/global/en/pages/financial-services/articles/banking-across-borders.html.

DiMaggio, J.P. and W.W. Powell (1983), 'The iron cage revisited: Institutional isomorphism and collective rationality in organizational fields', *American Sociological Review*, **48**(2), 147–60.

Dinc, S. (2005), 'Politicians and banks: Political influences on government-owned banks in emerging markets', *Journal of Financial Economics*, **77**(2), 453–79.

Epstein, G. (2015), 'Development central banking: A review of issues and experiences', *Working Paper No. 182*, International Labour Organization.

Fitch Ratings (2016a), 'Fitch downgrades Brazil to "BB"; outlook negative', *FitchRatings.com*, accessed 5 January 2017 at https://www.fitchratings.com/site/pr/1004065.

Fitch Ratings (2016b), 'Fitch reviews five state-owned Brazilian banks' ratings', *FitchRatings.com*, accessed 14 November 2016 at https://www.fitchratings.com/site/pr/1008129.

Fitch Ratings (2016c), 'Fitch affirms Cassa Depositi e Prestiti at "BBB+"; outlook stable', *FitchRatings.com*, accessed 14 November 2016 at https://www.fitchratings.com/site/pr/1004462.

Freshwater Action Network (FAN) (2007), *The African Development Bank and the Water and Sanitation Sector*, accessed 14 November 2016 at http://www.freshwateraction.net/sites/freshwateraction.net/files/The%20African%20Development%20Bank.pdf.

Fry, M. (1995), *Money, Interest, and Banking in Economic Development*, Baltimore, MD: Johns Hopkins University Press.

Hatch, M.J. (1997), *Organization Theory. Modern Symbolic and Postmodern Perspectives*, New York: Oxford University Press Inc.

Herr, H. and J. Priewe (2005), *The Macroeconomics of Development and Poverty Reduction: Strategies Beyond the Washington Consensus*, Baden-Baden: Nomos.

IBON International (2009), *Primer on ODA and Development Effectiveness: Can Aid be a Key Contribution to Genuine Development?*, accessed 6 July 2017 at www.dochas.ie/sites/default/files/Primer_on_oda_and_development_effectiveness.pdf.

International Finance Corporation (n.d.), 'Determining "the demonstration effects" of IFC's operations: A study', accessed 1 November 2016 at https://www.ifc.org/wps/wcm/connect/22b43a004fb4c9caa6c3ee0098cb14b9/IFC_EvaluationReport_DemonstrationEffects.pdf?MOD=AJPERES.

Kamps, J. and L. Polos (1999), 'Reducing uncertainty: A formal theory of organizations in action', *American Journal of Sociology*, **104**(6), 1774–810.

Kreditanstalt für Wiederaufbau (KfW) (1948), *Law Concerning Kreditanstalt für Wiederaufbau (1948)*, accessed 14 November 2016 at https://www.kfw.de/Download-Center/KfW-Gesetz-und-Satzung-sowie-Geschäftsordnungen/Law-concerning-KfW-and-KfW-By-laws/KfW_Gesetz_E.pdf.

Kreditanstalt für Wiederaufbau (KfW) (2007), *Management Report and Financial Statements of KfW 2007*, accessed 5 December 2016 at https://www.kfw.de/Download-Center/Finanzpublikationen/Financial-publications-PDFs/3_Finanzberichte-E/Jahresabschluss_und_Lagebericht_2007_EN.pdf.

Kreditanstalt für Wiederaufbau (KfW) (2014), *Management Report and Financial Statements 2014*, accessed 5 December 2016 at https://www.kfw.de/PDF/Download-Center/Finanzpublikationen/PDF-Dokumente-Berichte-etc./2_Jahresberichte/2014_Jahresabschluss-und-Lagebericht_DE-EN-2.pdf.

Kreditanstalt für Wiederaufbau (KfW) (n.d.), 'Responsible funding', accessed 14 November 2016 at https://www.kfw.de/KfW-Group/About-KfW/Arbeitsweise/Verantwortungsvolle-Refinanzierung/.

La Porta, R., F. Lopez-de-Silanez and A. Shleifer (2002), 'Government ownership of banks', *The Journal of Finance*, **57**(1), 265–301.

Lieberherr, E. (2016), 'Trade-offs and synergies: Horizontalization and legitimacy in the Swiss wastewater sector', *Public Management Review*, **18**(3), 456–78.

Maffioli, A. and C.M. Rodriguez (2013), 'The effectiveness of public development banks: Designing good impact evaluations', in F. de Olloqui (ed.), *Public*

Development Banks: Toward a New Paradigm?, Washington, DC: Inter-American Development Bank, pp. 39–66.

Mathur, K.B.L. (2002), 'Public sector banks in India: Should they be privatized?', *Economic and Political Weekly*, **37**(23), 2245–56.

Micco, A. and U. Panizza (2006), 'Bank ownership and lending behavior', *Economic Letters*, **93**(2), 248–54.

Moody's (2016), 'Black Sea Trade and Development Bank – A2 stable. Annual credit analysis', accessed 20 November 2016 at http://www.bstdb.org/investor-relations/credit-ratings/BSTDB_%20Moodys_Annual_Credit_Analysis_2016_11_16.pdf.

Nutt, C.P. (2010), 'An empirical test of Thompson's model of strategic choice', *International Journal of Business*, **15**(2), 159–82.

Rudolph, P.H. (2009), 'State financial institutions: Mandates, governance, and beyond', *Working Paper No. 5141*, World Bank, November.

Schmidt, V. (2010), 'Democracy and legitimacy in the European Union revisited: Input, output, and throughput', *Working Paper No. 21*, KFG, The Transformative Power of Europe, November.

Schmit, M., L. Gheeraert, T. Denuit and C. Warny (eds) (2011), *Public Financial Institutions in Europe*, Brussels: European Association of Public Banks.

Schroeder, M., P. Ekins and A. Power et al. (2011), 'The KfW experience in the reduction of energy use in and CO_2 emissions from buildings: Operation, impacts, and lessons for the UK', *UCL Energy Institute*, accessed 12 November 2016 at http://sticerd.lse.ac.uk/dps/case/cp/KfWFullReport.pdf.

Scott, H.D. (2007), 'Strengthening the governance and performance of state-owned financial institutions', *Working Paper No. 4321*, World Bank, August.

Smallridge, D. and F. de Olloqui (2011), 'A health diagnostic tool for public development banks', *Technical Notes IDB-TN-225*, Inter-American Development Bank, January.

Sriram, M.S. (2003), 'Commercialization of microfinance in India: A discussion of the emperor's apparel', *Economic and Political Weekly*, **45**(24), 65–73.

Standard and Poor's (2013), KfW, *Research*, accessed 14 November 2016 at https://www.kfw.de/PDF/Investor-Relations/Pdf-Dokumente-Investor-Relations/SP-Rating-Report-19-December-2013.pdf.

Standard and Poor's (2014), 'African Development Bank', *RatingsDirect*, accessed 20 November 2016 at http://www.afdb.org/fileadmin/uploads/afdb/Documents/Financial-Information/Standard_Poor_s_Rating_2014.pdf.

Standard and Poor's (2015), 'General criteria: Rating government-related entities: Methodology and assumptions', *RatingsDirect*, accessed 11 November 2016 at http://www.maalot.co.il/publications/GMT20150329155054.pdf.

Stiglitz, E.J. (1996), 'Some lessons from the East Asian Miracle', *The World Bank Research Observer*, **11**(2), 151–77.

Stiglitz, E.J. and M. Uy (1996), 'Financial markets, public policy, and the East Asian Miracle', *The World Bank Research Observer*, **11**(2), 249–76.

Stiglitz, E.J. and A. Weiss (1981), 'Credit rationing in markets with imperfect information', *The American Economic Review*, **71**(3), 393–410.

Thompson, D.J. (1967), *Organizations in Action: Social Science Bases of Administrative Theory*, New York: McGraw-Hill, Inc.

Thorne, J. and C. du Toit (2009), 'A macro-framework for successful development banks', *Development Southern Africa*, **26**(5), 677–94.

Tosi, L.H. (2009), *Theories of Organization*, Los Angeles, CA: Sage Publications.

UN (2015), 'The "raison d'etre" of state-owned development banks and recommendations for successful development banking', accessed 11 November 2016 at http://www.un.org/esa/ffd/ffd3/wp-content/uploads/sites/2/2015/07/Rais on-detre-of-DBs-nonpaper-Addis.pdf.

UN (n.d.), 'Goal 9: Build resilient infrastructure, promote sustainable industrialization and foster innovation', accessed 11 November 2016 at http://www.un.org/sustainabledevelopment/infrastructure-industrialization/.

Wan, M. (1995–96), 'Japan and the Asian Development Bank', *Pacific Affairs*, **68**(4), 509–28.

Ziai, A. (2014), 'Justice, not development: Sen and the hegemonic framework for ameliorating global inequality', *Global Justice: Theory Practice Rhetoric*, **7**, 28–38.

PART IV

Political attacks on public banks in Europe

9. Savings banks and *Landesbanken* in the German political economy: The long struggle between private and public banks

Daniel Seikel*

Public banks represent an important pillar of the German model of capitalism (Deeg, 1999). They play a central role in credit provision for small and medium-sized enterprises. From the point of view of competition policy, they constitute counterweight to the market power of private banks and ensure intensive competition in the German banking sector. Moreover, in the past they served as instruments for the federal states' (*Bundesländer*) regional economic and structural policies.

The politically promoted development of public banks towards full-fledged commercial banks that directly compete with private banks is the origin of the conflict between the public and the private economy in the German banking system. Ever since, political power networks have shielded regional state banks (*Landesbanken*) and savings banks from domestic political attacks of private banks. Attempts of private banks to challenge the privileges of public banks on a national level have constantly remained in vain. Only when the private banks made recourse to the European level, did they succeed in circumventing previously insurmountable political resistance and effecting a liberalization of the public banking sector using the cushion of European law. For many *Landesbanken* this was a devastating blow.

In this chapter I reconstruct the conflict between private and public banks from a historical perspective. The analysis rests on the theoretical approach of actor-centred institutionalism (Hix and Goetz, 2000; Knill

* This chapter is based on my dissertation, which was written at the Max-Planck Institute for the Study of Societies, Cologne, published in 2013 by Campus-Verlag ('Der Kampf um öffentlich-rechtliche Banken. Wie die Europäische Kommission Liberalisierung durchsetzt [The fight for public banks. How the European Commission enforces liberalization]). I thank Norma Tiedemann for the translation of the German manuscript.

and Lehmkuhl, 1999; Scharpf, 1997), with special attention given to the effects of the European integration process on societal relations of power at a national level.

In the following, I firstly discuss how the European integration process has changed the opportunity structures for private actors. Subsequently, I describe the main features of the German public banking sector and elaborate its functions for the German model of capitalism. The third section presents from a historical perspective the conflict between private and public banks and reconstructs how public banks integrated into prevalent regulatory conceptions about the organization of the state and the market. In the fourth section I illustrate the final confrontation between private and public banks, which eventuated in the demise of, amongst others, the WestLB, the former flagship of the German *Landesbanken*.

CHANGING SOCIAL RELATIONS OF POWER: THE EU AS A NEW OPPORTUNITY STRUCTURE FOR PRIVATE ACTORS

As the fourth section below will show, the European integration process has decisively shifted the power relations between public credit institutions and their networks on one hand, and private banks on the other. What are the institutional elements that improved the position of the liberalization advocates?

The institutional architecture of the European multilevel system generates a structural imbalance between liberalization and social regulation in favour of market-creating measures (see on this, at length, Scharpf, 1999), strengthening actors interested in liberalization. The market liberal bias is additionally enhanced by the strategic selectivity of European institutions. As neo-Marxist state theory has determined, institutions structure the access to political procedures and decision-making processes of different societal groups in an asymmetrical manner (Jessop, 1990, p. 100). This also holds true for European entities and procedures (Ziltener, 2000, p. 81). The European integration process influences the possibilities of actors to pursue their interests differently (Jessop, 1990, p. 117). According to Ziltener (2000, p. 82) the political system of the EU primarily privileges transnationally organized interest groups and enterprises. Stone, Sweet and Sandholtz (1998), for instance, ascribe the neoliberal bias of the internal market project to the lobbying activities, complaints and lawsuits of economic actors who conduct transactions across borders and thus expect advantages from European regulations. The European multilevel system thus particularly favours mobile factors (capital, enterprises) (Scharpf,

2010, pp. 221–2). As Smith (2001b, pp. 7–8) states in his study on the regional states bank case, the change of societal power relations due to European integration affects the position of public services:

> This political mobility of capital derives from the ability of private sector actors to move outside regional or national political arenas in order to combat government practices that privilege public enterprises or reserve entire sectors for public services and thereby exclude private competitors . . . This is a crucial development because however privileged the position of business in national political economies, that privilege stops when it encounters the autonomous preferences of the state. Political mobility gives business added leverage to challenge government practices that protect public sector economic activities at the expense of private sector competitors.

Hix and Goetz (2000) as well as Knill and Lehmkuhl (1999) have specified how the connection between institutional asymmetry and the shift of societal relations of power can initiate institutional rearrangements of national systems. The creation of a superordinate political and institutional arena generates new opportunities for actors to circumvent national-level restrictions. Hence, the European level represents a new opportunity structure. First, the EU offers an exit option – when, for example, governments are impeded in pursuing their goals on a national level by public opinion, veto players or institutional mechanisms, the supranational level offers them the possibility to bypass such resistance and eventually, through political initiatives at the European level, also to enforce their political aims domestically. Second, actors who have been defeated in disputes in the domestic arena and/or are excluded from political processes can appeal to the European Court of Justice or bring in the European Commission to halt practices breaching European law (veto option) (Hix and Goetz, 2000, pp. 13–14). These options change the rules of the political process within nation states. The internal market regime legally restricts the scope of political options; other political and institutional developments, on the other hand, are strengthened (Hix and Goetz, 2000, p. 12). Arrangements that are not compatible with the market-liberal European internal market rules have to be aligned. In the alignment process of national institutional settings governments come under pressure to take into account the changing power relations. This opens up 'windows of opportunity' for some actors to either feed-in their domestic policy interests again in the national policy arena or, alternatively, to pursue them via the cushion of the European level. As a consequence, the probability increases that actors who would benefit from the changes override existing institutionalized power relations (Knill and Lehmkuhl, 1999, p. 1).

This can also be observed in the liberalization of public banks in

Germany. The European integration process enabled German private banks to pursue and enforce their interests via the European level. European competition law offered a leverage to break up previously insurmountable domestic oppositions and therewith to finally force through own, previously blocked, interests after decades of political struggle. By resorting to European law, private banks were able to legally impose beforehand domestically blocked economic liberalization.

PUBLIC BANKS AND THE GERMAN MODEL OF CAPITALISM

The degree of governmental influence on the banking sector determines the state's 'depth of reach-through' in the economy. In the political economy of the Federal Republic, control over the banking sector is a specifically important resource. Germany is considered to be the typical example of a bank-based economic system (Zysman, 1983). The banking system constitutes the 'commanding heights' of the German model of capitalism. Public banks therein have a special significance for the state. They enable the state to pursue market-correcting policies such as (re-)distributive and regulatory policies and to directly influence economic development. Furthermore, by fostering public credit institutions the state can hedge the power of a few market-dominating private major banks. The latter in particular has always been of considerable importance in the German case due to the dominant position of private banks in the financial system (Zysman, 1983, p. 260; see the next section). Few other capitalist national economies have such a large public banking sector as Germany; nowhere else is the competition between private and public banks so pronounced. In Europe, Germany, next to Finland, has the biggest share of state-controlled credit institutions in the banking sector (Bluhm and Martens, 2009, p. 594).

The German banking system is subdivided into three groups: private banks, cooperative banks and public banks (Deeg, 1999, p. 19). The different bank institutions are in so-called group competition: banks of one group are legally shielded against takeovers of banks from other groups and compete as the entire banking group with the other groups. Public banks are in competition with private banks in all segments of the banking business (Deeg, 2001).

The public pillar consists primarily of savings banks and *Landesbanken*. Savings banks are usually in the possession of municipalities. In the case of most *Landesbanken*, the federal states are or have been the main owners: WestLB (North Rhine-Westphalia), BayernLB (Bavaria), LBBW

(Baden-Wuerttemberg), HSH Nordbank (Hamburg, Schleswig-Holstein), Helaba (Hessen, Thuringia), NordLB (Lower Saxony, Saxony-Anhalt), SachsenLB (Saxony), Bremer Landesbank (Bremen), LBB[1] (Berlin), LRP[2] (Rhineland-Palatinate) and SaarLB (Saarland). The remaining shares are usually held by the regional savings banks associations, as well as by other *Landesbanken*. Savings banks are public-law institutions as was the case with the *Landesbanken* prior to the liberalization of the public banking sector.

Moreover, savings banks are part of communal public services. They fulfil prescribed public tasks and are legally committed to benefit the public (Dieckmann, 1981, p. 16). This means that the generation of profits – although aimed for – is not a primary goal. Profits are normally ploughed back – that is, turned into own capital or channelled into non-profit projects (Eichhorn, 1992, p. 16). Part of the public mandate is credit supply for municipalities, the population and small and medium-sized enterprises, the support of municipal or the state's regional and structural policy, as well as the promotion of competition in the banking sector (Deutscher Sparkassen- und Giroverband, 2001). For that purpose, public banks, prior to the liberalization described below, were protected by two public liability guarantees: the guarantor liability (Gewährträgerhaftung) made sure that the guarantor would be liable for its credit institutions without limits on the liability amount; the institutional liability (Anstaltslast) obliged the guarantors to ensure the uninterrupted economic existence of the institution (Schorner, 2008, p. 95; Seubert, 2005, pp. 124–5). *Landesbanken* have therefore been rated with the same grades as the federal states, usually with an AAA or AA+ (no or minor default risk) rating. Thus, they were able to refinance themselves on the capital markets at very favourable interest rates (Grossman, 2006, p. 337; Smith, 2001a, p. 529).

Public banks play an important role in the funding of small and medium-sized enterprises, which are of central importance for the German model of capitalism (Berghoff, 2006; Bluhm and Martens, 2009). As Deeg (1999) shows, the relatively small savings banks compared to the 'big banks' (Deutsche Bank, Commerzbank, Dresdner Bank) have always been much more important for the SME-based German model than has been suggested by advocates of the 'financial capitalism' thesis such as Hilferding (1910 [1974]), the thesis of 'organized capitalism' such as Shonfield (1965 [1980]) or the 'Deutschland AG' thesis such as Beyer (2003). The savings bank sector contributes the largest share for the funding of German

---

[1] Sold in 2007 to the German Savings Banks Association (Deutscher Sparkassen- und Giroverband, DSGV).

[2] Sold in 1992 to the WestLB and merged in 2005 with the LBBW.

companies compared to the other banking groups. Public credit institutions have specialized in the long-term funding of medium-sized businesses (Deeg, 1999, pp. 113–14). The economic importance of medium-sized companies in Germany is exceptionally high. The so-called *Mittelstand* (SMEs)[3] comprises more than 99 per cent of all companies, transacts 44 per cent of all gross investments, employs two-thirds of all employees, generates almost half of the GDP and furthermore trains more than 80 per cent of all apprentices. Moreover, medium-sized firms contribute a considerable part to the export strength of the German economy. Due to their specialization they manufacture internationally competitive products and take a leading position in numerous technological niche sectors (Berghoff, 2006, p. 268). Small and medium-sized companies thus constitute the backbone of the German model of so-called 'diversified quality production' (DQP) (Streeck, 1991). Since for small and medium-sized enterprises a capital market funding is rarely an option, public banks occupy a key position in the credit supply of the *Mittelstand*. Public credit institutions hence represent an integral component of the DQP model: companies that produce customized, highly specialized technology goods are dependent on stable, long-term financial relations. Savings banks and *Landesbanken* in particular often maintain such permanent relationships to medium-sized enterprises. These relationships allow for long-term strategies, investments in research, development and skills. Thus, public credit institutions constitute a central element of the German model of capitalism.

THE CONFLICT BETWEEN PRIVATE BANKS AND PUBLIC BANKS AGAINST THE BACKGROUND OF REGULATORY CONCEPTIONS ABOUT THE ORGANIZATION OF STATE AND MARKET

The conflicts between private and public banks are a permanent side-effect of the politically promoted development of public banks. Under the protection of political actors, public banks have developed into full-fledged commercial banks, standing in competition to private banks. At no point were private banks able to weaken domestically the strong position of public banks.[4] The following sections illustrate that the special status of public banks inter-alia rested on regulatory functions that representatives

---

[3] This comprises enterprises with fewer than 500 employees and less than 50 billion euros annual turnover (Berghoff, 2006, p. 269).

[4] For a comprehensive depiction of the political struggles between both banking groups in the twentieth century see Seikel (2013, Chapter 5.1).

of ordoliberalism[5] as well as representatives of Keynesianism ascribed to public banks.

Public Banks in the Postwar Era: Between Financial Capital and Ordoliberalism

Up until World War II, the major private banks had coordinated and regulated the competition between corporations in the form of cartels (Beyer, 2003, p. 125). The role of monopolies and cartels in the takeover of state power by the National Socialists was a central aspect in the postwar critique towards concentration of power in the economy. Governmental interventions to regulate market power – and thus also the public banks as elements of competition policy – have been justified by reference to the superior objective of preventing the renewed emergence of cartels and economic power concentration. In order to break the dominance of the major banks, competition in the banking sector has been promoted politically after 1945 (Deeg, 1999, pp. 32–3). The philosophy of the 'Freiburg School' was enormously influential in this, not least since it constituted in the 1950s the basis for the concept of the 'social market economy' (Story and Walter, 1997, p. 163). Minister for economic affairs Ludwig Erhard (Christian Democratic Union of Germany – CDU) perceived medium-sized enterprises to be the central pillars of the economy. Erhard feared that the economic power of major companies could hamper the functioning of the markets (Berghoff, 2006, p. 281). The savings banks occupied in two respects an important position in the concept of the social market economy: as a counterbalance to private banks and as credit suppliers for the *Mittelstand*. The idea to intensify competition with the use of state banks corresponded with ordoliberal philosophy. The role of German cartels and monopolies in the two world wars had increased the consciousness of ordoliberal thinkers towards the negative consequences of economic concentration of power. From the perspective of ordoliberal thinkers the expansion of cartels, particularly in heavy industries, had led to the emergence of private power entities that had gained massive political weight (Eucken, 1952, p. 170–72). Major banks were involved in the funding and organization of these cartels (Beyer, 2003, p. 125). In the German Third Reich, private and state power eventually merged (Eucken, 1952, p. 173). For the representatives of ordoliberalism, public banks presented a possibility to intervene correctively in the economic process without having to resort to the means of nationalization or splitting up of banks.

---

[5] The German variant of social liberalism, which emphasizes the need for the state to ensure that the free market produces results close to its theoretical potential.

The left took a similar position. In the interwar period of the Weimar Republic, social democracy and trade unions had welcomed the economic power concentration of monopolies and cartels since they interpreted these conditions as being a step in the historic transition towards socialism. Of particular influence in this regard have been the works of Hilferding and Sombart. But after World War II, a reinterpretation of the assessment of corporate power concentration took place within the left (Höpner, 2004). The highly concentrated economy had not led to socialism but straightforwardly into fascism (cf. Höpner, 2004, p. 23). With this lesson learned, social democratic forces in the postwar era developed 'a positive relation to the market as the lesser evil compared to financial capital' (Höpner, 2004, p. 24, own translation). The divestiture of monopolies and anti-cartel policies found their ways into the political programmes of social democracy and trade unions (Höpner, 2004, p. 22).

The idea to counteract the monopolization of finance via competition from public credit institutions was therefore popular amongst liberals as well as amongst the left. Based on their traumatic historic experiences, both saw a need to counter what they perceived as natural tendencies towards monopolies. While liberals opposed nationalization, the left called for the collectivization of banks. Establishing public credit institutions, however, was reconcilable with both positions.

Public Banks during Keynesianism

The second half of the twentieth century was marked by an intensification of the competition between private and public banks. This was mainly due to the expansion of *Landesbanken*. The WestLB was deliberately established as a competitor for Deutsche Bank. Furthermore, *Landesbanken* became important instruments of the federal states' industrial policies. In the context of the rise of Keynesianism, *Landesbanken* and savings banks received an additional source of legitimization. The competition in the banking sector was now also perceived to be decisive for the effectiveness of demand side–oriented growth impulses. This phase represents the golden age of *Landesbanken* as political banks.

Since the end of the 1950s, significant changes occurred in the German banking system. The big private banks had again ascended to their former economic as well as political strength. They had been split up after the war into regional banks. By 1957, after the repeal of the Big Bank Law (*Grossbankengesetz*), these regional successor institutions merged to form Deutsche Bank, Commerzbank and Dresdner Bank (Lütz, 2000, p. 125). In addition, the domestic competition between domestic banking groups had changed (Deeg, 1999, p. 4). Due to the strong growth of savings accounts in the 1960s, the savings banks that had been dominating this segment of the banking business generated high revenues (Deeg, 1999, p. 50). The rise in saving deposits enabled banks to refinance and expand their lending activities at relatively attractive terms.

The special position of public banks was, as before, justified with the regulatory necessity to hedge against the potential danger of a one-sided market domination of private banks through the promotion of public banks (Dieckmann, 1981, p. 24). With the grand coalition in government in 1966, the economic policy orientation of Germany changed to a Keynesian-style anticyclical macroeconomic policy (Deeg, 1999, pp. 49–50). The new economics minister Karl Schiller (SPD) understood savings banks and regional state banks as *political* banks (cf. Schiller, 1969). For the federal government, public banks became instruments for the pursuit of macroeconomic goals. Next to the intensification of competition, *Landesbanken* were supposed to intensify their engagement in the equity funding of corporations. Moreover, *Landesbanken* ought to break up the cartel-like structures in some business branches such as the DM-denominated bonds in foreign markets (Schiller, 1969, pp. 141–3). One of Schiller's central projects was the liberalization of the debit and credit interest rates.[6] Schiller identified the lack of competition between banks as the reason for the limited impact of key rate reductions by the German central bank. The commercial banks did not pass on these reductions to their customers. Interest rate increases, on the other hand, were immediately implemented (Bundesministerium der Finanzen, 1979). The complete deregulation of interest rates was supposed to solve this problem (Dieckmann, 1981, p. 172) and a free price competition between the banks was thought to lead to the reduction of interest rates for loans and savings. Therefore, investment incentives were to be created, which were expected to trigger a cyclical upturn (Deeg, 1999, pp. 49–50; Dieckmann, 1981, p. 174). Fixed interest rates were abandoned in 1967. Also, the entrance of WestLB into the private banks' emission cartels of DM bonds can be understood in this context. In particular, the monopoly position of the Deutsche Bank in World Bank bonds placements was a particularly important target since – due to the World Bank's market position – the interest rate of these bonds virtually equalled a private key interest rate. The WestLB was supposed to participate in the issuing of World Bank bonds and thereby underbid the interest rate of the Deutsche Bank. And indeed, several times during the

---

[6] Since 1912, interest rates have been cartelized between the banking groups. The interest cartel was publicly sanctioned in 1932. Since 1961, interest rates were directly determined by the state (Dieckmann, 1981, pp. 171–3).

1970s, a reduction of the credit interest rate by as much as 0.75 percentage points was reached.[7]

The 1970s were also the heyday of the debate about the power of banks. The magazine *Der Spiegel*, for instance, accused the major private banks of controlling all key industries. Bankers were said to increasingly gain political influence. The entire economy would have become a 'secret holding which divides and rules via finely knitted nets of personal relationships' according to *Der Spiegel* (own translation). Even from the ranks of the CDU, critical voices were to be heard: the banks would be 'omnipotent' and more influential than the minister for economic affairs.[8] The power of banks was primarily an issue within the West German left. In the Social Democratic Party (SPD) and the trade unions, claims demanding nationalization of the banking system became prominent (Story and Walter, 1997, p. 292). This was particularly expressed in the debate about 'state-monopolistic capitalism'. Fascism was interpreted as a consequence of 'the imperialist aspirations to global power of German monopoly capital' (Czichon, 1970, pp. 200–201, own translation). At the centre of critique was the Deutsche Bank,[9] which was presented as the financial centre of the 'most powerful and most influential monopoly group' and as the 'biggest power concentration of West Germany' (ibid., own translation). In the eyes of some leftist critics, the domination of 'financial capital' would declassify 'the Bundestag virtually to a legislative body of impotence' (Czichon, 1970, p. 202, own translation).

This time marks the birth of *Landesbanken*. From 1969 on, several regional giro centres (central banks for the savings banks) merged to the *Landesbanken* (e.g., in 1969 Westdeutsche Landesbank, in 1970 Norddeutsche Landesbank, in 1972 Bayerische Landesbank). By then, the savings banks required more effective banks as cooperation partners to satisfy the medium-sized enterprises' increasing financial needs. Money lending to companies offered the new *Landesbanken* a profitable avenue in which to invest the savings banks' surplus liquidity. For the federal states the larger and financially more potent *Landesbanken* were more interesting for the pursuit of economic policy objectives (Deeg, 1999, pp. 51–2). The federal states were able to undertake structural assistance programmes via their own institutions; these procedures were less time consuming and less bureaucratic than the transactions via the ministerial bureaucracy.

---

[7]   Interview, Federal Ministry of Economy.

[8]   *Der Spiegel* (1971), 'Die Omnipotenten', [The omnipotent], 18 January.

[9]   'Quietly, consequently, only controlled by itself – this is how the bank, founded in 1870, established a network of money, spirit and mindset against which nothing works anymore in Germany', *Der Spiegel* (1985), 'Das Riesen-Monopoly der Deutschen Bank' [The giant monopoly of Deutsche Bank], 11 February (own translation).

Since timing is decisive for anticyclical measures for economic stimulation, the problematic time lags with which investment programmes used to be implemented could thus be reduced.[10] Many considered the *Landesbanken* to be the only actors who were able to limit the power of the major banks.[11]

The WestLB, measured in terms of total assets, was the biggest West German bank (Deeg, 1999, p. 52). In the 1970s, the WestLB evolved into the most important instrument of the federal state government's economic and industrial policy. As the flagship of the *Landesbanken*, the WestLB was regarded as a prime model for the pursuit of industrial policies by federal state governments carried out via *Landesbanken* (Deeg, 1999, p. 134). *Landesbanken* made use of the liquidity surpluses from private saving deposits of the savings banks to aggressively expand their own market share (Deeg, 1999, p. 22). In this way the WestLB conquered new branches of business: industrial financing, industrial holdings and international business (Reimann, 1992, p. 201). For the WestLB, industrial finance had a special significance, since North Rhine-Westphalia was an industrial site. Therefore, the regional government was interested in sufficient credit provision for its companies (Poullain, 1979, p. 84). The WestLB played a leading part in mastering the structural transformation of the Ruhr area. Through the purchase of company shares on a large scale by the WestLB, the federal state secured itself direct influence on entire economic sectors, primarily the coal, steel and energy industries (Deeg, 1999, p. 127). Thereby, the interests of the federal state government in strategic decisions of large companies were supposed to be protected. Between 1969 and 1975 the WestLB increased the value of its corporate shares from DM15 million to DM791 million. Thus, the WestLB was competing with the major banks also for influence on large industrial companies. The cartel-like practices of the three major banks in syndicated businesses were broken up (Deeg, 1999, pp. 135–40).

Due to the internationalization of medium-sized enterprises in the 1970s and 1980s the importance of savings banks for foreign business also increased. The growing world trade activities of German companies required that public banks would also engage in the international credit business (Poullain, 1979, pp. 278–9). Therefore, the WestLB and other *Landesbanken* purchased shares of foreign banks and built up a worldwide network of branch offices that encompassed the globally most important financial and trading sites (Reimann, 1992, p. 201). In addition, *Landesbanken* began to get involved on the euromarkets on a large scale.

---

[10] Interview, Savings Banks and Giro Association of the Rhineland (Rheinischer Sparkassen- und Giroverband, RSGV).

[11] *Der Spiegel* (1971), 'Die Omnipotenten' [The omnipotent], 18 January.

Landesbanken established subsidiary companies in Luxembourg, which used to be the most important off-shore place for DM transactions in the 1970s (Mura, 1994, p. 261). *Landesbanken* affiliates became the most important banking group at the Luxembourg financial centre and were leading business with DM loans (Mura, 1994, pp. 262–3).[12] In 1976, the WestLB conducted 25 per cent of all international transactions in Germany. The *Landesbanken* had eventually established themselves in the ranks of the large internationally active banks (Deeg, 1999, p. 53).

Why did the initially regionally oriented public banks develop into players on international financial markets? The credit substitute business presented one of the few remaining business branches in which savings banks were not involved. The international financial market business was, moreover, more profitable than the classic banking business, which was limited to the granting of credits and saving deposits. Due to the liability guarantees, *Landesbanken* were able to raise capital under favourable conditions on international capital markets. Therefore, they could compete domestically with private banks for SME clients. Eventually, the expansion of foreign business enabled *Landesbanken* to develop a functioning business model.[13] This led to a situation in which *Landesbanken* – torn between regional orientation on the one hand and the temptations of international investment banking on the other – continuously extended their international financial and credit business.

In the mid-1970s, private banks began to divest their holdings in companies and increasingly targeted *Mittelstand* business, which was dominated by public and cooperative banks. The reason for this reorientation was the decrease of large corporations' credit demand since bigger enterprises increasingly financed their investments through own capital reserves or engaged in capital market activities on their own. Hence, the share of bank credits in the entire capital of all German stock corporations decreased from 16.9 per cent in 1974 to 6.6 per cent in 1984. This, however, did not result in a general departure from the bank-based model of organized capitalism, since the importance of banks for the funding of small and medium-sized enterprises even increased and the extension of credits to mid-sized corporations became more important for banks (Deeg, 1999, pp. 4–5, 17–19, 57).

After this, the tensions between the banking groups increased further. The division of labour between the banking groups was eroding. Each banking group tried to gain a foothold in all financial businesses (Deeg, 1999, pp. 19–20). The federal states and the central state continued to

---

12   Interview, Helaba.
13   Interview, Helaba.

defend the market orientation of public banks, not least since they were dependent on the help of effective public banks in order to overcome the growing structural economic problems. While other banks reduced their industrial holdings, the WestLB raised its industrial portfolio systematically. In the 1980s, the value of shares rose to DM3.2 billion, thereby reaching a level that was comparable to the Commerzbank and Dresdner Bank. In addition, the WestLB further enlarged its international business and thus increasingly competed with other European banks (Deeg, 1999, pp. 56–7, 140–2; Smith, 2001b, p. 15). This development eventually resulted in a situation in which the *Landesbanken* increasingly departed from their original public mission; the combination of political banks and international investment banks would serve private banks and the European Commission as the gateway for their decisive assault on the *Landesbanken*.

EUROPEANIZATION, LIBERALIZATION AND FINANCIALIZATION: THE END OF THE *LANDESBANKEN*

Up until the 1990s, European law was irrelevant to the confrontations between private and public banks; it used to be a domestic conflict. Until the mid-1980s the coexistence of different varieties of capitalism – and also different mixing ratios of the public and the private economy – was not questioned by the European integration process (Höpner and Schäfer, 2010, p. 349). The 'peaceful' coexistence came to an end when the internal market project was launched. It exerted a strong adjustment pressure upon the various national forms of organizing the 'mixed economy'. The public service sectors became subject to a profound liberalization process (Bieling and Deckwirth, 2008). Against this background, the final dispute over the liberalization of the German public banking sector took place. As described in the following, private banks were able to Europeanize and in the end to win their domestic conflict with the public banks by bringing in the European Commission.

The Private Banks' Decisive Strategy: Playing at the European Level

Landesbanken, next to the liability guarantees, had another competitive advantage over private banks: they repeatedly received fresh capital from the federal states, which was refunded under terms that were considerably below the market-based capital costs. This enabled the *Landesbanken* to expand their business volume and take further market shares from private financial institutions.[14] In 1993, the Federal Association of German Banks (Bundesverband deutscher Banken, BdB) filed a complaint with the European Commission about the transfer of the public *Wohnungsbauförderanstalt* (home-building funding agency) (Wfa) of North Rhine-Westphalia to the WestLB (Grossman, 2006, p. 335; Smith, 2001a, p. 529). Also, other federal states had transferred their *Wohnungsbauförderanstalten* to *Landesbanken*. The Commission accepted the case with great interest since it sensed an opportunity to extend European competition law to national banking sectors. In the course of inquiring about the Wfa transfer, the liability guarantees attracted the Commission's attention as state aids, which potentially distorts competition. This was threatening for the *Landesbanken*: without guarantees their ratings were in danger of being downgraded. The business model of the *Landesbanken* would lose its foundations.[15]

The federal government tried by all means to defend the public credit institutions. During the European Council meeting in Amsterdam (1997) the German government attempted to introduce a safeguard clause into the Amsterdam Treaty, which was supposed to repel the Commission's attack on the German public banks,[16] but the German government did not succeed in winning the approval of the other member states. At the end, the federal government achieved only the inclusion of a general, legally non-binding declaration (Grossman, 2006, p. 339) that stated that, although the organization of the public banking sector would remain within the competence of the member states, this 'may not adversely affect the conditions of competition to an extent beyond that required in order to perform these particular tasks' (Treaty of Amsterdam, Declaration on Public Credit Institutions in Germany).

In October 1997, the Commission launched a proceeding concerning the Wfa transfer. In July 1999, the Commission determined the transfer as illegal state aid that had to be refunded (European Commission, 2000). Encouraged by this success, the European Banking Federation lodged a complaint with the Commission in December 1999 against the institutional and the guarantor liabilities (Grossman, 2006, p. 326; Smith, 2001a, p. 525), which was initiated by the BdB.[17] Thereby, the savings banks were also formally and directly targeted.

---

[14] Interviews, European Commission and Commerzbank.

[15] The solvency of the regional state banks without state liability was even graded below 'investment grade' (Sinn, 1997, p. 43): such investments are considered to be speculative with (a high) default probability (junk bonds).

[16] Interviews, RSGV, European Commission, WestLB, Landesbank Schleswig-Holstein (LSH), Legal Service of the Commission, BdB, Federal Ministry of Finance.

[17] Interviews, DSGV, European Commission and BdB.

In the conflict over institutional liability, the Commission was able to exert considerable pressure.[18] The economic advantage of the guarantees was estimated at 1 billion euros per year since the coming into force of the Treaty of Rome (Moser et al., 2002). Since a potential recompense of the aid including interest had to be immediately effective, this would have led to a bankruptcy of the institutions and would have also posed enormous financial problems for the liable owners.[19]

In March 2000, the Commission offered to differentiate between the transnationally active *Landesbanken* and the almost exclusively regionally active savings banks (Smith, 2001b, pp. 26, 36).[20] The Commission declared that the guarantees would be unproblematic when trade between member states were not impaired. This was a signal that the savings banks, which were not transnationally active, could be kept out of the conflict (Smith, 2001, pp. 20–21). This was the wedge that was driven between the regional state banks and the savings banks.

Up until this point, the German position had remained in fundamental opposition and had contested the competence of the Commission to intervene in national banking sectors,[21] but under increasing pressure from Brussels, the public bank camp got into difficulties. Due to the Commission's success in the Wfa proceeding and the failure of the Amsterdam attempt, the savings banks began to re-evaluate the situation. Both events had demonstrated the assertiveness of the Commission.[22] Compared to the *Landesbanken*, the guarantees were of little economic interest for the savings banks. The guarantees did indeed also apply to the savings banks, but with the exception of a few large savings banks these hardly benefitted from the guarantees since they refinanced themselves with account deposits and not via the capital market. The savings banks tried to find a negotiated solution that would maintain their legal form as public-law institution. In return, the savings banks were willing to give up the guarantees – in other words, to sacrifice the *Landesbanken*. At the end of 2000, the WestLB, too, realized that the guarantees could not be defended and that a Commission decision would be stricter than a possible compromise. In November 2000, the WestLB split into the WestLB AG commercial bank and the NRW. BANK development bank. The guarantees were supposed to remain in

---

[18] For an analysis of the Commission's strategies with which it overcame the opposition of the German side, see in detail Seikel (2013, p. 198–206) as well as Seikel (2014, pp. 181–2).

[19] Interview, DSGV.

[20] Interview, European Commission.

[21] Interview, European Commission.

[22] Interviews, DSGV and WestLB.

force for the NRW.BANK so that at least developmental bank activities would remain under the protection of the state's liability.[23] The camp of the public banks proposed a compromise to the Commission. The guarantees were supposed to be abolished. In return, periods of transition would be granted to make it possible for banks to prepare for the change. The Commission eventually accepted the proposal.[24] The guarantees were removed. A retroactive compensation was cancelled. In return, the Commission granted public banks a transition period of four years before the guarantees would expire. All liabilities that would be taken up in this period remained under the guarantor liability until 2015, for all obligations taken up before the guarantee would persist without limitations (European Commission, 2002, pp. 2–3).

The Demise of the *Landesbanken*

For the *Landesbanken* the consequences of the loss of the guarantees were catastrophic. Their business model, resting on the associated refunding advantages, lost its basis. The rating of the WestLB immediately dropped close to the margin of the investment grade.[25] The WestLB was thus no longer competitive.[26]

Before the guarantees expired the *Landesbanken* used the transition period to acquire as much cheap capital as possible. In the four years prior to the guarantee's termination they took up more than 100 billion euros (Müller, 2010, p. 36). Nevertheless, low-interest-paying liabilities also had to be serviced. Eventually, the *Landesbanken* did not succeed in developing a viable business model. There were no sufficient investment opportunities in the credit business for the money that was taken up during the transition period. The *Landesbanken* had no option but to channel the surplus capital into the credit substitute business such as subprime products and CDOs (collateral debts obligations) – and thus financed long-term liabilities with short-term businesses.[27] Although this strategy indeed proved profitable for some time, it was also high risk. In the course of the financial crisis, it directly brought ruin on the *Landesbanken*. WestLB, HSH Nordbank, BayernLB, LBBW and

---

[23] Interviews, LSH, DSGV, WestLB, Financial Ministry Hessen, Financial Ministry NRW and European Commission.

[24] Interviews, European Commission, LSH and Financial Ministry NRW.

[25] Institutional investors are only allowed to purchase bonds with an 'investment grade'. In case this grading is undercut, all contracts with the investor become invalid; the bank is threatened with insolvency.

[26] Interview, WestLB.

[27] Interview, RSGV.

SachsenLB had to be bailed out with multibillion rescue packages to avoid bankruptcy. NordLB and Helaba remained to the largest extent unencumbered by the crisis.[28]

The Commission approved bailouts for the heavily affected *Landesbanken* only on strict conditions. The WestLB was to split in half its transaction volume and sold before 2011. The federal state and the savings banks were to be ruled out as owners – which de facto implied a privatization. Moreover, the remaining part of WestLB was forced to confine itself to its core activities (handling of payment transactions, loans to SMEs, association banking for the savings banks, capital market business and funding of large projects).[29] After another state aid investigation against WestLB bad bank[30] 'Phoenix', the WestLB even had to shrink to the size of a purely regional association bank for the savings banks with a balance sheet of 45 billion euros. At the time of this decision the WestLB possessed total assets of 191 billion euros and 4200 employees. All other business segments were to be sold.[31] Since no buyer could be found, a major part of the WestLB was liquidated. Only a financial services provider (Portigon AG) with 1432 employees remained, which continues to be in the possession of the federal state. The association banking business with 400 employees was affiliated to Helaba. Presumably before mid-2018, HSH Nordbank has to be split into a holding and an operational company which has to be privatized. If no buyer can be found, the bank has to be liquidated.[32] The BayernLB had to pay back 5 billion euros of state aid and, similar to the WestLB, had to sell substantial business segments,[33] but continues to exist as a public-law institution. Also, the LBBW was obliged to concentrate on its regional core business and to reduce its capital market business as well as its proprietary trading. The balance sheet total had to be decreased by 40 per cent.[34] The Commission initially determined that the LBBW was to be converted from a public-law institution into a stock company, but later

---

[28] NordLB and Helaba had, as a consequence of spectacular losses during the 1970s, minimized their foreign business and concentrated on regional activities (Seikel, 2013, p. 127).

[29] *Spiegel-Online* (2009), 'EU-Auflagen für Staatshilfen: *WestLB* muss sich drastischer Schrumpfkur unterziehen', 12 May.

[30] A 'bad bank' is a financial institution established to liquidate highly problematic assets of another financial institution. For this purpose, 'bad' assets are removed from the balance sheet of the founding institution and transferred to the 'bad bank'.

[31] Interview, European Commission.

[32] European Commission, Press Release, accessed 6 July 2017 at www.europa.eu/rapid/press-release_STATEMENT-15-5866_de.htm.

[33] *Spiegel-Online* (2012), 'Nach jahrelangen Verhandlungen: EU besiegelt Schrumpfkur für BayernLB', 9 July.

[34] European Commission, Press Release, accessed 6 July 2017 at www.europa.eu/rapid/press-release_IP-09-1927_de.htm.

revoked this requirement.[35] The bankrupt SachsenLB was merged with the LBBW.

While savings banks are still of great importance to the German production regime, the industrial and economic competition policy functions of the formerly powerful German *Landesbanken* had to be abandoned. The era of the *Landesbanken* as political banks is definitely over.

CONCLUSION

The liberalization of the public banking sector in Germany illustrates that the European integration process effected a structural change of the German banking system – the core of the German production regime – which was hardly thought possible. As shown above, the control over the banking system represents a decisive power resource in the political economy of the Federal Republic. This means that the involvement of the European level has shifted the economic power relations at the heart of the German political economy.

The case at hand also shows that the European multilevel system offers possibilities for actors to bypass strong opposition in national arenas by activating European institutions. However, European law is not neutral regarding its compatibility with the interests of different groups of actors. In particular, European competition law is 'charged' with a normative concept of a certain model of economic organization which obliges all economic actors including the state to act like profit-maximizing private investors. Politically defined objectives that are alien to market logics and that imply a business practice that is non-profit-maximizing and that occasionally even involves losses are thus subordinated to the guiding principle of undistorted competition. Therefore, European competition law excludes economic organization principles that conflict with undistorted markets and free competition. In other words, European law entails 'sleeping liberalization options' that can be activated by actors with an interest in liberalization but cannot be used by actors with an interest in defending market-correcting regulations.[36]

---

[35] *Stuttgarter-Zeitung.de*, accessed 6 July 2017 at www.stuttgarter-zeitung.de/inhalt.eu-kommission-hat-entschieden-lbbw-muss-keine-aktiengesellschaft-werden.dc7e3224-f794-4aa6-b75b-0a10197d6a4d.html.

[36] On the concept of 'sleeping liberalization options' in European law and their activation see Seikel (2013), Chapter 6.

REFERENCES

Berghoff, H. (2006), 'The end of family business? The Mittelstand and German capitalism in transition, 1949–2000', Business History Review, 80(2), 263–96.

Beyer, J. (2003), 'Deutschland AG a.d: Deutsche Bank, Allianz und das Verflechtungszentrum des deutschen Kapitalismus' [Deutschland AG a.d: Deutsche Bank, Allianz and the interweaving centre of German capitalism], in W. Streeck and M. Höpner (eds), Alle Macht dem Markt? Fallstudien zur Abwicklung der Deutschland AG, Frankfurt: Campus, pp. 118–46.

Bieling, H.-J. and C. Deckwirth (2008), 'Die Reorganization der öffentlichen Infrastruktur in der Europäischen Union – Einleitung' [The reorganization of public infrastructure in the European Union – Introduction], in H.-J. Bieling, C. Deckwirth and S. Schmalz (eds), Liberalisierung und Privatisierung in Europa. Die Reorganization der öffentlichen Infrastruktur in der Europäischen Union, Münster: Westfälisches Dampfboot, pp. 9–33.

Bluhm, K. and B. Martens (2009), 'Recomposed institutions: Smaller firms' strategies, shareholder value orientation and bank relationships in Germany', Socio-Economic Review, 7, 585–604.

Bundesministerium der Finanzen (1979), Bericht der Studienkommission: 'Grundsatzfragen der Kreditwirtschaft' [Report of the Study Commission: 'Principal Issues of the Banking Industry'], Bonn: Stollfuss.

Czichon, E. (1970), Der Bankier und die Macht. Hermann Josef Abs in der deutschen Politik [The Banker and the Power: Hermann Josef Abs in German Politics], Köln: Pahl-Rugenstein.

Deeg, R. (1999), Finance Capitalism Unveiled: Banks and the German Political Economy, Ann Arbor, MI: University of Michigan Press.

Deeg, R. (2001), 'Institutional change and the uses and limits of path dependency: The case of German finance', MPIfG Discussion Paper No. 01/06.

Deutscher Sparkassen- und Giroverband (2001), 'Stellungnahme des Deutschen Sparkassen- und Giroverbandes zu der gegen Anstaltslast und Gewährträgerhaftung in Deutschland gerichteten Beschwerde der Europäischen Bankenvereinigung' [Statement by the German Savings Banks and Giro Association on the complaint lodged by the European Banking Association against Anstaltslast and Gewährträgerhaftung in Germany], Berlin: Deutscher Sparkassen- und Giroverband.

Dieckmann, J. (1981), Der Einfluss der Deutschen Sparkassenorganisation auf die staatliche Wirtschaftspolitik in der historischen Entwicklung: Eine empirische Untersuchung zur Theorie der Verbände [The Influence of the German Sparkassen Organization on State Economic Policy in Historical Development: An Empirical Study on the Theory of Associations], Frankfurt: Rita G. Fischer Verlag.

Eichhorn, P. (1992), 'Privatisierung von Sparkassen: Wachsende Bankenmacht' [Privatization of savings banks: Growing bank power], Zeitschrift für das gesamte Kreditwesen, 45(24), 11–16.

Eucken, W. (1952), Grundsätze der Wirtschaftspolitik [Principles of Economic Policy], Tübingen: J.C.B. Mohr.

European Commission (2000), 'Commission Decision of 8 July 1999 on a measure implemented by the Federal Republic of Germany for Westdeutsche Landesbank – Girozentrale (WestLB): 2000/392/EC', Brussels.

European Commission (2002), 'State Aid No. E 10/2000 – Germany. Institutional Liability and Guarantors Liability: C(2002) 1286', Brussels.

Grossman, E. (2006), 'Europeanization as an interactive process: German public banks meet EU state aid policy', Journal of Common Market Studies, 44(2), 325–48.

Hilferding, R. (1910 [1974]), Das Finanzkapital [Financial Capital], Frankfurt: EVA.

Hix, S. and K.H. Goetz (2000), 'Introduction: European integration and national political systems', West European Politics, 23(4), 1–26.

Höpner, M. (2004), 'Sozialdemokratie, Gewerkschaften und organisierter Kapitalismus, 1880–2002' [Social democracy, trade unions and organized capitalism, 1880–2002], MPIfG Discussion Paper No. 04/10.

Höpner, M. and A. Schäfer (2010), 'A new phase of European integration: Organized capitalisms in post-Ricardian Europe', West European Politics, 33(2), 344–68.

Jessop, B. (1990), State Theory. Putting the Capitalist State in its Place, Cambridge, UK: Polity Press.

Knill, C. and D. Lehmkuhl (1999), 'How Europe matters: Different mechanisms of Europeanization', European Integration Online Papers, 3(7), accessed 6 July 2017 at https://pdfs.semanticscholar.org/c7af/83f50463c0c33e489bafec75e1a86eeab6bb.pdf.

Lütz, S. (2000), 'From managed to market capitalism? German finance in transition', MPIfG Discussion Paper No. 00/2.

Moser, S., N. Pesaresi and K. Soukup (2002), 'State guarantees to German public banks: A new step in the enforcement of state aid discipline to financial services in the Community', Competition Policy Newsletter, June, 1–11.

Müller, L. (2010), Bank-Räuber: Wie kriminelle Manager und unfähige Politiker uns in den Ruin treiben [Bank Robber: How Criminal Managers and Incapable Politicians Drive Us into Ruin], Berlin: Econ.

Mura, J. (1994), Entwicklungslinien der deutschen Sparkassengeschichte [Lines of Development of Sparkassen History], Stuttgart: Deutscher Sparkassenverlag.

Poullain, L. (1979), Tätigkeitsbericht [Progress Report], Stuttgart: Seewald.

Reimann, W. (1992), Öffentliche Banken in der Zeit [Public Banks in Time], Bonn: VöB-Service Gesellschaft.

Scharpf, F.W. (1997), Games Real Actors Play. Actor-centered Institutionalism in Policy Research, Oxford: Westview Press.

Scharpf, F.W. (1999), Governing in Europe: Effective and Democratic?, Oxford: Oxford University Press.

Scharpf, F.W. (2010), 'The asymmetry of European integration, or why the EU cannot be a "social market economy"', Socio-Economic Review, 8(2), 211–50.

Schiller, K. (1969), 'Sparkassen in der Industriegesellschaft' [Savings banks in industrial society], Sparkasse, 86(5), 137–43.

Schorner, F. (2008), Privatisierung kommunaler Sparkassen. Aktuelle Entwicklungen in historischem und internationalem Kontext [Privatization of Municipal Savings Banks: Current Developments in Historical and International Context], Hamburg: Verlag Dr. Kovac.

Seikel, D. (2013), 'Der Kampf um öffentlich-rechtliche Banken. Wie die Europäische Kommission Liberalisierung durchsetzt' [The fight for public-law banks. How the European Commission enforces liberalization], Frankfurt: Campus.

Seikel, D. (2014), 'How the European Commission deepened financial market integration. The battle over the liberalization of public banks in Germany', Journal of European Public Policy, 21(2), 169–87.

Seubert, W. (2005), Die Brüsseler 'Verständigung' zu Anstaltslast und Gewährträgerhaftung: Eine Betrachtung aus europarechtlicher und mitgliedstaatlicher Sicht [The Brussels 'Understanding' about Anstaltslast and Gewährträgerhaftung: Considerations from Both the European and National Levels], Frankfurt: Peter Lang.

Shonfield, A. (1965 [1980]), Modern Capitalism, Oxford: Oxford University Press.

Sinn, H.-W. (1997), Der Staat im Bankwesen [The State in Banking], München: C.H. Beck.

Smith, M.P. (2001a), 'In pursuit of selective liberalization: Single market competition and its limits', Journal of European Public Policy, 8(4), 519–40.

Smith, M.P. (2001b), 'Who are the agents of Europeanization? EC competition policy and Germany's public law banks', RSC Working Paper No. 2001/39.

Stone Sweet, A. and W Sandholtz (1998), 'Integration, supranational governance, and the institutionalization of the European polity', in W. Sandholtz and A. Stone Sweet (eds), European Integration and Supranational Governance, Oxford: Oxford University Press, pp. 1–26.

Story, J. and I. Walter (1997), Political Economy of Financial Integration in Europe: The Battle of the Systems, Manchester: Manchester University Press.

Streeck, W. (1991), 'On the institutional conditions of diversified quality production', in E. Matzner and W. Streeck (eds), Beyond Keynesianism: The Socio-Economics of Production and Full Employment, Aldershot, UK and Brookfield, VT, USA: Edward Elgar Publishing, pp. 21–61.

Ziltener, P. (2000), 'Die Veränderung von Staatlichkeit in Europa – regulations – und staatstheoretische Überlegungen' [The change of statehood in Europe – regulations – and state-theoretical considerations], in H.-J. Bieling and J. Steinhilber (eds), Die Konfiguration Europas: Dimensionen einer kritischen Integrationstheorie, Münster: Westfälisches Dampfboot, pp. 73–101.

Zysman, J. (1983), Governments, Markets, and Growth: Financial Systems and the Politics of Industrial Change, Oxford: Martin Robertson.

10. Marginalizing the German savings banks through the European Single Market

Halyna Semenyshyn

In the years before the financial crisis, the European Commission pursued the creation of a single liberalized European financial market. The crisis brought the liberalization push to a halt, as it had discredited policies of financial liberalization. However, once the immediacy of the crisis was overcome, the European Commission and the European Central Bank (ECB) resumed the process of financial market integration with the aim of finalizing the European Monetary Union (EMU). Besides creating a capital markets union (CMU), the renewed push for financial market integration has focused on the establishment of a banking union consisting of three pillars: a single supervisory mechanism (SSM), a single resolution mechanism (SRM), and a deposit insurance scheme (EDIS). The last pillar, euro area–wide deposit insurance, has not been finalized as of 2016. By not treating the alternative banks differently, the envisaged banking union threatens the existence of public savings banks as well as cooperative banks in the eurozone.

Deeg and Donnelly (2016) emphasize that the alternative banks are in danger due to the cost of new supervision, restrictions on the size and nature of their balance sheets, and pressure on them to look to outside investors, which in the end could change their model. The authors conclude that the banking union is generally a threat to alternative banking via 'crisis-induced liberalization', but they state optimistically that the project is not a threat to the German savings banks model. On the contrary, I argue that the banking union has the potential to squeeze the savings banks in the future, especially when the common deposit insurance mechanism is adopted. This last pillar of the banking union will force savings banks to abandon their own joint liability scheme.

This chapter focuses on the case of German savings banks that fared relatively well in the crisis, but still could not avoid the impact of the banking union project. The major puzzle is why the traditional model of public savings banks is becoming marginalized in EU financial regulations, even though it has proven to be stable. The aim of this chapter is to understand why savings banks were not able to position their model as an alternative within the European space. In addition, it explores how the savings banks are responding to the new challenges of the supranational financial regulatory policy-making processes, and why they take a defensive position against the banking union project in the political struggles within the EU. It begins with a brief overview of the structure of German savings banks.

STRUCTURE OF GERMAN SAVINGS BANKS

One of the key features of the German banking system with regard to other European countries is the high degree of public ownership. The regional public banking sector is represented by savings banks that are members of the German Savings Banks Association (Deutscher Sparkassen- und Giroverband, DSGV) (DSGV, 2016c). In addition, they belong to the Savings Banks Finance Group, which comprises approximately 580 institutions: 409 savings banks, 7 state bank groups (*Landesbanken Gruppen*), 9 regional building societies (*Landesbausparkassen*), 11 public primary insurance groups, and a number of asset management, leasing, and factoring companies with overall combined total assets of €2800 million in 2015 (DSGV, 2016a).

The guiding principle of a savings bank is the promotion of the common good and fostering close relationships between local government institutions and the cities and communities in the region; therefore, its main targets are small and medium-sized enterprises (SMEs) in its own specific regional area (Döring, 2003). Savings banks function on the basis of a regional principle that does not allow them to compete amongst each other (Dietrich, 2009; Gärtner, 2009; Hessiches Sparkassengesetzt, 2008, §1, cl. 3[1]). Since profit maximization is not the primary objective (Hessisches Sparkassengesetz, 2008, §2, cl. 1, 6), they are not engaged in speculations in the global financial markets.

Until 2005, the savings banks enjoyed institutional and guarantor liability (Staats, 2005, p. 70; see also Seikel, Chapter 9 in this volume). Unlike the *Landesbanken*, the removal of these public guarantees did not threaten their business model because in the 1970s they established among themselves common institutional protection (*Institutssicherung*) and joint liability schemes (*Haftungsverbünde*). The latter are used as 'a special form

---

[1] Each state in Germany has its own savings banks law. I am referring to the Hessisches Sparkassengesetz, which covers the savings banks in the state of Hessen.

of deposit insurance with an institutional guarantee' and can be compared to an insurance tool (Käfer, 2015, p. 6). For example, if a savings bank has depleted its own deposit insurance, other savings banks would help with their deposit insurance. This institutional protection has been modified most recently in response to the EU Directive on Deposit Guarantee Schemes (DGS). The savings bank institutional protection scheme (IPS) is organized into 13 guarantee funds for (1) the regional savings banks associations, (2) the regional building societies, and (3) the *Landesbanken* and giro centers. In addition to institutional protection, the IPS provides deposit protection – it can cover customer claims related to savings deposits, savings certificates, time deposits, sight deposits, and bearer bonds, and allows the customer to claim up to €100 000 of their deposits.

Landesbanken also belong to the decentralized structure of the Savings Banks Finance Group. Historically, they have developed as the clearinghouses (*Girozentrale*) of the savings banks, and assumed the function of a central financial intermediary, thus becoming the key advisors and support for financial issues to the savings banks (Pohl and Freitag, 1994, p. 447). Since the late 1960s, the *Landesbanken* have also served large corporate customers and are active on international financial markets (see Seikel, Chapter 9 in this volume). The respective German states (*Länder*) and regional savings banks own *Landesbanken*, which are represented by the regional associations of savings banks (DBRS, 2006, p.2). The *Landesbanken* have their own safeguard funds; however, if they exhaust these funds, the savings banks can theoretically use their deposit insurance to bail out the *Landesbanken* in their group (interview, BaFin – the Federal Financial Supervisory Authority).

PERFORMANCE OF THE SAVINGS BANKS BEFORE AND AFTER THE CRISIS

This section describes how the savings banks managed to perform relatively well before and after the crisis. As argued by Deos et al. in Chapter 4 of this volume, savings banks have acted and can act as stability anchors for the financial system.

Strong, long-term customer ties contribute to the good performance of savings banks during a financial crisis as well as in stable times. This is due to the concept of a relationship in which savings banks are able to collect information beyond accessible public information, so they can share and assess risks better. The main aim of the smaller banks is to build long-term credit relationships with their customers, which explains higher returns on equity and lower volatility in the crisis. Analyzing a bank-level panel dataset from 1995 to 2007, Beck et al. (2009) find that the cooperative and savings banks are more stable and further from insolvency than the privately owned banks, even though the latter enjoy higher profits.

The German savings banks did not directly experience the financial crisis in credit business, securities business, special funds, or liquidity provision.[2] The crisis has influenced them through the real economy and through the level of interest rates. Financial strength was in decline due to an increase in unemployment and a fall in production in firms. However, as their business partners recovered quickly, so did the savings banks. In addition, they were not exposed to the securitization process. In contrast to the big private banks and *Landesbanken*, the savings banks managed to act as a stabilizing factor due to their operations in lending and their strategy in providing credit to SMEs (interview, BaFin). The savings banks could also refinance through deposits from retail customers, whereas *Landesbanken* had problems refinancing in the capital market.

The savings banks' commitment to the *Landesbanken* is, however, one external risk that is difficult to manage. Many savings banks were influenced indirectly by the difficulties in their *Landesbanken* during the time of the crisis. When the *Landesbanken* are not able to generate additional capital, it creates a systemic risk impacting the smallest savings bank, which might have to absorb the losses of the *Landesbanken* caused by their involvement in risky financial operations (interview, BaFin). However, there was no need for the savings banks to tap into their reserve funds, as the *Landesbanken* were supported through guarantees by the state and the Special Financial Market Stabilization Fund (Sonderfonds Finanzmarktstabilisierung, SoFFin).

According to the assessment of the DSGV, the decentralized business model of the Savings Banks Finance Group proved to be more resistant to the financial crisis than the centralized models of the large banking groups (DSGV, 2010a). As international banks withdrew many of their activities from the market, savings banks obtained more space to expand their business. In 2009, savings banks and *Landesbanken* developed business relationships with around three-quarters of German companies, granting 42.6 percent of loans to companies and self-employed individuals (Figure 10.1).

In 2009, the savings banks made 62.1 billion new credit commitments to enterprises, and thus loan offers increased by 5.5 percent in comparison to 2008 (DSGV, 2010a). Additionally in 2009, the savings banks were able

---

[2] The exceptions are some savings banks, e.g., Südholsteiner and Nord-Ostsee-Sparkassen in Schleswig-Holstein, that were also involved in trading on the international market (interview with Dr Mechthild Schrooten, Professor of Economics at Bremen University of Applied Sciences; Drost, 2010).

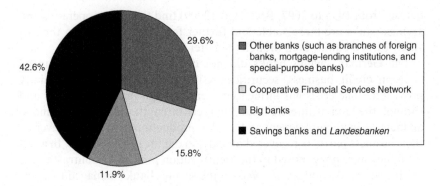

Note: a. Cooperative Financial Services Network is a consolidated banking group, which comprises the National Association of German Cooperative Banks (BVR), regional associations, DZ Bank (central bank), cooperative service organizations and local cooperative banks (BVR, 2017; Cupei, 2016, p. 3).

Source: DSGV (2010a).

Figure 10.1 Market share for loans to businesses and self-employed persons, by banking group, 2009 (excluding loans to financial enterprises)

to increase the deposit base by €9.6 billion to just under €752 billion, which created a steady foundation for providing investments to local customers in the region (DSGV, 2010b).

In 2009, savings banks continued to be the market leader for deposit-taking businesses with a market share of 40.4 percent of business with private customers (DSGV, 2010a, p. 20). The savings banks' market share in deposit-taking from business amounted to only 10.5 percent, but this is still more than before the crisis (DSGV, 2010a).

Savings banks proved to be stability anchors during the financial crisis. Nevertheless, the banking union initiative of the European Commission does not acknowledge their contribution to financial stability. By treating all banks the same, the banking union in its current state threatens the business model of the savings banks.

BANKING UNION INITIATIVE AS PART OF THE SINGLE MARKET AGENDA

The origins of the European Economic and Monetary Union (EMU) and financial integration are rooted in the Single Market program. The aim of this program is to eliminate all national or subnational obstacles to the free movement of goods, services, capital, and labor among the European Union's member states (Story and Walter, 1997). It is regarded as 'the most far-reaching and ambitious regulatory project in the world' (Young, 2006, p. 374). The EU Single Market has expanded into the EMU, which 'involves the coordination of economic and fiscal policies, a common monetary policy, and a common currency, the euro' (European Commission, 2016b).

Neoliberal ideas have guided the construction of the Single Market and the EMU (Bugaric, 2013; Drahokoupil et al., 2009). The EMU fits into three analytical dimensions of neoliberalism: as the regulatory experiment, which embraces 'place-, territory- and scale-specific projects designed to impose, intensify or reproduce market-disciplinary modalities of governance'; as a system of inter-jurisdictional policy transfer of neoliberal policy prototypes; and as a transnational rule regime that determines the 'rules of the game' on EU policy experimentation and regulatory reorganization (Brenner et al., 2010, p. 335).

In 2001, the so-called Lamfalussy Process started the liberalization of national financial markets as well as their integration and governance, and these processes can be understood as 'one integrated project of market-building in Europe' (Mügge, 2006, p. 991). The Lamfalussy Process shifted the competencies of rule-making and supervision from a national to a multilevel and networked arrangement (Posner, 2010, pp. 43–50). The liberalization also entailed the revocation of state guarantees for public banks (see Seikel, Chapter 9 in this volume).

The financial crisis emanating from the United States led the European Commission to suspend further financial liberalization. By the year 2012, however, the European Commission had resumed its single financial market agenda. This time the Commission justified its agenda by pointing out the need for more harmonized regulation in order 'to break the link between the sovereign debt and bank debt, and the vicious circle' that led to the use of taxpayer money for rescuing the banks (European Commission, 2012, p. 3). The publicly stated primary goals of the banking union are to limit the use of public funds for stabilization purposes, to develop the control rules for the 'highly vulnerable and interconnected banking system', and to construct an institution responsible for rescuing the banks through a common mechanism at EU level (Bieling, 2013, p. 293).

The first steps to harmonize the regulation and supervision of bank activities in the EU had been realized in two pillars of the banking union by 2014: the single supervisory mechanism (SSM) and the single resolution mechanism (SRM). The third pillar proposed by the European Commission, a euro area–wide deposit insurance scheme (EDIS), is currently being negotiated among the EU member states. The efforts to finalize the banking union are articulated in the *Five Presidents' Report: Completing Europe's Economic and Monetary Union*[3] (Juncker et al., 2015). Thus, the banking union can be defined as a major institutional post-crisis reform that changes the competencies of national institutions, creates new agencies and institutions, and puts pressure on the old banking structures within the EU member states.

Most commentators on the banking union see the project as the best solution to the financial crisis and the means to avoid future crises (Flassbeck and Lapavistas, 2013; Lannoo, 2015; Verón, 2015). As Howarth and Quaglia (2013) put it, the banking union is seen 'as an alternative route to stability: a European holy grail' (p. 120). For the proponents of the banking union, the new institution, with its uniform deposit insurance, uniform resolution mechanism, and additional banking monitoring, is a strong mechanism implying that 'one Euro-zone country would have to commit public funds to rescuing the banks of another member country' (Flassbeck and Lapavistas, 2013, p. 21).

THE DRIVING FORCES OF THE BANKING UNION

Many actors involved in the process see the European Commission as the main driver of the banking union idea (interviews, ASBA,[4] DSGV Brussels, EAPB,[5] EFBS,[6] ESBG[7]). It was able to secure the support of the president of the Eurogroup, the president of the European Central Bank, and even the social democratic president of the European Parliament (see Juncker et al., 2015). Being a strong actor within the European arena and while exercising its agenda-setting power, the Commission allies closely with the ECB to steer the debate on financial regulation in its favor. It keeps consultation with the financial industry rather short, thereby limiting the possibilities for industry feedback (interview, ESBG).

Nevertheless, the associations of the European banking industry have a significant influence on regulation. Instead of taking policies, the banking industry routinely makes policies (Pagliari and Young, 2014, p. 577). The EU institutions offer access to lobbyists via their formal institutional context (e.g., the mandate of regulatory agencies, their internal governance

---

[3] The report presents deliberations and discussions of the five presidents: Jean-Claude Juncker (European Commission), Donald Tusk (Euro Summit), Jeroen Dijsselbloem (Eurogroup), Mario Draghi (ECB), and Martin Schultz (European Parliament).

[4] Austrian Savings Banks Association.

[5] European Association of Public Banks.

[6] European Federation of Building Societies.

[7] European Savings and Retail Banking Group.

structure, or the opaque and discretionary environment) and via the informal institutions of 'revolving doors'. This gives rise to the emergence of new networks and policy communities, which in turn share similar beliefs and values (Mügge, 2006, p. 999; Pagliari and Young, 2014, pp. 577–8). The banking sector's main lobby association at the European level is the European Banking Federation (EBF) for the private banks. It supports the creation of a fully completed banking union with its third pillar, a euro area–wide deposit insurance scheme (EDIS), and emphasizes that the EDIS should not grant any exceptions for specific banks as defined by their membership in a particular group of the banking sector (EBF, 2015). This exception is favored by the European Savings Bank and Retail Group[8] (ESBG) and the European Association of Cooperative Banks (EACB) (see below). In terms of financial yearly expenses on lobbying, the association of private banks, the EBF with €4 375 000, significantly outweighs the financial potential of the ESBG (€275 000) and EACB (€225 000) (Wolf et al., 2014, p. 18).

IMPACT OF THE BANKING UNION ON THE GERMAN SAVINGS BANKS

Since the launch of the banking union project, the German savings banks have opposed its imposition on small banks. So far, they have only won the concession that they are classified as less-significant institutions (LSIs) to be supervised by the German financial supervisory agency, BaFin, and not directly by the European Central Bank (ECB) (Deutsche Bundesbank, 2016b). They feel most threatened by the European Commission's proposal for a European deposit insurance scheme (EDIS), which was announced on 24 November 2015. The EDIS is supposed to replace the national deposit guarantee schemes of the European Union's member states. Starting in 2017, the goal is to create a centralized European deposit insurance fund (DIF) in three stages by 2024 with fully mutualized deposit insurance: a reinsurance scheme, a co-insurance scheme, and a full insurance for participating in national deposit guarantee schemes (DGSs) (European Commission, 2015). While the association of private banks supports the Commission's projects (EBF, 2015), the small banking sector, including savings and cooperative banks, opposes a uniform EDIS because it wants to maintain its institutional protection scheme (IPS), which has been in place for decades.

---

[8] ESBG brings together savings banks and retail banks with savings bank characteristics such as local commitment (interview, ESBG).

The IPS of savings banks functions in the following way: if a member institute in the group is facing economic difficulties, it can get support from the corresponding guarantee fund, thus securing the solvency and liquidity of the institute. The fund might consider measures such as increasing equity capital, providing guarantees, and fulfilling third-party claims. The guarantee funds of IPS are interrelated; therefore, they can provide supraregional and system-wide compensation. In the first case, for example, if a guarantee fund of the regional savings banks association cannot supply enough means, all 11 guarantee funds will share their resources. The regional building societies, the *Landesbanken*, and giro centers have their own independent funds that can also be tapped should one of the other funds be depleted. Such IPS is primarily based on prevention, which involves structured risk monitoring aimed at identifying potential risks and applying prevention measures. For this reason, the legally prescribed deposit protection of up to €100 000 is a fall-back solution that can be used should the savings bank IPS fail (DSGV, 2016b).

The Association of Cooperative Banks (BVR) as well as the Association of Savings Banks in Germany (DSGV) emphatically reject any form of common liability for deposits in the EU or the euro area and claim that the abolition of IPS would cause irreparable damage to the decentralized structures of the German banking market. The cooperative and savings banks fear a double burden of additional costs, as they will need to pay the contributions to their own IPS as well as provide funds to the European deposit insurance fund (DIF) under the European deposit insurance scheme (EDIS) (BVR and DSGV, 2015, 2016). In addition, they will need to replenish the DIF if funds have been used up for compensation and resolution. The small banks are convinced that their own IPS is functioning well and thus secures the stability of the banks. Taking into account their resources, size, and risk averseness, a two-layer protection system would be too costly for them and impair their competitiveness. Forced to comply with the EDIS, a savings bank might have to give up its own well-established protection system, which offers prevention measures and secures safeguard funds for restructuring a savings bank in need. A policy brief from the Centre for European Policy Studies (CEPS) acknowledges the importance of IPSs and thus sees no grounds for abolishing them, as the system has proven to work well so far (Gros, 2013, p. 3).

SAVINGS BANK DEFENSIVE STRATEGIES

Even though the German savings banks have not experienced the credit crunch, they are not able to present their model as an alternative in the financial world. On the contrary, they are placed in the same situation as the large private banks and have to take the defensive position of lobbying against pressure from the regulatory burden, thus 'defending their success against a challenging environment' (DSGV, 2014 p. 3).

There are some reasons why the German savings banks model has not been able to win strong support in the financial reform debates. First, German savings banks belong to the Savings Banks Finance Group, which has a decentralized and heterogeneous structure. A savings bank or a *Landesbank* in the group shares a common perspective, but might pursue different interests in banking policy or regulatory law due to the size, mission, and specificities of a business model or involvement in the international financial markets. Thus, European financial policy-makers find it difficult to understand what kind of banking model the German Savings Banks Finance Group actually speaks on behalf of (interview, ESBG). Second, some *Landesbanken* in the group lost severely in the crisis and have gone through the winding-down (WestLB) or restructuring (HSH Nordbank) processes that were approved by the European Commission. Savings banks have partial ownership of *Landesbanken*; therefore, they can exercise oversight over the *Landesbanken*. The *Landesbanken*, where the savings banks did not use this right to the fullest, ended in the crisis as in the example of the WestLB. Still, as in the case of Helaba, the performance of the *Landesbanken* proved to be more prudent when savings banks had a greater say in their governance structure (see Polikhronidi and Scherrer, Chapter 11 in this volume).

Third, German savings banks have lost many of their European allies such as Belgium, France, Italy, and Spain, where savings banks have been restructured, privatized, or completely eliminated (Ayadi et al., 2009; Butzbach, 2007; Ordóñez, 2011). The privatization process of Italian savings banks started in 1990 with the Amato legislation, which declared the reorganization of the state-owned banks into joint-stock companies and change of ownership rights. This carried on with the 1993 Consolidated Law on Banking, which paved the way for the consolidation of savings banks into new corporate forms (Ayadi et al., 2009, pp. 157–8). In the 1990s, France also confronted mergers and acquisitions (M&As) among savings banks as the number of savings banks shrank from 450 to around 40 within a few years (Butzbach, 2007, p. 149). After the financial crisis, the Spanish banking system faced sharp adjustments in the form of restructuring, mergers, concentration processes, and reduction in capacity, thus reducing the number of savings banks from 45 to 17 (Ordóñez, 2011, p. 26). The lack of allies of the same nature and model makes it harder for savings banks to establish strong coalitions. Thus, the interests of a small bank are marginalized in the agenda-setting and decision-making phase of European financial market politics.

Since German savings banks were less dependent on EU regulations before, they have focused on lobbying within their national channels. However, with the increased influence of EU regulation on national banking systems, they have to mobilize and enter the European lobbying channels.

Savings banks are aware that it is impossible to lobby against the banking union project as a whole. After losing their traditional allies, they have to adapt strategically to the new environment and establish new alliances. The overlap between the positions of savings banks and cooperatives allows them to build stronger alliances at the European level, even though the two groups are competitors at the national level (interviews, ASBA, ESBG and DSGV Brussels). Another partner is the European Association of SMEs (UEAPME), which had previously supported the public banks in fighting the DG Competition's agenda of removing state guarantees for public banks (interview, UEAPME).

At the national level, savings banks are better positioned to lobby for their interests. At home, where their model is rooted, there are more favorable opportunities to lobby the national government and to develop strong alliances. Since German savings banks are located in almost every municipality where they have strong ties to local government, they can effectively lobby the national government from the bottom up. Inasmuch as savings banks are still present in other European countries, they can equally try to influence the national governments and financial ministers (interviews, ASBA and EFBS), thus strengthening their voice within the Council of Europe. This channel gives national associations of savings banks a complementary entry point for influence that is missing for the European associations, as 'the Council members look at their respective stakeholders, including interest groups, in member states' (Coen and Richardson, 2009, p. 10).

The debate over the banking union has gained visibility at the national level and German savings banks have actually been able to win a broader coalition of support. In the case of the European deposit insurance scheme (EDIS), the German Banking Industry Committee (Deutsche Kreditwirtschaft, DK), which collectively represents the interests of the German financial industry, supports the demands of the small and cooperative banks and criticizes the new European initiative (DK, 2016). These small banks have also managed to win support from representatives within the German business community – the Association of German Chambers of Commerce and Industry and the German Confederation of Skilled Crafts – as well as from the financial services department of the German trade union ver.di (DWN, 2016; ver.di, 2016). However, the Federation of German Industries (BDI), the association dominated by large corporations, supports the establishment of a common deposit insurance scheme as a part of the banking union and emphasizes its relevance for the industry and real economy (BDI, 2016).

In turn, the government coalition of two German parties, CDU/CSU and SPD, supports the national IPS and has been arguing against the EDIS. The parliamentarians criticize the *Five Presidents' Report*, and claim that 'harmonization of bank risks through a common EDIS brings no trust in security of savings deposits in Europe and does not contribute to the stability of banks' (*Bundestag*, 2015). The German politicians argue on the grounds of the subsidiary principle, which allows member states to claim that the EU Commission exceeds its competencies with the offered provisions, and emphasizes that the member states can better regulate the issue (*Bundestag*, 2016).

Their efforts seem to bear some fruit. The European Commission plans to amend the Capital Requirements Regulation and Directive as well as the Bank Recovery and Resolution Directive in favor of banks with a simple business model. The Greens member of the European Parliament, Sven Giegold, interprets this as the European Commission's departure from the 'one-size-fits-all' approach (Giegold, 2016; interview, ESBG). However, the European Commission continues to pursue the completion of the banking union and an agreement on a common EDIS (European Commission, 2016a).

CONCLUSION

The financial crisis made it possible for the European Commission to pursue its integration agenda in financial policies and has been used by policy-makers to reinforce and restructure the Single Market agenda. Following the line of the *Five Presidents' Report*, the Commission aims to finalize the new banking union project, which reflects the idea of fully integrated markets. This new initiative has been the most contested during the process of crisis management, as it marginalizes an alternative savings bank model oriented towards the regions and constrains the protection and promotion of alternative banks (Deeg and Donnelly, 2016).

The banking union forced the savings banks to employ defensive strategies in order to protect their business model, even though they were minimally exposed to the threats of the international financial crisis and were able to restore consumer confidence in the performance of financial markets (DSGV, 2010a). Still, finding allies to support their own model and winning a position as an alternative banking type on the EU level has been a challenging task for savings banks.

The identity of the savings bank model is perceived differently in the national and European context. While it is still strong in Germany by securing support from the German banking industry, it loses its discursive power at the European level. Ultimately, the lack of understanding of the savings bank model, which is able to protect savings banks via the IPS, makes them policy-takers rather than policy-makers in the European financial domain. The project remains an uncomfortable compromise, not only because of German opposition to the mutual support for the banks throughout the eurozone, but also because it ignores the complexity of the banking systems in each member state and their role in national economies. Thus, savings banks are pleading for fragmented oversight regulation and preservation of their own protective system.

One can conclude that due to strong political will from European institutions and lack of coalition partners within the European arena, the fight of the small public banks is almost lost at the EU level. They will face future privatization pressure from the Commission, notwithstanding the fact that the system of local and regional savings banks contributes to maintaining the social market economy (Smith, 2001, p. 28). With the adoption of EDIS, their own joint liability system is in danger, because even in a successful case, it might be abandoned in the end.

REFERENCES

Ayadi, R., R.H. Schmidt and S. Carbo Valverde et al. (2009), 'Investigating diversity in the banking sector in Europe: The performance and role of savings banks', accessed 7 July 2017 at https://www.ceps.eu/publications/investigating-diversity-banking-sector-europe-performance-and-role-savings-banks.

BDI (2016), 'Europäische Einlagensicherung: Besser gründlich als schnell!', in *BDI Fokus Finanzmarkt, No. 8*, accessed 7 July 2017 at http://bdi.eu/media/themen felder/konjunktur_und_finanzmaerkte/publikationen/20160411_Newsletter_Fok us_Finanzmarkt.pdf.

Beck, T., H. Hesse, T. Kick and N. von Westernhagen (2009), 'Bank ownership and stability: Evidence from Germany', unpublished working paper, accessed 7 July 2017 at http://voxeu.org/article/bank-ownership-and-stability-evidence-germany.

Bieling, H.-J. (2013), 'European financial capitalism and the politics of (de-) financialization', *Competition & Change*, 17(3), 283–98.

Brenner, N., J. Peck and N. Theodore (2010), 'After neoliberalization?' *Globalizations*, 7(3), 327–45.

Bugaric, B. (2013), 'Europe against the left? On legal limits to progressive politics, *LSE Europe in Question Discussion Paper Series No. 61*, accessed 7 July 2017 at http://www.lse.ac.uk/europeanInstitute/LEQS%20Discussion%20Paper%20Serie s/LEQSPaper61.pdf.

Bundestag (2015), 'Gegen Europäische Einlagensicherung' [European counterparty protection], accessed 7 July 2017 at https://www.bundestag.de/presse/hib/2015-1 1/-/394266.

Bundestag (2016), 'Nein zur europäischen Einlagensicherung' [No to European deposit guarantee], Berlin, accessed 11 July 2017 at https://www.bundestag.de/dokumente/textarchiv/2016/kw08-de-einlagenversicherung/409570.

Butzbach, O. (2007), 'Varieties within capitalism? The modernisation of French and Italian savings banks, 1980–2000', *Perspectives*, accessed 7 July 2017 at http://www.savings-banks.com/SiteCollectionDocuments/Perspectives%2054.pdf.

BVR (2017), 'Cooperative Financial Network', accessed 11 July 2017 at https://www.bvr.de/About_us/Cooperative_Financial_Network.

BVR and DSGV (2015), 'Volksbanken und Sparkassen gegen Vergemeinschaftung der Einlagensicherung' [Volksbanken and Sparkassen against communitization of the deposit guarantee scheme], *Press Release No. 71*, accessed 7 July 2017 at https://www.dsgv.de/de/presse/pressemitteilungen/151110_PM_BVR_DSGV_Einlagensicherung.html.

BVR and DSGV (2016), 'Credible, sustainable deposit protection', accessed 7 July 2017 at https://www.bvr.de/p.nsf/0/67986E91756806B2C1257F39003DD0CF/$file/EDIS%20Positionspapier%20ENGLISCH%20.pdf.

Coen, D. and J. Richardson (eds) (2009), *Lobbying the European Union: Institutions, Actors, and Issues*, Oxford: Oxford University Press.

Cupei, D. (2016), 'La riforma del Credito Cooperativo e i riflessi sul territorio' [Reform of cooperative credit and reflections on the territory], accessed 11 July 2011 at http://www.issirfa.cnr.it/regioni_sistemacreditizio/attachments/article/385/Cupei.pdf.

DBRS (2006), 'German Landesbanken: Analytical background and methodology', accessed 11 July 2017 at http://www.dbrs.com/research/208732/german-landes banken-analytical-background-and-methodology-archived.pdf.

Deeg, R. and S. Donnelly (2016), 'Banking union and the future of alternative banks: Revival, stagnation or decline?' *West European Politics*, **39**(3), 585–604.

Deutsche Bundesbank (2016b), 'The supervision of less significant institutions in the single supervisory mechanism', accessed 7 July 2017 at https://www.bundesbank.de/Redaktion/EN/. . .Articles/. . ./2016_01_supervision.pdf.

Dietrich, B.H. (2009), *German Banking Structure, Pricing and Competition: Implications and International Policy Perspectives*, Frankfurt: Peter Lang.

DK (2016), 'Deutsche Kreditwirtschaft lehnt Kommissionsvorschlag zum einheitlichen Europäischen Einlagensicherungssystem ab' [Deutsche Kreditwirtschaft rejects Commission proposal on the single European deposit guarantee scheme], *Bankenverband.de*, 26 January, accessed 7 July 2017 at https://bankenverband.de/newsroom/presse-infos/dk-lehnt-kommissionsvorschlag-zum-einlagensicherun gssystem-ab/.

Döring, T. (2003), 'German public banks under the pressure of the EU subsidy proceedings', *Intereconomics*, **38**(2), 94–101.

Drahokoupil, J., B. van Apeldoorn and L. Horn (2009), 'Introduction: Towards a critical political economy of European governance', in B. van Apeldoorn, J. Drahokoupil and L. Horn (eds), *Contradictions and Limits of Neoliberal European Governance: From Lisbon to Lisbon*, London: Macmillan, pp. 1–17.

Drost, F.M. (2010), 'Die Schleswig-Holsteinische Idylle trügt', *Handelsblatt*, 29 April, accessed 7 July 2017 at http://www.handelsblatt.com/unternehmen/banken-versicherungen/kreditwirtschaft-in-der-krise-die-schleswig-holsteinische-idylle-tr uegt/3423512.html.

DSGV (2010a), *Financial Report 2009: Winning Through Trust*, accessed 7 July 2017 at https://www.dsgv.de/_download_gallery/Publikationen/Finanzbericht2009_E. pdf.

DSGV (2010b), *Profile: Winning Through Trust*, accessed 7 July 2017 at https:// www.dsgv.de/_download_gallery/Publika. . .Finanzbericht2009_E.pdf.

DSGV (2014), *Finanzbericht 2013: Unser Ergebnis – Unser Beitrag* [Financial Report 2013: Our Results – Our Contribution], accessed 7 July at http://docplayer. org/6210839-Deutscher-sparkassen-und-giroverband-finanzbericht-2013-unser-ergebnis-unser-beitrag.html.

DSGV (2016a), 'Finanzbericht 2015' [*Financial Report*], accessed 7 July 2017 at https://www.dsgv.de/en/facts/annual_report/financial_report.html.

DSGV (2016b), 'So funktioniert das Sicherungssystem' [How the backup system works], accessed 7 July 2017 at https://www.dsgv.de/de/sparkassen-finanzgruppe/ sicherungssystem/funktionsweise_sicherungssystem.html.

DSGV (2016c), 'Sparkassen: Geschäfte, die man versteht, mit Kunden, die man kennt' [Savings banks: Shops that you understand, with customers you know], accessed 7 July 2017 at https://www.dsgv.de/de/sparkassen-finanzgruppe/organisation/spark assen.html.

DWN (2016), 'Deutsche Wirtscahft bildet massive Front gegen EU-Einlagensicherung' [German economy forms massive front against EU deposit guarantee], *Deutsche Wirtschafts Nachrichten*, 7 June, accessed 7 July 2017 at http:// deutsche-wirtschafts-nachrichten.de/2016/06/07/deutsche-wirtschaft-bildet-mass ive-front-gegen-eu-einlagensicherung/.

EBF (2015), 'EBF position on the European Commission proposal for a European deposit insurance scheme', accessed 7 July 2017 at www.ebf-fbe.eu/wp-content/ uploads/2016/04/EBF_020198J-Position-on-COM-Proposal-for-a-European-Dep osit-Insurance-Scheme-EDIS-v10-final.pdf+&cd=1&hl=en&ct=clnk&gl=uk.

European Commission (2012), 'Communication from the Commission to the European Parliament and the Council: A Roadmap towards a Banking Union', Brussels, accessed 7 July 2017 at http://eur-lex.europa.eu/legal-content/EN/TXT/ ?uri=CELEX:52012DC0510.

European Commission (2015), 'Proposal for a Regulation of the European Parliament and of the Council Amending Regulation (EU) 806/2014 in Order to Establish a European Deposit Insurance Scheme', accessed 7 July 2017 at http:// eur-lex.europa.eu/legal-content/EN/TXT/?uri=CELEX%3A52015PC0586.

European Commission (2016a), 'Communication from the Commission to the European Parliament, the Council, the European Economic and Social Committee and the Committee of the Regions – Commission Work Programme 2017: Delivering a Europe that Protects, Empowers and Defends', accessed 7 July 2017 at http://eur-lex.europa.eu/legal-content/en/TXT/?uri=CELEX:52016DC0710df.

European Commission (2016b), 'Economic and Monetary Union', accessed 7 July 2017 at http://ec.europa.eu/economy_finance/euro/emu/index_en.htm.

Flassbeck, H. and C. Lapavistas (2013), *The Systemic Crisis of the Euro – True Causes and Effective Therapies*, Berlin: Studien.

Gärtner, S. (2009), 'Balanced structural policy: German savings banks from a regional economic perspective', *Perspectives*, No. 58, Brussels: European Savings Group, accessed 7 July 2017 at https://www.wsbi-esbg.org/About-us/History/Pages/Gart ner.aspx.

Giegold, S. (2016), 'Endlich offene Ohren: EU-Kommission will an einfachen Regeln für risikoarme, kleine Banken arbeiten' [Finally open ears: EU Commission wants to work on simple rules for low-risk small banks], accessed 7 July 2017 at http://www.sven-giegold.de/2016/endlich-offene-ohren-eu-kommission-will-an-einfachen-regeln-fuer-risikoarme-kleine-banken-arbeiten/.

Gros, D. (2013), 'Principles of a two-tier European deposit (re-) insurance system', *CEPS Policy Briefs No. 287*, accessed 7 July 2017 at www.ceps.eu/system/files/PB%20No%20288%20DG%20Deposit%20Reinsurance.pdf.

Hessiches Sparkassengesetzt (2008), 'Hessisches Sparkassengesetz in der Fassung vom 24. February 1991, Zuletzt geändert durch Gesetz vom 29' [Hessen Savings Bank Act as amended on 24 February 1991, as last amended by Law of 29 October 1991.

Howarth, D. and L. Quaglia (2013), 'Banking union as Holy Grail: Rebuilding the Single Market in financial services, stabilizing Europe's banks and "completing" Economic and Monetary Union', *JCMS: Journal of Common Market Studies*, **51**(S1), 103–23.

Juncker, J.-C., D. Tusk and J. Dijsselbloem et al.(2015), *The Five Presidents' Report: Completing Europe's Economic and Monetary Union*, accessed 7 July 2017 at https://ec.europa.eu/priorities/sites/beta-political/files/5-presidents-report_en.pdf.

Käfer, B. (2015), 'The value of a joint liability scheme: Estimating group support for German Landesbanken', *Joint Discussion Paper Series in Economics No. 25-2015*, accessed 7 July 2017 at https://www.uni-marburg.de/fb02/makro/forschung/magkspapers/paper_2015/25-2015_kaefer.pdf.

Lannoo, K. (ed.) (2015), *The Great Financial Plumbing: From Northern Rock to Banking Union*, London: Rowman & Littlefield.

Mügge, D. (2006), 'Reordering the marketplace: Competition politics in European finance', *JCMS: Journal of Common Market Studies*, **44**(5), 991–1022.

Ordóñez, M.F. (2011), 'The restructuring of the Spanish banking sector and the Royal Decree-Law for the reinforcement of the financial system', accessed 7 July at http://www.bde.es/f/webbde/GAP/Secciones/SalaPrensa/InformacionInteres/Reestructuracion SectorFinanciero/Ficheros/en/mfo210211e.pdf.

Pagliari, S. and K.L. Young (2014), 'Leveraged interests: Financial industry power and the role of private sector coalitions', *Review of International Political Economy*, **21**(3), 575–610.

Pohl, M. and S. Freitag (eds) (1994), *Handbook on the History of European Banks*, Aldershot, UK and Brookfield, VT, USA: Edward Elgar Publishing.

Posner, E. (2010), 'The Lamfalussy Process: Polyarchic origins of networked financial rule-making in the EU', in C.F. Sabel and J. Zeitlin (eds), *Experimentalist Governance in the European Union: Towards a New Architecture*, Oxford: Oxford University Press.

Smith, M.P. (2001), 'Who are the agents of Europeanization? EC competition policy and Germany's public law banks', *EUI Working Papers No. 2001/39*.

Staats, S. (2005), *Fusionen bei Sparkassen und Landesbanken: Eine Untersuchung zu den Möglichkeiten der Vereinigung öffentlich-rechtlicher Kreditinstitute* [Mergers in Sparkassen and Landesbanken: An Investigation into the Possibilities of Assocation of Public-Law Credit Institutions], Berlin: Duncker & Humblot.

Story, J. and I. Walter (1997), *The Political Economy of Financial Integration in Europe: The Battle of the Systems*, Cambridge, MA: MIT Press.

ver.di (2016), 'Unterstützung der Unterschriften Aktion gegen die EU-Pläne zur Vergemeinschaftung des Sparkassen-Einlagen-Sicherungssystems' [Supporting signatures action against the EU plans for the coordination of the savings bank deposit guarantee scheme], briefing, accessed 7 July 2017 at https://fidi.verdi.de/

++file++57233a887713b80752001bb8/download/1604_Brief_BR%2BPR_S-Fina
nzgruppe.pdf.

Verón, N. (2015), 'Europe's radical banking union', *Bruegel Essay and Lecture Series*,
5 May, accessed 7 July 2017 at http://bruegel.org/2015/05/europes-radical-bank
ing-union/.

Wolf, M., K. Haar and O. Hoedeman (2014), *The Fire Power of the Financial
Lobby*, Corporate European Observatory, accessed 7 July 2017 at https://corpor
ateeurope.org/sites/default/files/attachments/financial_lobby_report.pdf.

Young, A.R. (2006), 'The politics of regulation and the internal market', in K.E.
Jørgensen, M.A. Pollak and B. Rosamond (eds), *Handbook of European Union
Politics*, New York: Sage, pp. 373–89.

PART V

Keeping public banks accountable to the public

11. Governance makes a difference: A case study of the German *Landesbanken* Helaba and WestLB

Xeniya Polikhronidi and Christoph Scherrer

The extraordinary losses of the *Landesbanken* in the global financial crisis tarnished the reputation of German public banks (see Semenyshyn, Chapter 10 in this volume). Their longtime leader, WestLB, co-owned by the most populous German state, North Rhine-Westphalia, incurred such high losses that it ceased to exist (see Seikel, Chapter 9 in this volume). Part of its business was taken over by the considerably smaller Helaba, the *Landesbank* of the German states Hessia and Thuringia. Helaba was one of the few *Landesbanken* that passed through the crisis rather unscathed. WestLB's and Helaba's different fates in the crisis give reason to question the popular verdict against state ownership. It raises the question of why Helaba did not suffer the same fate as most other German *Landesbanken*. The common answer is that Helaba pursued a more prudent business policy than WestLB. This answer, however, does not explain why Helaba was more risk-averse. By examining and comparing the governance of these two banks, we hope to shed light on the reasons for Helaba's better performance. The insights gained from this inquiry may also guide further discussion on how to ensure the prudent behavior of public banks.

Our approach to explaining the different performance of *Landesbanken* by looking at governance structure differs from previous attempts (see Gubitz, 2013; Hau and Thum, 2009; König and Wruuck, 2011; Trampusch et al., 2014) by taking a multi-theoretical perspective. Our analysis is founded upon the integration of five governance theories into a single framework: principal–agent theory, contingency theory, strategic choice theory, stakeholder theory, and sociological new institutional theory. Each of these theories on its own provides a valuable contribution to the in-depth study of specific governance issues in an organization. However, none of these theories is encompassing enough to account for the wide spectrum of aspects in the governance of a bank as a whole. We find that the governance of Helaba and WestLB differed remarkably, which may, to a large extent, explain the different fate of these two *Landesbanken*.

Our contribution is structured as follows. First, we briefly present the theories and bring them into an overall framework. Then we apply this multi-paradigm approach to the comparison of Helaba and WestLB.

THEORETICAL FRAMES

Most of the literature looks at corporate governance through the lens of the principal–agent theory (prototypical: Shleifer and Vishny, 1997; specifically for *Landesbanken*: Hau and Thum 2009; König and Wruuck, 2011). This approach, however, has increasingly evoked criticism (e.g., Aguilera et al., 2008; Fiss, 2008). By abstracting away from the complexities of the environment and by taking a strictly rational and contractarian approach toward business relationships, this theory cannot provide a full and adequate picture of the governance dynamics within a firm. Therefore, other approaches, mainly developed in the organizational studies of sociology, have become more prominent in research on corporate governance. But again, taken individually, none of these theories provide a broad enough view on the complexity of the governance issue. Each, though to a different extent, illuminates only some particular aspects within the complex puzzle of governance (Cornforth, 2004). By following the familiar 'either-or approach' (Letza and Sun, 2002, p. 53), a great deal of the research critical of principal–agent theory is equally narrow (ibid.).

For a more comprehensive view on the governance of a firm, an integrated multi-theoretical framework proves more promising. Of course, such an approach is not without its own problems. The ontologies of the integrated theories may not always be compatible and the multi-theoretical approach may lack the depth that is usually easier to achieve via frameworks relying on a single theory. Nevertheless, a multi-theoretical framework based on principal–agent theory, contingency theory, strategic choice theory, stakeholder theory, and sociological neoinstitutionalism seems to capture the complexity of *Landesbanken* governance most adequately.

Principal–agent theory has been a dominant perspective on corporate governance in academic research as well as in policy development. The theory approaches a corporation by placing the interests of shareholders at the center of concern, where the maximization of the owners' welfare and creation of value are the main objectives of a firm (Shleifer and Vishny, 1997). In general, research within this perspective is centered on the model of the relationship between a principal delegating work and an agent working on behalf of a principal (Eisenhardt, 1989). At the core of this relationship Jensen and Meckling (1976) identify the 'agency problem', comprising two types of concerns (Eisenhardt, 1989). First, the principal and agent might have different goals and interests. This issue turns into a problem because of the asymmetry of information between the principal and the agent, making it difficult for the former to monitor and verify the behavior of the latter. Second, the principal and the agent might have different attitudes toward risk and uncertainty that can ultimately lead to different preferences in actions and outcomes. The general idea of agency theory is that all social relations in economic interaction can be reduced to a set of contracts and, thus, the key solution to agency problems can be found in optimal contracting (ibid.).

Considering a firm as a 'nexus of contracts' neglects its environment. Contingency theory tries to fill this gap. It is often referred to as 'the organization in its environment approach' (Donaldson, 1996, p. 61). It claims that there is no single organizational structure that would effectively fit all organizations. This theory emphasizes that organizational performance is not determined by any given structure per se. Rather, performance is conditional on varying influences known as 'contingency factors' (ibid.), which stem from the broader organizational environment (external) as well as from the organization itself (internal; Currie and Suhomlinova, 2007). For instance, Mintzberg (1979) identified environmental contingencies such as complexity, diversity, hostility and stability.

The supporters of the strategic choice theory accept that contingencies play a role in the formation of organizational structures. However, this role may depend on the strategic choice of those who have the power to exert influence on the organization's design and structure. Actors might diverge in their responses to similar contingencies due to different preferences, interests, values, or power resources (ibid.). A 'dominant coalition' (Cyert and March, 1963) might also form. Members of such a dominant coalition are not necessarily identical with the holders of formal authority within an organization (Child, 1972).

Stakeholder theory approaches a firm from the open-system actor-level perspective. It takes into account the diversity and multiplicity of interests involved. Stakeholders are 'any group or individual who is affected by or can affect the organization's objectives' (Freeman and McVea, 2001, p. 3). For instance, stakeholders can include stockholders, managers, employees, suppliers, customers, local communities and the general public (Hill and Jones, 1992). In contrast to principal–agent theory, which is centered on the interests of shareholders, stakeholder theory promotes a shared vision of a firm. It considers survival, not the maximization of shareholder wealth, as a firm's central objective. Proponents of the theory claim that the stakeholder perspective provides a flexible strategic framework for a firm that operates in a turbulent and unstable environment. Success in managing the complex nature of the diverse stakeholder relationships depends on the long-term set of values that they share (Freeman and McVea, 2001). This theory highlights the importance of a cooperative attitude, where stakeholders are not set against one another in a zero-sum game, but rather act as contributors to a win-win situation.

In the theory of sociological new institutionalism, legitimacy requirements are primary factors explaining individual and collective behavior. Institutionalized practices may deviate from the principles of efficiency or rationality. Particularly under the conditions of insecurity and competition, it is expected that actors strongly orientate their behavior toward others. DiMaggio and Powell (1983) identify three types of institutional isomorphism – coercive, mimetic and normative. Coercive isomorphism happens through force, persuasion or invitation to join. Mimetic isomorphism takes place when an organization itself initiates the mimicking of other organizations. Often organizations model themselves after other organizations that are operating in their field and that they consider to be more successful or legitimate. The normative form of isomorphism commonly results from the phenomenon of professionalization. Members of a 'profession' tend to have similar attitudes and approaches to doing their job. Relying on the processes of isomorphism, DiMaggio and Powell (1983, pp. 154–5) develop several predictors, including the following:

- The more an organization is dependent on another organization, the more similar its structures, climate and behavioral focus will be to that organization.
- The greater the uncertainties in the means and ends, the more an organization will mimic other organizations that it considers successful.
- The more ambiguous and unclear the technologies and goals of an organization are, the more it will depend on appearances for legitimacy and, therefore, the more it will mimic other organizations that it considers successful.
- The greater the participation of members of an organization in professional associations or other networks, the more the organization will be like other organizations involved.

In addition, neoinstitutionalism distinguishes between the day-to-day activities of an organization and its formal design. It might often be the case that the two do not necessarily represent a coherently integrated whole (Meyer and Rowan, 1977).

THE MULTI-PARADIGM APPROACH

Each of the theories discussed above makes an important contribution to the understanding of an organization's behavior. Principal–agent theory highlights the importance of structuring the relationship between owners and managers through optimal contracting and control within a bank. Contingency theory accounts for the internal and external environments as well as general tangible characteristics of a bank. Strategic choice theory emphasizes the complexity of the strategic and power relations of actors in their concrete environments. Stakeholder theory acknowledges the variety of these actors. Finally, neoinstitutionalism helps to explain the emergence of specific organizational forms.

As each of the above theories illuminates only a certain aspect of an organization's complexity, we assemble these theories in a more comprehensive model, as done by Polikhronidi (2012). Figure 11.1 maps the governance process by categorizing the potential factors of influence on organizational governance in three major groups: actors, organizational contingencies, and institutions. The levels at which this influence originates range from the particular organization to the broader world.

As stakeholder theory suggests, owners and managers do not represent all of the actors that might influence a firm. Therefore, the first group includes a variety of possible actors. According to strategic choice theory, it is important to keep in mind that the governance of an organization might be influenced by strategic decisions, behavior, and views of these stakeholders. Actors may also form 'dominant coalitions' and differ in their importance or power within the organization. However, the interests and influence of the same actor may vary in different contexts and according to a set of contingencies. Therefore, the second group of factors is organizational contingencies. Contingency theory suggests that each organization has its own set of internal characteristics, which are embedded in the broader environment. Yet, these tangible characteristics of a firm might be to a large extent determined by processes that are not always readily visible. Thus, institutions represent the third group. Despite their less tangible nature, they may often significantly affect the governance structure of an organization through processes of institutionalization and institutional isomorphism.

This model also depicts the nature of influence processes. First, the factors of influence are all directly and indirectly interconnected, further influencing one another. Second, two types of arrows (light and dark) represent the influence process between the governance of an organization and the influencing factor. The solid arrows represent influences exercised upon governance structures, while dashed arrows indicate influences

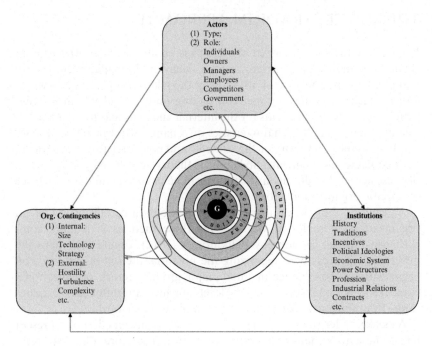

Figure 11.1　The multi-paradigm perspective on the study of organizational governance

exerted by governance structures. These processes constantly interact with each other. In other words, the influence of a single factor on governance might not originate and happen in an isolated space. Therefore, unintended consequences are also possible. Figure 11.1 depicts this complex relationship, shown through the intersections of lines and the circular interactions between processes of influence.

The theories embedded in Figure 11.1 illuminate governance as a nexus of complex relationships between different factors of influence at different levels. Of course, this particular model is neither universal nor exhaustive. Additionally, such a broad approach lacks an in-depth perspective on concrete issues. Yet, it may better structure the investigation into the role governance practices played in the diverging fates of *Landesbanken*.

THE CASE STUDY OF HELABA AND WESTLB

At the end of June 2012, WestLB, the Düsseldorf-based *Landesbank* of North Rhine-Westphalia, ceased to exist. For a few decades, the once largest German *Landesbank* had competed successfully against such private rivals as Deutsche Bank in domestic and international capital markets. But by the end of the 2000s, it had consumed billions in state aid and was therefore liquidated at the behest of the European Commission. A small part of WestLB, the savings bank business, was integrated into the previously considerably smaller Landesbank Hessen-Thüringen, known as Helaba (see Seikel, Chapter 9 in this volume). Situated in the financial capital of Germany, Frankfurt am Main, Helaba required no state aid during the financial crisis of 2007/08. Between 2001 and 2010, Helaba had earned €2.2 billion, while WestLB had accumulated losses of €4.6 billion before taxes. In fact, very few private German banks survived the crisis as unscathed as Helaba (Gubitz, 2013, pp. 176, 183, 191).

For an inquiry into the reasons of these two banks' different fates, we will rely on the above-developed multi-paradigm perspective.

Governance: The History of Experiences and Personalities

Once postwar reconstruction was completed, the German savings banks and *Landesbanken* association, Deutscher Sparkassen- und Giroverband (DSGV), began to promote a more competitive and market-oriented model for the public banking sector (Deeg, 2002). The success of this policy, however, was not lasting and the negative consequences of these 'promising' business strategies arose already by the mid-1970s, when three large *Landesbanken* – WestLB, NordLB, and Helaba – incurred heavy losses (ibid.). Forty years later, in hindsight, it seems that this early crisis was the decisive event in the destiny of some of these banks. Namely, it led Helaba to become much more cautious in its expansion, while WestLB continued its way forward into aggressive competition with ambitious profit targets (interviews with Helaba,[1] SGVHT,[2] and Seikel, 2011).[3]

Helaba and its Crisis

Helaba suffered significant losses in the period 1973–76. Its owners, the Savings Banks Association of Hessia (SGVH) and the government

---

[1] Interview, representative of Helaba (28 November, 2011), Frankfurt am Main.

[2] Interview, representative of Sparkassen- und Giroverband Hessen-Thüringen (18 November 2011), Frankfurt am Main.

[3] Interview, Daniel Seikel, doctoral student at International Max Planck Research School (20 October 2011), whose dissertation was published in 2013 by Campus-Verlag ('Der Kampf um öffentlich-rechtliche Banken. Wie die Europäische Kommission Liberalisierung durchsetzt [The fight for public banks. How the European Commission enforces liberalization]).

of Hessia, had to inject about DM3 billion. The decisions that led to these losses were made under the leadership of Wilhelm Hankel. He became president of Helaba in 1972, but had to leave the position soon after at the end of 1973. Inspired by the 'new era' of competitive public banking, Hankel pursued risky but seemingly profitable large investments in both domestic and foreign markets. However, he neglected the formal procedures of decision-making, relying more on friends and state political officials. The then Prime Minister of Hessia, Albert Osswald, lost his position in the wake of the crisis (*Der Spiegel*, 1974, 1977).

This early crisis of Helaba delivered a lesson to the local state government and the Savings Banks Association. They learned this lesson well, switching to a risk-averse business model and reducing the political and other informal influences to a minimum (Gubitz, 2013, p. 252). The Charter of Helaba (Helaba, 2009) was amended to provide the owners with stronger supervision mechanisms. When, in the end of the 1980s, Helaba again faced financial difficulties, the government of Hessia reduced its stake in the bank in favor of the Savings Banks Association of Hessia. In 1991, shortly after German unification, the savings banks of the neighboring state of Thuringia joined the Savings Banks Association of Hessia. Afterwards, the Association of Savings and Giro Banks Hessen-Thuringia (SGVHT) owned 85 percent, the state of Hessia 10 percent and the state of Thuringia 5 percent. Ever since, Helaba has not faced any financial difficulties that could threaten its existence. After the takeover of parts of WestLB, the shares of the two states were slightly reduced (interviews with Helaba, SGVHT, Schmidt[4] and Seikel in 2011; *Der Spiegel*, 1989; Helaba, 2012).

WestLB and its Leaders

If Helaba seems to have learned something from its crises, then WestLB represents the reverse case. In the course of its history, WestLB produced one scandal after another. Why? In contrast to the organizational learning that took place at Helaba, dominant individuals at the helm of WestLB seem to have left their stamp on its history.

Ludwig Poullain was the first chairman of the newly established Westdeutsche Landesbank Girozentrale, the precursor of WestLB. Appointed in 1969, he persuaded the North Rhine-Westphalia's state government of the need for a large and commercially active *Landesbank*. Poullain believed that 'Landesbanks were sleepy, provincial banks that faced a bleak future' (Deeg, 2002, p. 135). He justified the enlarged role by

---

[4] Interview, Prof. Dr. R.H. Schmidt (9 November 2011), Chair of International Banking and Finance, House of Finance, Goethe University. Frankfurt am Main.

noting both the prospect of higher profits and the increased market competition in favor of large industrial customers of financial services.

However, the success of Poullain's policy was short-lived. WestLB faced its first financial difficulties in 1974, when it lost DM250 million in currency trading (Deeg, 2002, p. 137). Despite all the criticism from the opposition party and the public, the bank did not reduce the scope of its activities. The only 'enhancement' in its governance was the increased number of governmental representatives on its administrative board. Poullain tried to resist any upturn in government intervention. On charges of corruption he was dismissed in 1978 (Hertl, 1979).

WestLB did not seem to learn from that episode. Concerns were raised, but its business model did not change. In 1981, its ambitious course was further intensified with the appointment of Friedel Neuber as head of the bank. The government of North Rhine-Westphalia was highly supportive of his desire to make the bank a 'global player'. It increased its share of ownership from 33 percent to over 43 percent (Deeg, 2002, p. 141). Governmental officials were only concerned about the right balance between their interest in using WestLB as an instrument for regional economic policy and their keenness on having a strong and profitable bank in their region (interview, Seikel, 2011).

Well connected to the Social Democratic Party that long-ruled the state of North Rhine-Westphalia (NRW), Friedel Neuber managed to head WestLB for 20 years. It earned him the nickname 'Red Godfather' (Bönisch and Dohmen, 2001; Taylor, 2010). His tenure ended with the so-called 'Flugaffäre' ('Flight Affair') when it was discovered that NRW's top politicians had used WestLB's jets for flights for questionable purposes (Bönisch et al., 1999; Bönisch and Dohmen, 2001).

Following lengthy disputes with the EU Commission (see Seikel, Chapter 9 in this volume), WestLB was reorganized in 2002. It was split into two banks: WestLB AG, operating under private law as a commercial bank, and Landesbank NRW (now NRW.BANK), responsible for public banking functions (WestLB, 2012). In 2011, each of the two savings banks associations in NRW held a stake of 25 percent in WestLB. The other half of the bank's shares (48.62 percent) was distributed between the NRW. BANK (30.86 percent) and the state of North Rhine-Westphalia (17.76 percent). Despite the seemingly minor share of the NRW government in the WestLB AG, it actually held almost the entire second half of the shares indirectly since it owned 98.6 percent of NRW.BANK (ibid.).

In sum, contrary to Helaba, the history of WestLB reminds one rather of a Greek tragedy, with its colorful protagonists, impressive plot and lack of a happy ending. After Neuber's 20-year rule, WestLB was chaired by six different CEOs until it was dissolved (WestLB *Annual Reports*, 2001–10).

Governance: Stakeholders, Ownership Structure, and Governance Design

The respective histories of Helaba and WestLB impacted not only their informal governance style but also such formal aspects as ownership and governance structures. After the crisis in the 1970s, the governance structure of Helaba was considerably altered. It serves as a benchmark against which one may evaluate WestLB's weak governance structure. Interestingly, while WestLB adopted a corporate governance code in 2002, Helaba did without it (Gubitz, 2013, p. 264).

The owners
In response to Helaba's 1970s' crisis, a 'Board of Owners' was established in addition to the Supervisory Board and the Board of Managing Directors. This governance structure is unique to this bank and contributes considerably to the notion of the 'special case of Helaba' (interviews with DSGV,[5] Helaba, SGVHT, 2011).WestLB had a structure common to German companies under private law: Managing Board and Supervisory Board. At first glance, the Board of Owners seems to be simply a more formally institutionalized version of a shareholders' meeting with the major difference being that Helaba as a public bank does not have shareholders but has owners instead (interview, Helaba 2011). However, the Board of Owners in Helaba differs significantly from the shareholders' meeting at WestLB (interview, DSGV, 2011). There is reason to believe that the Board of Owners at Helaba has a comparatively stronger role than that of the Shareholder Meeting at WestLB since the 'responsibilities' of the former are officially spelled out, whereas the latter is assigned 'voting rights' (Helaba, 2009, §9; WestLB, 2010, §16).

For decision-making, a member of the Board of Owners is expected to be well informed and prepared. As suggested by interviews with the representatives of Helaba and its majority owner SGVHT, they are well informed about almost everything that happens in the bank. The Board of Owners officially meets three to four times per year (interview, Helaba, 2011). In the case of decisions on particularly big loans or investments, SGVHT receives 'exactly the same papers the board of directors gets. Not a summary – the complete papers' (interview, SGVHT, 2011). The department of control at SGVHT examines the received information and then decides on it. Besides the formal channels, there are many less formal communication opportunities between the management of Helaba and the owners. Several staff members of SGVHT are assigned to work directly

---

[5] Interview with a representative of Der Deutsche Sparkassen- und Giroverband (28 November 2011).

with the bank. They sometimes call their colleagues at Helaba every day and, when needed, it takes them '300 meters to go' from SGVHT to the bank (ibid.). However, it is important to note that Helaba has this particularly close relationship only with the representatives of its majority owner – SGVHT (interviews with Helaba, SGVHT, 2011). The Board of Owners and the Supervisory Board members, who are appointed by the two states, as well as employee representatives, are limited to their official duties (interview, DSGV, 2011; Gubitz, 2013, p. 279). Helaba considers itself an 'apolitical' and 'professional bank' (interview, Helaba, 2011).

This close relationship between a *Landesbank's* management and its owners was not found at WestLB or many other *Landesbanken* (interview with DSGV, 2011). While at Helaba the savings banks association as owners constrained the risk-taking of management, the critique of WestLB's foray into derivatives was limited to individual, smaller savings banks in North Rhine-Westphalia. Therefore, the belated takeover of WestLB by the savings banks was not able to change the course at WestLB (Gubitz, 2013, pp. 286, 304).

The supervisory boards
Helaba has a supervisory board composed of 36 members, while that of WestLB was made up of 20 (Helaba, 2009, §11; WestLB, 2010, §6). At both institutions, the Supervisory Board is (was) assisted by the work of such committees as: (1) Credit Committee, (2) Participation Committee, (3) Audit and Risk Committee, and (4) Personnel Committee. In the Articles and Bylaws of WestLB, however, only two of these committees were explicitly mentioned: the Guarantors Committee, which dealt with questions of the liabilities of the bank that were still covered by the liability guarantee schemes, and the committee that should have been established in accordance with the Codetermination Act (WestLB, 2010, §§10.1 and 12a). The Charter of Helaba, apart from the general provisions similar to many firms, unambiguously states that the members of the Supervisory Board should form the Credit Committee. Moreover, it describes in detail all the procedures and functions related to its work (Helaba, 2009, §15). This 12-member committee, which deals with the issues of loans and the question of their approval, is in fact one of the central decision-making bodies in the business of the bank. It also performs the functions of the risk committee and meets at least every month (interview, Helaba, 2011; Helaba, 2009, §15.3).

During Neuber's long rule at WestLB, state politicians were sitting on the Supervisory Board; thereafter, the state appointed finance experts. However, after fresh scandals, the savings banks associations took a larger share in WestLB and placed their own representatives on the board.

Their influence was limited by the transformation of WestLB into a stock company. Under German corporate law the management of a stock company is quite free in its decisions with regard to the Supervisory Board (Kirchhoff, 1987, p. 149) and the law of corporate codetermination stipulates the representation of the corporation's employees on the board. In the case of WestLB, representatives of the employees occupied half the seats on the board (Gubitz, 2013, p. 198).[6]

The management boards

The statutes of WestLB left its management ample discretion (WestLB, 2010, §5.4). The reason given for not specifying the responsibilities of the Board of Managing Directors was that: 'WestLB AG refrains from specifying fixed responsibilities for its Managing Board members in the rules for conducting business in order to ensure *maximum flexibility*' (Declaration of Conformity, 2007–10, emphasis added). In contrast, the Board of Managing Directors at Helaba has limited competences. For instance, decisions on the acquisition or liquidation of participations have to be approved by the Supervisory Board. Moreover, in case these participations involve stakes larger than 25 percent, the Board of Owners also has to be asked. The same applies to loans. The Board of Managing Directors can approve loans only within concrete limits unless there is a situation of urgency. However, even then, management has to present to the members of the Supervisory Board all the details of the loans. In general, Helaba has 'very restrictive and very clear guidelines' toward the competences of the Board of Managing Directors in the bank (interview with Helaba, 2011; Gubitz, 2013, p. 244).

While the charter allows for majority votes (Helaba, 2009, §17.3), in practice if there is one single person on the management board that has doubts about a business decision, the final decision will not be made until full consensus is reached. Therefore, even when the Board of Managing Directors makes a decision that does not require the direct approval of the Supervisory Board or of the Board of Owners, such a decision has to receive the full and anonymous support of every member on the board (interview, Helaba, 2011).

The Independence of the Members of the Boards and Mission Creep

The ownership structure, that is, dominance of the savings banks association SGVHT, shields Helaba from undue political influence, not only

---

[6] The chairperson not being an employee's representative has two votes in case of a tie.

in its commercial, but also in its public business. Helaba's subsidized activities in support of regional development are placed in a separate division, Wirtschafts- und Infrastrukturbank Hessen (WIH). The Charter of Helaba lists in detail the competences of WIH (Helaba, 2009, §25.1). The Supervisory Board's special committee for WIH includes Supervisory Board members representing the interests of owner-governments and has as its chairman the Hessian minister for economics. This is the space in the bank where politicians are given an opportunity to promote their concerns related to the state economic development policies (interviews with Helaba, SGVHT and DSGV in 2011).

In North Rhine-Westphalia, a separate bank, which is predominantly owned by the state, the NRW.BANK, carries out the subsidized activities. Before the dissolution of WestLB, NRW.BANK was its owner. In contrast to Helaba, the state government could influence WestLB policies much more directly.

CONCLUSION

This case study of the two *Landesbanken*, Helaba and WestLB, illustrates that despite their common origin and similar nature, the two banks are quite different. Helaba, the smaller and less ambitious bank, came out of the crisis relatively unharmed and today it continues to successfully perform the functions that it has been assigned. WestLB, once a renowned and ambitious bank, failed. Why and how did these two banks become so different? The multi-paradigm perspective approaches this question by looking at the three major types of influences on the governance of banks – actors, institutions and contingencies and their complex interaction at different levels (Table 11.1).

The contingencies of innovative and turbulent developments in the banking sector together with increased competition from savings banks were the environmental influences to which the ambitious and strong leader of WestLB, Ludwig Poullain, responded in the late 1960s. He made the strategic choice of moving a public bank onto commercial and international terrain. He thereby mimicked the goals and behavior of private banks, which at this time were considered to be the role model for banking. After ten years as the head of WestLB, he left a lasting legacy that was reinforced by another strong leader with strong political connections, Friedel Neuber. The significant coercive and normative influence of the NRW government, which was interested in a strong and competitive *Landesbank*, was further strengthened under his rule.

As discussed above, a public bank can suffer from significant governance

Table 11.1   The major influencing factors on the governance of Helaba and WestLB

	Helaba	WestLB
Influential actors	Savings banks association SGVHT	Managers NRW government
Contingencies	State liability guarantees and their removal	Hostility/turbulence/complexity of the business environment
Organizational structure and design	Stable performance of the SGVHT	
Institutions	Risk-averse attitude	'Competitive rival' attitude
	Moderate profit ambitions	'Global player' ambitions
	Organizational history	Cronyism
	Organizational memory	Clientelism
	Organizational learning	Legacy of the former leaders and their leadership

problems stemming from its state ownership. The agency problem, inten-sified by the complexity of environmental contingencies and the institu-tional nature of the owner, can lead a public bank to make opportunistic decisions. Such a setting requires particularly careful and effective con-tracting that could structure and control the relationships. Yet, in compari-son to Helaba, WestLB did not seem to have a strong system of control and oversight. If there were powerful actors, who were interested in a 'flexible' approach to decision-making in the bank, then the governance structure of WestLB could well have been a result of their strategic choices and negotiations with one another. Optimal contracting can be a solution to the governance problems only if there are parties that are interested in setting up such a contract in the first place. In the history of WestLB and its ownership structure there were stakeholders, such as local savings banks, business clients and taxpayers, who could have been interested in increased oversight. But the savings banks were more interested in keeping WestLB out of their business realm, the business clients were interested in additional competition with private banks, and taxpayers were apparently more interested in other issues.

Since 2000, the broader environmental factors, such as the abolishment of the state liability guarantees; the increased frequency and intensity of financial crises; and the increasing pressure from the EU Commission have turned into a survival test for many state-owned banks. In this environment, WestLB rushed into models of doing business, which at the time seemed to be legitimate: the risky, but profitable and promising models of private banks. However, with the legacy of its historical performance and with the lack of solid corporate governance structures, WestLB failed.

The case of Helaba is different because its majority owner, the local savings banks association, was interested in the stability of the bank first and foremost. In its early years, Helaba made a painful mistake. The memory of this failure continues to guide Helaba and its owners. These owners have learned that individuals and their influence can prove problematic. Therefore, to limit the agency effect, they set up a governance structure characterized by strict control and monitoring mechanisms. Closely connected to savings banks, who are known for their more prudent business practices, this *Landesbank* absorbs their style not only through the coercive pressures of its owners but also via the processes of normative and mimetic isomorphism. Therefore, when the external contingency turned into a general financial crisis, Helaba was well prepared with the help of its business model and governance structure.

REFERENCES

Aguilera, R., I. Filatotchev, H. Gospel and G. Jackson (2008), 'An organizational approach to comparative corporate governance: Costs, contingencies, and complementarities', *Organization Science*, **19**(3), 475–92.

Bönisch, G. and F. Dohmen (2001), 'Bitterer Abgang' [Bitter ending], *Der Spiegel*, 13 May.

Bönisch, G., T. Darnstädt, B. Schmid and A. Stuppe (1999), 'Wie eine grosse private Party' [Like a big private party], *Der Spiegel*, 20 December.

Child, J. (1972), 'Organizational structure, environment and performance: The role of strategic choice', *Sociology*, **6**(1), 1–22.

Cornforth, C. (2004), 'The governance of cooperatives and mutual associations: A paradox perspective', *Annals of Public and Cooperative Economics*, **75**(1), 11–32.

Currie, G. and O. Suhomlinova (2007), 'Organizational contingencies', in G. Ritzer (ed.), *Blackwell Encyclopedia of Sociology*, Wiley-Blackwell, accessed 11 December 2011 at http://www.blackwellreference.com/public/tocnode?id=g9781405124331_yr2011_chunk_g978140512433121_ss1-19#citation.

Cyert, R. and J. March (1963), *A Behavioral Theory of the Firm*, Englewood Cliffs, NJ: Prentice-Hall.

Deeg, R. (2002), *Finance Capitalism Unveiled: Banks and the German Political Economy*, Ann Arbor, MI: The University of Michigan Press.

Der Spiegel (1974), 'Landesbanken: Kaum zu bremsen' [Landesbanken: Hard to slow down], 11 November.

Der Spiegel (1977), 'Hinter Zäunen' [Behind the fences], 18 April.

Der Spiegel (1989), 'Rückschlag für Helaba' [Setback for Helaba], 11 September.

DiMaggio, P.J. and W.W. Powell (1991), 'Introduction', in P.J DiMaggio and W.W. Powell (eds), *The New Institutionalism in Organizational Analysis*, Chicago, IL: University of Chicago Press, pp. 1–40.

Eisenhardt, K. (1989), 'Agency theory: An assessment and review', *Academy of Management Review*, **14**(1), 57–74.

Fiss, P. (2008), 'Institutions and corporate governance', in R. Greenwood, C. Oliver, R. Suddaby and K. Sahlin-Andersson (eds), *The Sage Handbook of Organizational Institutionalism*, London: Sage, pp. 389–410.

Freeman, E. and J. McVea (2001), 'A stakeholder approach to strategic management', *Darden Business School, University of Virginia, Working Paper No. 01-02*, accessed 2 December 2011 at http://ssrn.com/abstract=263511.

Gubitz, B. (2013), *Das Ende des Landesbankensektors: Der Einfluss von Politik, Management und Sparkassen* [The End of the Landesbanken Sector: The Influence of Politics, Management and Savings Banks], Wiesbaden, Springer Gabler.

Hau, H. and M. Thum (2009), 'Subprime crisis and board (in-)competence. Private versus public banks in Germany', *Economic Policy*, **24**(60), 701–52.

Helaba (2009), *Charter of Landesbank Hessen-Thüringen Girozentrale*, accessed 11 July 2017 at https://www.helaba.com/blob/com/helaba/about-us/. . ./dl-charter--english--en-data.pdf.

Helaba (2012), website, accessed 20 December at https://www.helaba.de/helaba/.

Hertl, R. (1979), 'Verurteilt vor dem Urteil. Das politische Ränkespiel um den Fall des früheren Landesbankchefs Poullain' [Sentenced before judgement. The political play about the case of the former Landesbank chief Poullain], *Die Zeit*, 1 June, accessed 8 July 2017 at http://www.zeit.de/1979/23/verurteilt-vor-dem-urteil.

Hill, C. and T. Jones (1992), 'Stakeholder-agency theory', *Journal of Management Studies*, **29**(2), 131–54.

Jensen, M. and W. Meckling (1976), 'Theory of the firm: Managerial behavior, agency costs and ownership structure', *Journal of Financial Economics*, **3**(4), 305–60.

Kirchhoff, U. (1987), *Zielwandel bei öffentlichen Unternehmen, aufgezeigt am Beispiel der Banken des Bundes,* Schriften zum Genossenschaftswesen und zur öffentlichen Wirtschaft, Bd. 20 [A Change in the Goal of Public Enterprises, Illustrated by the Example of the Federal Banks], Berlin: Duncker & Humblot.

König, T. and P. Wruuck (2011), 'Aufsichtsratskontrolle und strategische Agenda-Setzung in Landesbanken' [Supervisory board control and strategic agenda-setting in Landesbanken], *Perspektiven der Wirtschaftspolitik*, **12**(4), 397–412.

Letza, S. and X. Sun (2002), 'Corporate governance: Paradigms, dilemmas and beyond', *Poznan University of Economics Review*, **2**(1), 43–64.

Meyer, J. and B. Rowan (1977), 'Institutionalized organization: Formal structure as myth and ceremony', *The American Journal of Sociology*, **83**(2), 340–63.

Mintzberg, H. (1979), *The Structuring of Organizations*, Englewood Cliffs, NJ: Prentice-Hall.

Polikhronidi, X. (2012), 'The link between the corporate governance of the German Landesbanken and their performance during the recent financial crisis: The case study of Helaba and WestLB', unpublished Master's thesis, Fachbereich Gesellschaftswissenschaften, Universität Kassel.

Shleifer, A. and R. Vishny (1997), 'A survey on corporate governance', *Journal of Finance*, **52**(2), 737–81.

Taylor, E. (2010), 'Stress tests dredge up past at WestLB, Landesbanks', *Reuters News*,

27 July, accessed 18 January 2012 at http://www.reuters.com/article/2010/07/20/us-landesbanks-idUSTRE66J5IJ20100720.

Trampusch, C., B. Linden and M. Schwan (2014), 'Staatskapitalismus in NRW und Bayern: Der Aufstieg und Fall von WestLB und BayernLB' [State-Capitalism in NRW and Bavaria: The rise and fall of WestLB and BayernLB], *Z Vgl Polit Wiss*, **8**, 129–54.

WestLB (2010), *Articles and Bylaws of WestLB AG*.

WestLB (2012), 'Chronology of WestLB', WestLB official website, accessed 2 January 2012 at http://www.westlb.de/cms/sitecontent/westlb/westlb_de/en/wlb/ueber_uns/chronologie.standard.gid-N2FkNDZmMzU4OWFmYTIyMWM3N2Q2N2Q0YmU1NmI0OGU_.html.

12. Changing structure of non-performing loans: The case of Indian public banks

Meenakshi Rajeev*

It has been argued by a number of economists that a well-developed financial system enables the smooth flow of savings and investments, and hence supports economic growth (see Goldsmith, 1969; King and Levine, 1993). A healthy financial system can help allocate resources across time and space by reducing inefficiencies from market frictions and other socioeconomic factors. Amongst the various desirable characteristics of a well-functioning financial system, a low level of non-performing assets/loans (NPAs/NPLs)[1] is undoubtedly important. NPAs beyond a certain level are indeed a cause for concern, as they affect efficient delivery of credit, hamper the recycling of credit and thereby also adversely impact productive investment and eventually growth. In addition, NPAs affect the profitability of financial institutions, since higher NPAs require higher provisioning. This means that a large part of the profit needs to be kept aside as provision against bad loans.

In India, bank nationalization took place in 1969 and public banks came to play a major role in the economy. Subsequently, there was a large-scale expansion of public bank networks in the rural areas and an introduction of prescribed lending norms for priority sectors such as agriculture and small industries. Due to such social banking, the problem of bad loans did not initially receive priority from policy-makers. NPAs came into play after reforms in the financial sector were introduced, as recommended by the *Report of the Committee on the Financial System* (Narasimham, 1991), and an appropriate accounting system was put in place.

* This chapter benefited from an earlier project carried out under the South Asia Network of Economic Research Institutes (SANEI). The author is grateful to SANEI for its support and thanks the Reserve Bank of India (RBI) for its support to the Institute for Social and Economic Change (ISEC). Part of the chapter is presented at the ISEC-SASS joint conference at the Sichuan Academy of Social Sciences (SASS), China and support from ISEC is acknowledged. The usual disclaimer applies.
[1] In this chapter, NPA and NPL are used interchangeably.

Broadly speaking, an NPA is defined as an advance where payment of interest or repayment of principal instalments (in case of term loans) remains unpaid for a certain period.[2] In India, the definition of NPAs has changed over time. According to the Narasimham Committee Report (1991), assets (advances, bills discounted, overdrafts, cash credits) for which the interest remains due for a period of 180 days should be considered NPAs. Subsequently, this period was reduced, and from March 1995 onwards the assets for which interest has remained unpaid for 90 days have been considered NPAs.

After the introduction of the Basel norms, most countries are now adhering to NPA norms across the globe. Consequently, the subject has received attention from researchers, leading to a substantial amount of literature on the subject, a complete review of which is beyond the scope of the current chapter.

In the Indian context, Rajan (1994) argues that not addressing the problem in time can lead to crisis later while Ghosh (2005), Mor and Sharma (2003) and Rajaraman et al. (1999) subsequently discuss the problem of high NPAs and the crisis that may arise in Indian banks. It is worth mentioning that though the NPA issue has received considerable attention in the post-reform period and subsequently in media and political circles in 2015–16 after a rise in NPA levels of the public banks, academic work on the subject has not kept pace with such developments (see D'Silva et al., 2012; Lokare, 2014; Thiagarajan et al., 2011). While Lokare (2014) attempts to capture the current changes in NPAs, his analysis is primarily based on NPA levels. However, it is important to consider NPAs as a percentage of gross advances to obtain an appropriate assessment of the problem, as an increase in total advances almost always leads to an increase in the level of NPAs as well. This expository chapter attempts to provide an overview of the NPA problem in India by concentrating on its various dimensions and highlighting the structural changes it has undergone in different phases of economic development. Insights from various field experiences are brought together to understand the reasons for the NPA problem in Indian public banks as well as possible measures to combat it.

The next section provides a brief historical perspective on Indian public banks and subsequent financial sector reform measures. The chapter then moves on to discuss NPA experiences in Indian banks: reforms to reduce NPAs in the 1990s, a decline in NPAs until the 2000s and NPAs in priority and non-priority sectors in the 2000s. Recent trends show a deteriorating picture for NPAs, and these are discussed in the fifth section followed by

---

[2] The duration given for an asset to be considered an NPA varies from country to country and can change over time within a particular country.

causes and possible measures. The role of self-help groups in ensuring credit delivery to the poor and ensuring proper recovery is discussed in the penultimate section followed by a concluding section.

BANK NATIONALIZATION AND LIBERALIZATION IN INDIA: A HISTORICAL PERSPECTIVE

After bank nationalization in 1969 (see Chavan, Chapter 7 in this volume),[3] certain welfare measures were initiated in the Indian banking sector where the first and most significant was to ensure the presence of banks in rural and remote regions. The second was to ascertain the flow of credit to selected priority sectors such as agriculture and small-scale industries. These initiatives led to a significant increase in the number of bank offices from 8262 in 1969 to 59752 in 1990. Consequently, the number of customers served per branch declined from 64000 in 1969 to 14000 in 1990, but the share of rural deposits increased steadily. Although bank nationalization was successful in terms of expanding the banking network as well as mobilizing deposits and providing bank credit to the general population, it affected the financial health of the nationalized commercial banks. As a result of the expansionist policy adopted by the Reserve Bank of India (RBI), the number of loss-making branches increased due to high NPA levels, especially in rural areas (Rajeev, 2008b).

While financial sector reforms were initiated as early as 1985 based on recommendations made in the *Report of the Committee to Review the Working of the Monetary System* (Chakravarty, 1985), it was not until 1992, with the recommendations of the Committee on the Financial System (CFS; Narasimham, 1991), that a real drive to restructure the Indian financial system could be observed.

Twofold measures were initiated to improve the functioning of the banking sector, which consisted of a set of deregulation measures together with the introduction of certain institutional and legal reforms. Noteworthy deregulation measures introduced during the period included: the reduction of statutory pre-emption to release more funds for commercial lending; greater operational autonomy to banks; the

---

[3] The Government of India holds majority stakes (more than 50 per cent) in Indian public sector banks. Shares in these banks are also listed on stock exchanges. For example, the State Bank of India (SBI) is an Indian multinational, public sector banking and financial services company. The SBI is ranked 232nd on the *Fortune Global 500* list of the world's biggest corporations as of 2016. The Government of India held around 58.59 per cent of SBI shares as of 31 March 2014 (www.wikipedia.org).

introduction of a market-determined interest rate; and liberalization of entry norms for financial intermediaries to increase competition in the banking sector. Statutory pre-emption requires two types of reserve ratios to be maintained by Indian commercial banks: cash reserve ratio and statutory liquidity ratio, where the latter refers to the proportion of total liabilities that commercial banks must hold in the form of government securities and other approved securities to provide funds for state activities.

Reform measures attempted to improve the competitive environment, and it has been boosted by allowing new private sector banks and more liberal entry by foreign banks. In the post-liberalization period, commercial banks face competition both from within the banking sector and from the outside. Our computation of the Herfindahl-Hirschman Index (HHI), which is a widely used measure of competition, also shows that market concentration declined in the deposit market (from 0.48 in 1992 to 0.37 in 2005) as well as in the credit market (from 0.46 to 0.34 in the same period) (see Rajeev and Mahesh, 2014), which proves that competition increased substantially over the period.

REFORMS TO REDUCE NON-PERFORMING ASSETS IN THE 1990s

The concept of classifying bank assets based on their quality began as early as 1985–86. This was when the RBI introduced critical measures to comprehensively and uniformly monitor credit via the Health Code System. Subsequently, the Narasimham Committee (1991) felt that the classification of assets according to health codes was not in accordance with international standards. The usual practice is that an asset is treated as non-performing when interest is due for at least two quarters and in respect of such non-performing assets, interest is not recognized on an accrual basis but is booked as income only when it is actually received. The committee suggested that a similar practice be followed by banks and financial institutions in India, and recommended that interest on NPAs be booked as income on an accrual basis.

In 1993, based on the recommendations of the Tiwari and Narasimham Committees, Debt Recovery Act was passed and tribunals were established in various parts of the country to assist banks in the speedy recovery of NPAs of Rs1 million or more (www.rbi.org). In addition to these institutional reforms introduced to speed up recovery, various measures taken to reduce NPAs included compromise settlements, rescheduling and restructuring bank loans (by the Asset Reconstruction Companies), and corporate debt restructuring and recovery through Lok Adalats[4] and the civil courts. In this context, it should be noted that one factor responsible for the increasing level of NPAs in the Indian banking industry is a weak legal system (Kapila and Kapila, 2000). Subsequently, based on the recommendations of the Andhyarujina Committee (1999), the SARFAESI Act (Securitization and Reconstruction of Financial Assets and Enforcement of Security Interest) was passed on 17 December 2002, which provided for the enforcement of the security factor without recourse to civil suits. This act was passed with the aim of enabling banks and financial institutions to realize long-term assets, manage liquidity problems, reduce asset liability mismatches, and improve recovery by taking possession of securities, selling them and thereby reducing NPAs.

DECLINE IN NPAs UNTIL THE FIRST DECADE OF THE 2000s

While efforts were ongoing for NPA classifications along with refinement of the accounting system and measures to reduce NPAs in the initial phases of the reform period (i.e., in the 1990s), proper implementation of these norms took time. Systematic data on NPAs started to become available in usable form only in 1998. Though the total gross NPA ratio increased significantly between 1998 and 2002, it started to decline subsequently. Starting from as high as 15.7 per cent in 1996–97, the Indian banking sector was able to reduce it to 2.4 per cent by 2009–10, which can be considered a significant achievement (RBI, 2014).

In an interconnected global world it is of interest to look at India's performance vis-à-vis the other nations. Compared to OECD countries, NPA ratios in India as well as other Asian nations were at a relatively higher level at the beginning of this century. In 2001, the Indian ratio was 11.4 per cent while corresponding figures for the UK and the USA were only 2.6 per cent and 1.3 per cent, respectively (Table 12.1). By 2009, however, India had reduced its NPA ratio to 2.21 per cent (a trend seen for many other Asian nations as well), while for the UK and the USA it increased to 3.51 and 5 per cent, respectively.

At the bank group level, we observe that the track record of public sector banks is as good as their counterparts in the private sector (Table 12.2) and in some cases, public sector banks are actually performing better than

---

[4] Lok Adalat is a system of alternative dispute resolution established in 1987. It roughly translates as 'People's Court', under which both parties in a dispute should agree to settlement (see www.gktoday.in/lok-adalat/, last accessed 8 July 2017).

Table 12.1   NPA by total advances ratio for selected countries and selected years

Countries	2001	2009	2015
Bangladesh	31.5	–	9.3
Brazil	5.6	4.2	3.3
China	29.8	1.6	1.5
Germany	4.6	3.3	2.3
Hong Kong	6.5	1.6	0.7
India	11.4	2.2	5.9
Indonesia	31.9	33.0	2.4
Japan	8.4	2.4	1.6
Malaysia	17.8	3.6	1.6
Philippines	27.7	3.5	1.9
Singapore	8.0	2.0	0.9
Sri Lanka	15.3	–	3.2
Thailand	11.5	5.2	2.7
United Kingdom	2.6	3.5	1.8
United States	1.3	5.0	1.5

Source: Global Financial Stability Report, various issues, IMF.

established Indian private sector banks. Indeed, if we examine the growth of loans vis-à-vis NPAs, after the reforms, it appears that the public sector banks were able to address the NPA problem more effectively than Indian private banks (especially that of the old private banks). However, they do not fare so well (except for 2009) when compared to foreign banks, maybe partly because foreign banks are long accustomed to NPA norms in their parent countries. Further, various credit-related welfare programmes are carried out through public sector banks, and public banks have maximum reach in rural areas where foreign banks are absent. It is econometrically shown that a higher number of rural branches significantly increase the share of NPAs in total advances (Rajeev, 2008b).

NPAs IN PRIORITY AND NON-PRIORITY SECTORS IN THE 2000s

One important question raised in the case of NPAs in Indian commercial banks is whether credit policy in line with the government social banking motto led to an increase in NPAs. To examine this, we consider sector-wise NPAs in the priority sectors (agriculture, small-scale industries and some

Table 12.2 Bank group wise NPAs of Indian commercial banks, 2002–09

	Gross NPAs of Scheduled Commercial Banks (Nominal Values, Rs million)							
	2002	2003	2004	2005	2006	2007	2008	2009
Public sector banks								
Gross NPAs	564 730	540 900	515 370	483 990	413 580	389 680	404 520	449 570
% to gross advance	11.1	9.4	7.8	5.5	3.6	2.7	2.2	2.0
Old private banks								
Gross NPAs	48 510	45 500	43 980	42 000	37 590	29 690	25 570	30 072
% to gross advance	11.0	8.9	7.6	6.0	4.4	3.1	2.3	2.4
New private banks								
Gross NPAs	68 110	72 320	59 830	45 820	40 520	62 870	104 400	138 540
% to gross advance	8.9	7.6	5.0	3.6	1.7	1.9	2.5	3.1
Foreign banks								
Gross NPAs	27 260	28 450	28 940	21 920	19 280	22 630	28 590	64 440
% to gross advance	5.4	5.3	4.6	2.8	1.9	1.8	1.8	3.8

Source: Computed using RBI data: https://rbi.org.in/scripts/PublicationsView.aspx?id=15854.

other sectors) vis-à-vis non-priority sector loans. Our analysis of data reveals that the share of NPAs in the priority sector vis-à-vis the share of total advances for the sector is indeed higher than the corresponding NPAs shares in the non-priority sector, and this trend has continued over the years (Figure 12.1).

According to our analysis of bank group wise sectoral NPA data, the average share of priority sector NPAs in the total NPAs was around 46.2 per cent, 47.9 per cent and 23.9 per cent for the State Bank of India and its associate banks,[5] other nationalized public banks and private banks, respectively, in 2005. While lower share of priority sector NPAs (less than 50 per cent) have been highlighted by some observers, a point often missed is that the priority sector constitutes about 40 per cent of total lending. Further, the decline in NPAs in agriculture from 2008 to 2009 (Figure 12.1) may have partly been due to the loan waiver policy adopted by the government for the priority sector, under which non-performing loans to farmers were waived.

Computation of sector wise NPAs to total advances using data from RBI reveals that while the NPA ratio for the agricultural sector was about 12.7 per cent in 2002 (6 per cent in 2005) for public sector banks, it was as high as 18.8 per cent in 2002 (11 per cent in 2005) for small-scale industry. For the non-priority sectors together, NPAs as a percentage of total advances declined from about 8 per cent to 4 per cent from 2002 to 2005, showing a steady sector-wise decline.

Thus we observe certain important features of NPA for Indian public banks in this period. First, there was a significant reduction in NPA levels after the impacts of financial sector reforms began to be felt, especially in the last decade. It has come down from double digits to about 2 per cent (from 2006–07 to 2009–10). Second, performance of public banks is noteworthy as they show a lower ratio of NPAs to gross advances. Third, priority sectors like small-scale industries show a higher share of NPAs for the public banks. Our analysis using bank-level data in a panel data framework (see Rajeev, 2008b) also shows that having more rural branches adversely affects NPA levels. Thus it appears that in spite of having to adhere to welfare norms (such as mandatory priority sector lending or opening rural branches), public banks have fared fairly well in combating bad loans. The important question that arises is whether this trend continued over time?

---

[5] Such as the State Bank of Mysore and the State Bank of Travancore, some of them now merged with the State Bank of India.

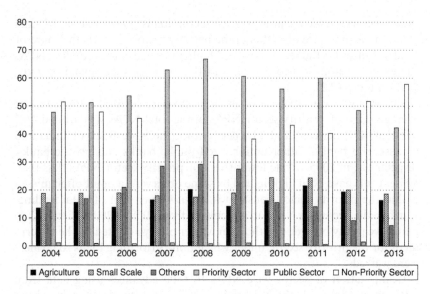

Source: Compiled from RBI *Reports on Trends & Progress of Banking in India* (2004–13).

Figure 12.1   Sector contribution to NPA in percentage of total NPA, 2004–13

RECENT INCREASES IN NPAs

After 2010, the Indian banking sector experienced changes on three important fronts. First, the previous steady decline in NPAs as a percentage of gross advances has reversed in recent years, especially for the public banks. While globally the ratios of NPA have continued to decline or show a minor increase for many Asian nations like China, Japan, Indonesia and Malaysia, it reached nearly 6 per cent for India (Table 12.1). This gives an indication that in addition to global factors, certain domestic factors are responsible for India's recent poor performance.

Second, public sector banks with two major subgroups, the State Bank and its associates and other nationalized banks, now show a higher NPA percentage than private and foreign banks. As of 31 March 2015, the State Bank and its associates and other nationalized banks showed NPA ratios of 4.28 and 5.26 per cent, respectively; but for private and foreign banks the corresponding figures were 2.1 and 3.2 per cent (Reserve Bank of India, 2015).

Third, the share of the priority sector has come down significantly. Even though loan default in the priority sector remains a concern, it is currently the non-priority sector, mainly the corporate sector, that has turned out to be a major contributor to bad loans. If we take all the stressed assets of public banks together, it was at an all-time high of 14.1 per cent as of September 2015, followed by private banks at 4.6 per cent and foreign banks at 3.4 per cent (Reserve Bank of India, 2015).

Sectoral data as of June 2015 indicates that among the broad sectors, industry continued to record the highest ratio of NPAs to total advances at about 19.5 per cent, followed by services at 7 per cent and the retail sector at just 2 per cent. In terms of size, medium and large industries each had an NPA ratio of 21 per cent, whereas for micro-industries the ratio stood at over 8 per cent. Five major subsectors (mining, iron and steel, textiles, infrastructure and aviation), which together constituted 24.2 per cent of the total advances of state commercial banks (SCBs), contributed 53 per cent of total NPAs (as of June 2015; Reserve Bank of India, 2015). Importantly, the GNPA ratios of the large borrowers among public banks increased from 6.1 per cent in March 2015 to 8.1 per cent in September 2015.

UNDERSTANDING THE CAUSES OF LOAN DEFAULT

The 2015–16 Ministry of Finance *Annual Report* attributed the performance of public banks with regard to non-performing loans primarily to exogenous factors such as global slowdown and continuing uncertainty in the global markets, leading to lower exports of various products like textiles, engineering goods, leather items and gems. In addition to the external factors, it said that: 'the ban in mining projects, delay in clearance of projects in power and steel sector, volatility in prices of raw material and a shortage of power have impacted operations in infrastructure sectors, which were aggressively funded by the banks in the past' (*Annual Report*, Ministry of Finance, 2015–16). Infrastructure projects also face substantial delay at times due to the problems of environmental clearance and land acquisition.

Besides the infrastructure sector, the steel industry in particular is increasingly unable to repay its loans (interviews with bank officials) as the international price of steel is on a downward curve and China, with excess capacity, is dumping its steel into many markets including India. Thus certain exogenous changes in the business environment are one major cause of enhanced risk and bad loans.

However, experts from the Reserve Bank of India also highlight three important internal causes for the deteriorating situation: corporate imprudence, corporate misdemeanour, and faulty risk assessment and lack of cautiousness on the part of the banks (Mundra, 2016). It is felt that some corporations are expanding their business without assessing its viability and eventually defaulting on their loans.

While many may engage in such activities due to lack of judgement (bounded rationality), some borrowers can be termed as wilful defaulters. Proper risk assessment by banks in selecting borrowers is a necessity, and Indian banks appear to have failed in this regard to some extent. Many believe that bank officials are also to be blamed for collusive behaviour. An example of this is the Kingfisher Airlines default case, where some officials are under investigation (Press Trust of India, 2016).

Banks claim that they adhere to standard risk assessment procedures. As far as risk assessment of loan applications is concerned, a bank assesses various risk parameters including management risks (adequacy of knowledge), business risks (demand fluctuations, competition), political risks (change in state policies), operational risks, and marketing risks. These risks are assessed based on a standard questionnaire and scores are assigned accordingly. Subsequently, a risk assessment model (RAM) is used to finally arrive at a decision. This exercise is usually carried out by specialized bank officials and is not outsourced. In the past, individual officers made decisions to sanction a project based on risk ratings, but today a committee takes the final call for most banks. Because NPAs have risen in recent times although banks follow the same procedures to assess potential borrowers, they have become much stricter in sanctioning loans, thereby creating some amount of credit rationing. To reduce moral hazard, information about defaulters is also made easily available so that a bank can make an informed decision (interviews with public bank recovery departments).

Rules concerning the declaration of an account as an NPA have also become stricter in recent times. For example, even if a loan granted by a bank is serviced properly by a borrower, the loan has to be declared an NPA if the borrower is not repaying his or her loan on time, taken at another bank. Today all these activities are system driven, and hence there is less scope for concealing information, leading to higher levels of declared NPAs.

Though the legal process to recover a bad loan has been modified (see the second section above), it still has not been able to provide the required support to banks. Enacted in 2002, the SARFAESI Act (Securitization and Reconstruction of Financial Assets and Enforcement of Security Interest) was intended to help banks deal with the recovery process faster and stay out of the civil courts; however, the recovery rates have remained dismally low, even in recent times (Table 12.3).

Table 12.3   NPAs of state commercial banks recovered through various channels, selected years

	One-time Settlement/ Compromise Scheme	LokAdalats	Debt Recovery Tribunals	SARFAESI Act
2003–04				
No. of cases referred	139 562	186 100	7 544	2661
Amount involved	1510	1063	12 305	7847
Amount recovered	617	149	2117	1156
2008–09				
No. of cases referred	–	548 308	2004	61 760
Amount involved	–	4023	4130	12 067
Amount recovered	–	96	3348	3982
2012–13				
No. of cases referred	–	840 691	13 408	190 537
Amount involved	–	6600	31 000	68 100
Amount recovered	–	400	4400	18 500

Source: RBI *Reports on Trends & Progress of Banking in India* (2002–13); https://rbidocs. rbi.org.in/rdocs/Publications/PDFs/67311.pdf Page 89 for 2003–04.

In agriculture, a specific form of state intervention aggravates the NPA problem. From time to time and especially near election times, some state governments declare loan waivers for farmers. Our field survey in the state of Karnataka (see Rajeev and Vani, 2012) shows that such waivers help rich farmers more than poor farmers, as poor farmers have less access to formal credit. Further, the fact that the farmers who repay loans on time get no waiver benefits, creates moral hazard problem for the prompt repayer and these farmers could thus be less willing to repay on time subsequently and instead wait for a waiver (see also Bhattacharjee and Rajeev, 2013).

From corporate and agriculture, we now turn to the small industries sector which was the highest source of NPAs in the last decade and still continues to contribute to bad loans. Firms in the sector face specific operational and marketing problems and many a times cannot repay loans on time due to funding constraints. These firms often produce intermediary goods that are purchased by other large producers and/or the government and in recent times due to lower economic activities, buyers including the government do not pay on time leading to default by these firms (revealed from our interview with bank officials).

Wilful defaulters are also present among small producers. Our survey of the small-scale sector (see Rajeev, 2008a) reveals that though banks usually do not designate borrowers as wilful defaulters, bank officials can assess the cases during field visits. From our discussions with bank officials, wilful defaulters can be classified into three categories: (1) people with political influence; (2) negligent borrowers who feel (for whatever reason) that they need not repay; (3) and borrowers who divert funds for other purposes. The second case usually occurs with loans under certain government schemes (from our observations, in the case of borrowers, e.g. youth or women getting loans under special schemes and so on). In the third case, some borrowers rightly understand that they can earn a higher return by diverting their funds to other businesses such as real estate. By the time the bank confiscates their security, which usually takes a considerable amount of time, they would have earned a return much higher than the lost security. Our survey revealed a particular group of wilful defaulters in micro-industries. These borrowers obtain loans under well-planned government schemes introduced to buy certain capital goods (for example, a sewing machine) to provide livelihood support to women or other vulnerable sections of the population. A well-organized intermediary network prepares, in collusion with the potential borrowers, documents for availing loans under a government scheme. However, rather than investing in the stated purpose, both parties share the loan amount. Even if a bank pays the supplier of the capital good directly, it can happen that this intermediary network establishes collusive agreements with the machine suppliers as well. While only a small proportion of firms are such wilful defaulters, this issue is important from a bank's perspective

In order to address the NPA situation, the central government has recently taken sector-specific measures in areas such as road, steel, power and textiles. It is also setting up six new Debt Recovery Tribunals to facilitate the recovery of bad loans (see also Gandhi, 2015). Further, to maintain an adequate capital-to-risk-asset ratio, the central government has also put substantial funds into public banks (*Annual Report* of the Ministry of Finance 2015–16).

The RBI, as a regulatory body, released a comprehensive 'Framework for Revitalizing Distressed Assets in the Economy' in January 2014. This framework encompasses a corrective action plan that ensures early appraisal and recognition of bad assets, and an assurance that unviable accounts will be dealt with promptly. Rajan (1994) discusses the problem of reluctance on the part of the banks to declare a loan as an NPA to maintain reputation and the above framework can help to address the problem. Therefore, the Central Repository of Information on Large Credits (CRILC) was established to collect, store and disseminate credit data to lenders. Banks are required to report credit information to CRILC, especially if an account with more than Rs50 million shows signs of distress (RBI, 2013–14).

Several legal reforms have also been introduced, most notably the recent Insolvency and Bankruptcy Code, 2016. The *Gazette of India* describes the purpose of this code, which is to consolidate and amend laws relating to insolvency resolution by establishing the Insolvency and Bankruptcy Board of India (28 May 2016).

SELF-HELP GROUPS: AN INSTITUTION THAT MAKES THE POOR BANKABLE

Potential borrowers in priority sectors (both agriculture and micro- and small industries) are mostly poor; banks, in an attempt to reduce NPAs, often shun these borrowers. These borrowers then turn to informal lenders with unfavourable terms such as high interest rates. Interestingly, however, these lenders face a much lower risk of default from poor borrowers which shows that poor people are somehow able to repay.

The self-help group is an institution that has indeed proven even to the formal institutions that the poor are bankable. In India, a self-help group (SHG) refers to a small group of 10–20 individuals (usually women) who come together for saving and lending activities amongst themselves. According to the National Bank for Agriculture and Rural Development (NABARD, 2015), SHGs are 'small, economically homogeneous affinity groups of usually rural poor, voluntarily formed to save and mutually contribute to a common fund to be lent to its members as per the group members' decision'. In India the NABARD assisted groups formed under the self-help group bank linkage programme (SBLP) are of particular importance as SBLP links the groups to the bank whereby the women members deal with banking sector directly. Savings are collected in small amounts at frequent intervals, usually once a week or a fortnight, during group meetings. The group meeting also acts as a forum in which it is decided who gets credit and how much, usually in a collaborative process. The most important feature is that the group takes joint liability for loan recovery.

The provision of hassle-free access to financial services and products through the formal sector at low interest rates has a number of benefits for the poor. First, an SBLP provides consumption as well as production loans without any collateral. Second, it enables SHG members to reap economic benefits from mutual help, solidarity and joint responsibility. The programme also ensures long-term help for a number of activities, most notably income-generating activities. Constant dealings with the banking sector help the members to be more at ease with formal lending institutions. At the same time it helps the formal banking sector identify rural needs and provide assistance accordingly. In other words, capacity building takes place at both ends. Account maintenance on a regular basis helps the group members understand how to handle financial resources.

As of 2015, the NABARD programme reported more than 7.5 million self-help groups linked to banks (NABARD, 2015). About 6 million groups have accessed credit under the programme, and the repayment rate is quite high. Thus the self-monitoring mechanism has worked well to ensure low NPAs for banks and made the poor bankable. During our field survey in the state of Karnataka (Rajeev et al., 2015), we observed that the repayment rate is above 80 per cent, and in certain districts it is as high as 95 per cent. However, certain observations from field research regarding repayment are noteworthy. Loan waivers given to the agriculture sector, as mentioned above (especially during the election in 2008), created a feeling of discrimination in the groups. It was revealed that some groups were misinformed by social workers in their village that the government also waived their loans. Thus with the hope of getting loan waivers, these members stopped paying instalments and consequently within a few months, the loan burden grew to the extent that it became unaffordable.

Currently, it is women who mainly form self-help groups in India. NABARD is presently in the process of forming farmer groups on the same principle. If such endeavours become successful, it will not only solve the problem of loan non-repayment, but also improve credit accessibility for the poor.

In the case of the small industries sector, we also observed that self-monitoring mechanisms are used to address the NPA problem to some extent in small firms in Kerala (Rajeev, 2008a). Small firms often become members of small industry associations to obtain various benefits or facilities. Banks often opt to ally themselves with small-scale industry associations, with the guarantee that the bank will provide small borrower loans without security/collateral. In case of non-repayment, the industry association is expected to put pressure on the borrower. The potential borrowers have to be members of the industry association, so that both the association and the bank stand to gain. Such models are not yet widespread in the small industries sector, but they certainly have great potential.

CONCLUSION

The problem of non-performing assets, which was long ignored in India, received considerable attention of the policy makers after the liberalization of the financial sector in the 1990s. Accounting norms have been modified substantially and mechanisms were put in place for reducing the amount of bad loans. Our discussions with banks revealed that the decline in NPAs during the first decade of the 2000s was mainly due to increased awareness at the bank level (see Rajeev and Mahesh, 2007) leading to strict self-monitoring. At first, NPA levels (as a percentage to advances) were higher in the priority sector than in the non-priority sector where within the priority sector, loan performance in the small industries sector was the worst. But even this sector has shown a reduction in bad loans over time.

However, in the most recent decade, structural changes in NPAs are noticeable in Indian public banks and three important features are noteworthy here. First, the steady decline in NPAs as a percentage of gross advances seen in the previous decade began to change in the last few years, especially for the public banks. Second, public sector banks, which consist of two major subgroups (the State Bank together with its associates and nationalized banks), now show a higher percentage of NPAs than private and foreign banks. Third, large businesses are contributing more to bad loans than the priority sectors. From the demand side, corporate imprudence is one major reason for this adversely changing scenario, and from the supply side, risk analysis processes of the banks are in question. The Reserve Bank of India has taken a number of measures to improve the health of the banking sector. The central government has also introduced legal reforms to address the problem. In the near future, public banks in India have to be more prudent and vigilant to improve their deteriorating health.

In India, banks often attempt to reduce bad loans by shunning poor borrowers. In this context, the self-help group model can be adapted in some of the priority sectors much more extensively to help the poor access loans and ensure bank repayment.

REFERENCES

Andhyarujina, T.R. (1999), *Report of the Committee on Legal Reforms in Banking Sector*, Mumbai: Reserve Bank of India.

Bhattacharjee, M. and M. Rajeev (2013), 'Modeling loan repayment behavior in developing countries', *Applied Economic Perspectives and Policy, Agricultural and Applied Economics Association*, **35**(2), 270–95.

Chakravarty, S. (1985), *Report of the Committee to Review the Working of the Monetary System*, Mumbai: RBI Press.

D'Silva, S., B. D'Silva and R.A. Gandhi (2012), 'Evaluation of non-performing assets in public and private sector banks in India: A comparative study', *Indian Journal of Economics & Business*, **11**(2), 561–69.

Gandhi, R. (2015), 'Asset reconstruction & NPA management summit', Keynote Address delivered by Shri R. Gandhi, Deputy Governor, RBI, at the Economic Times ReModel in India – Assets Reconstruction and NPA Management Summit, Mumbai on 15 September 2015, accessed 8 July 2017 at https://rbi.org.in/scripts/BS_SpeechesView.aspx?Id=974.

Ghosh, S. (2005), 'Does leverage influence banks' non-performing loans? Evidence from India', *Applied Economic Letters*, **12**(15), 913–18.

Goldsmith, R.W. (1969), *Financial Structure and Development (Studies in Comparative Economics)*, New Haven, CT and London: Yale University Press.

Kapila, R. and U. Kapila (2000), *Ongoing Developments in Banking and Financial Sector*, New Delhi: Academic Foundation.

King, R.G. and R. Levine (1993), 'Finance and growth: Schumpeter might be right', *Quarterly Journal of Economics*, **108**(3), 717–37.

Lokare, S.M. (2014), 'Re-emerging stress in the asset quality of Indian banks: Macro-financial linkages', *RBI Working Paper Series, No. WPS (DEPR) 03/2014*.

Ministry of Finance (2015–16), *Annual Report*, Ministry of Finance, Government of India.

Mor, N. and B. Sharma (2003), 'Rooting out non-performing assets', paper presented at the 5th Annual Conference on Money and Finance in the Indian Economy, Indira Gandhi Institute of Development Research, Mumbai.

Mundra, S.S. (2016), 'Asset quality challenges in India – diagnosis and prognosis', Keynote Address by Mr S.S. Mundra, Deputy Governor of the Reserve Bank of India, at the Edelweiss Credit Conclave, Mumbai, 28 April 2016.

Narasimham, M. (1991), *Report of the Committee on Banking Sector Reform*, Mumbai: RBI Press.

National Bank for Agriculture and Rural Development (NABARD) (2015), *Annual Report*, Mumbai: NABARD.

Press Trust of India (2016), 'Standard Chartered Bank alleges Mallya colluded with banks led by SBI', *The Economic Times*, 15 June accessed 3 November 2016 at http://economictimes.indiatimes.com/news/politics-and-nation/standard-chartered-bank-alleges-mallya-colluded-with-banks-led-by-sbi/articleshow/52769726.cms.

Rajan, R.G. (1994), 'Why bank credit policies fluctuate: A theory and some evidence', *The Quarterly Journal of Economics*, **109**(2), 399–441.

Rajaraman, I., S. Bhaumik and N. Bhatia (1999), 'NPA variations across Indian commercial banks: Some findings', *Economic and Political Weekly*, **34**(03–04), 161–8.

Rajeev, M. (2008a), 'Small-scale industries sector in India', in N. Ndubisi (ed.), *SME Development and Practices in Asia Pacific RIM*, Malaysia: Arah Publishers.

Rajeev, M. (2008b), *Asset as Liability? Nonperforming Assets in the Indian Commercial Banks, Project Report*, submitted to the South Asia Network of Economic Institutes.

Rajeev, M. and H.P. Mahesh (2007), 'Assets as liabilities: Non-performing assets in commercial banks of India', *Research Monitor, Global Development Network*, No. 3, 17–19.

Rajeev, M. and H.P. Mahesh (2014), 'The Indian banking system: Reforms and beyond', in J. Zajaczkowski, J. Schottli and M. Thapa (eds), *India in the Contemporary World: Polity, Economy and International Relations*, Abingdon, Oxford: Routledge.

Rajeev, M. and B.P. Vani (2012), *Farm Sector in Karnataka: Farmers' Indebtedness and*

Risk Management, Project Report, Bangalore: Institute for Social and Economic Change.

Rajeev, M., B.P. Vani and Veerashekharappa (2015), 'Financial inclusion through SHGs: Understanding quality and sustainability of SHGs in Karnataka State', *ISEC Monograph No. 40*, Bangalore: ISEC.

Reserve Bank of India (RBI) (2013–14), 'Framework for revitalising distressed assets in the economy – Guidelines on Joint Lenders' Forum (JLF) and Corrective Action Plan (CAP)', RBI/2013-14/503DBOD.BP.BC.No.97/21.04.132/2013-14, ac cessed 8 July 2017 at https://www.rbi.org.in/scripts/NotificationUser.aspx?Id=875 4&Mode=0.

Reserve Bank of India (RBI)(2015), *Financial Stability Report*, December 2015, accessed 8 July 2017 at https://rbi.org.in/Scripts/PublicationReportDetails.aspx? UrlPage=&ID=835.

Thiagarajan, S., S. Ayyappan and A. Ramachandran (2011), 'Credit risk determinants of public and private sector banks in India', *European Journal of Economics, Finance and Administrative Sciences*, **34**, 147–54.

13. The stakeholder governance of microfinance

Magdalena Dieterle

The link between public banks and microfinance may seem less than obvious, but when examined with respect to alternatives to the casino capitalism of commercial banking today, the link is clear. There is no need to enumerate the ways and lengths in which the standard commercial banking system has failed in recent times. However, many are beginning to see that where the 'profit-maximizing approach falls short the stakeholders' approach turns out to be more adequate' (Périlleux, 2010, p. 2). It is the experience of ownership that ties together microfinance institutions and financial credit cooperatives and juxtaposes their stakeholder nature to the shareholder nature of the more classic banking sector.

The time for examining alternatives to the standard commercial banking model is now. In the aftermath of a global banking crisis, we have reached a point at which the make-up and culture of the banking system can be more openly discussed. In addition, the merits of a stakeholder approach or a banking system built on the savings of the community served, are that they are profitable and grow, but at a stable rate. To look for models that can sustain themselves over the long run and not merely the next boom–bust cycle, it makes sense to consider those models that have already endured throughout the centuries. Therefore, I will provide examples from history to illustrate just how microfinance and financial credit cooperatives have been a stable alternative to commercial banks. I will show that microfinance is more than merely a small loan scheme, but rather financial intermediation for the poor. I will show that microfinance is not a new phenomenon, but has a long history that offers many lessons for us to learn, especially the merit of supportive external governance structures and internal governance policies that allow the financial institutions to exist and flourish. Supportive external governance structures in the form of legislation allow microfinance and financial credit cooperatives to compete with commercial banks, for example by offering competitive interest on deposits. In the case of Germany, the governance structure became a part of the banking culture, making alternatives such as financial credit cooperatives a part of the norm, changing and stabilizing the banking culture for its communities. We cannot export a banking culture ad hoc, but we can look at alternatives that have worked in many different cultures, such as microfinance and credit cooperatives, and examine what external and internal governance structures contribute to their success. We can examine what alternatives have existed throughout history and what tools they used to survive crisis – namely, how savings and community ownership can act as ballast during turbulent times and external governance structures, often supported by political interest, can give alternative banking models space to exist.

THE DEFINITION(S) OF MICROFINANCE

Regarding microfinance, even experts on the subject misuse the term, interchanging it with microcredit (Boudreaux and Cowen, 2008). Although usually stemming from expedience, this interchanging use is not only erroneous, but also actually damaging to the notion of what microfinance is. Simply put, microfinance is financial intermediation for the poor. Hans Dieter Seibel first coined the term in 1990, defining it as 'the part of the financial sector which comprises formal and informal financial institutions small and large that provide small sized financial services to the poorer sections of the population as well as larger sized financial services to agroprocessing and other small and medium rural enterprises' (Seibel, 2005, abstract). The term that was meant to include financial intermediation between borrowers and savers was taken up by the Consultancy Group to Assist the Poor (CGAP) in the mid-1990s and used in the microcredit revolution (championed by Muhammad Yunus), after which the terminology became expanded and muddled (Seibel, 2005). The innovative practice of focusing microloans primarily on women in Bangladesh was exciting and garnered much attention to the relatively small field. The confusion between microcredit and microfinance became further muddled and was used interchangeably more and more often. This is dangerous because it excludes much of what microfinance encompasses, most notably savings.

Savings are a huge and vital element of microfinance, also historically speaking. The indigenous financial institutions of the sixteenth and seventeenth centuries evolved into what we now know as microfinance institutions. 'Almost from the onset, microfinance meant financial intermediation between microsavings and microcredit, and was powered by that' (Seibel, 2005, p. 1).

Currently, the CGAP defines microfinance institutions (MFIs) broadly as 'licensed and unlicensed financial institutions that include nongovernmental organizations, commercial banks, credit unions, and cooperatives and agricultural, development and postal savings banks. They range from specialized microfinance providers to programs with larger multipurpose development organizations' (Isern et al., 2008).

Since the scope of microfinance institutions is so broad, it is important to establish limits for the purposes of this chapter. Although it is true that there is no best practice in microfinance and different models often serve different communities with their own unique challenges, it is also true that one could easily get lost in the exceptions and lose focus on the bigger picture. Therefore, I will focus on MFIs that are based on the stakeholder model, in which the institution is steeped in the community it serves and is funded in part or completely by clients' savings. The most classic examples of the stakeholder model are savings and credit cooperative associations (SACCOs) and rotating savings and credit associations (ROSCAs), popular throughout Africa. Also included are self-help groups (SHGs), popular throughout India, and to a certain extent group-lending models popularized by the Grameen Bank.

Distinguishing Features of Microfinance

There are several features that set microfinance apart from the classic conception of for-profit banking. A closer examination of those features and how they are exhibited in both past and present MFI models helps clarify their differences:[1]

- *Small loan size:* On the surface, this may be the simplest feature of microfinance to accept. After all, it is the least challenging to the conventional wisdom of what microfinance is: miniscule loans to the poor. However, it is critical to put loan size in the context of time and place, and emphasize that although the media have inundated us with stories of Bangladesh, the loan size must be considered small only for its particular context. For example, ACCION US, a leading MFI that has been lending within the United States since 1991, estimates its average loan at US$5100, but its loan range is from US$700–50 000 (ACCION US, 2017).

---

[1] When defining the fundamental features of microfinance, I have left out the focus on women or included it as one of many possible missions. This is because the focus on gender is a more recent and innovative feature that has not been a marker throughout the evolution of microfinance. My purpose is to look back and see what microfinance and financial credit cooperatives have in common to see what lessons can be learned in terms of better governance. Although the focus on gender is a critical innovative step in recent times, it is not critical for this comparison.

- *Purpose or mission:* For MFIs, there is usually a clear mission to reach the poor, sometimes with a more specific target such as poor women, rural areas, internally displaced people, and persecuted people within a region, ethnic or religious group. There is never a single best practice in microfinance and the plurality of purpose is a clear demonstration of why that is the case. But for the vast majority, there is a purpose or mission: to provide financial services to the unbanked poor (Mersland, 2011). Targeting the poor does not mean excluding wealthier or less poor clients. In fact, their inclusion could help bring stability to an MFI and allow for the continued provision of services to their poorer clients (ibid.).
- *Joint liability/limited liability:* Achieved in many ways, shared liability is a typical aspect of microfinance loans. Whether it is achieved through group loans as in the Grameen model or through loaning out pooled resources as in the ROSCA and SACCO models, it achieves the goal of limiting risk. Group liability also leads to group reporting, thereby easing the burden of monitoring but also increasing accuracy by reducing moral hazard (Banerjee et al., 1994).
- *Uncollateralized:* Because microfinance loans are not collateralized in the traditional sense, MFIs often rely on what is commonly referred to as social collateral. This can encompass many different dynamics from group pressure to repay to actually trading on reputation or social standing within the community (Banerjee et al., 1994; Wenner, 1995). Due to the fact that loans secured through social collateral rely so heavily on community ties, these techniques are especially effective in MFIs that are a part of the community, such as locally based MFIs and cooperatives directly owned by the community (Banerjee et al. 1994).
- *Savings:* As mentioned before, savings are a critical aspect of microfinance. Although it is not always legally allowed for small non-profit or NGO MFIs to take deposits, many forms of microfinance exist mostly or solely based on member deposits. ROSCAs and SACCOs are excellent examples of this. Savings not only allow them to operate, but their members also have ownership of the association, providing greater institutional and financial stability (Hollis and Sweetman, 1998; Périlleux et al., 2010).

  Another aspect of savings discussed with greater frequency is the notion of implicit savings through microfinance loans. Although seemingly contradictory, Boudreaux and Cowen (2008) clearly illustrate how loans alleviate the social pressures on microfinance client savings by removing accessibility. This is often true because the same tight-knit community that provides support to microfinance clients can also be the greatest source of pressure. Events and circumstances such a neighbor's wedding, the illness of a friend's child, or school fees for a cousin can create very urgent short-term demand for funds. Yet when the savings are removed and replaced by a loan, which is a known obligation, it is much easier to decline. The loan itself acts as savings, but instead of saving up for something as is ingrained in Western culture, loans allow microfinance clients to save down, or save by paying down their loan (Roberts, 2011).

- *Skill training:* Skill training is an important function of MFIs. Building financial literacy, even on the smallest scale, is one of the key aspects of microfinance. This can be achieved in a myriad of simple ways. Having a formalized, yet simplified process for filling out loan contracts is not merely for the benefit of the institution, but also for making their clients more accustomed to common banking procedures so they are more prepared to graduate to commercial banks. Even wait times for loans can be used to instill in clients the need to plan ahead. In addition to the many subtle and not so subtle indirect skill trainings, MFIs often offer basic business skills training courses and require client attendance as a condition for the loan. Training courses typically cover various topics from basic accounting skills to record keeping or basic financial planning. Some MFIs, such as Grameen Bank, Pro Mujer and Opportunity International, cover topics that go beyond basic business skills and cover broader life skills such as basic hygiene and health as well as the importance of education.

EARLY MICROFINANCE INSTITUTIONS

Often portrayed as only 40 years old or new in terms of financial institutions, the concept that we call microfinance is not a new phenomenon; it has a long and rich history going back centuries or longer (Guinnane, 2011; Hollis and Sweetman, 1998; Périlleux, 2010; Seibel, 2005). Even though the term 'microfinance' itself is relatively recent, the concept can be traced back centuries in Europe and so far back in regions such as India that searching for the first instance would be a largely futile endeavor (Guinnane, 2011). 'Microfinance is not a new concept and historical analyses are especially relevant for cooperatives, which are the "single most enduring and wide spread form of MFIs in the world"' (Hollis and Sweetman, 1998, in Périlleux, 2010, p. 2). Seibel clearly outlines why it is critical to acknowledge and look at the history of microfinance:

(i) Attributing the origin of microfinance to recent initiatives misses the histori-cal depth and scale of microfinance. As a consequence, centuries of experience, of learning from trial and error, failure and success in the past are being missed. (ii) Conducive policies in several European countries have created an environ-ment where small microfinance beginnings have evolved into vast networks of local and financial institutions which are now part of the formal banking system. (iii) This may present a vision to those who may think that microfinance is a poor solution for poor countries to be replaced by large commercial banks once development takes off. (iv) Informal finance and self-help have been at the origin of microfinance in Europe. Realizing how informal finance evolved into a major part of the banking system and contributed to poverty alleviation and development may induce policymakers, donors, and researchers to take a fresh look at indigenous and informal finance in the developing world. (Seibel, 2005, p. 1)

The History of Irish Loan Funds

There were many versions of microfinance institutions in Ireland's history, and most of them are typically illustrated as cautionary tales or lessons to be learned where others have failed. I will briefly illustrate the ways in which the Irish models were successful, as well as some of the reasons why that success was short-lived and ultimately dismissed as unsustainable.

Irish loan funds first emerged in the 1720s. They started out as a charity but quickly became financial intermediation between savers and borrowers (Seibel, 2005). Peer monitoring was used to enforce repayment. They grew very slowly until changes in regulations created a boom. A law passed in 1823 allowed the collecting and paying of interest on loans and deposits. In 1836, the Loan Fund Board was established for regulation and supervision (Hollis and Sweetman, 1998; Seibel, 2005). By 1840, 300 funds were self-sustaining institutions[2] that eventually covered 20 percent of the house-holds in Ireland (ibid.). They were successful, in part because they offered three times the commercial interest rates to their depositors, giving them a competitive advantage (Seibel, 2005). However, they eventually became too competitive and commercial banks successfully lobbied the government to put a cap on their interest rates in 1843. This marked the beginning of their decline. There was also a dramatic downturn in this time period due to the Potato Famine, which cost Ireland a quarter of its population around 1848, 12 percent due to death and another 12–13 percent due to emigration (Hollis and Sweetman, 2003, p. 2). However, Hollis and Sweetman (2003) show that strong Irish loan funds were able to survive the Potato Famine

---

[2] 'Although the funds received no government funding, they were exempt from paying the "stamp tax" on contracts, which saved them as much as 2 percent annually on the amount outstanding' (Hollis and Sweetman, 1998, p. 1879).

with some success, illustrating clearly that it was not the crisis caused by the famine that dictated the eventual disappearance of the Irish loan funds in the 1950s, but rather poor governance and mismanagement.

Towards the end of the nineteenth century, 'profiteers' began to exploit the loan funds. Fund managers extracted profits from the funds in terms of high salaries, which were made possible by two policies. First, funds had quick access to the Justice of the Peace and could seize the assets of defaulters, giving them a competitive advantage over other moneylenders. Second, the Regulatory Board relied on funds for financing and was therefore reluctant to shut them down, even when they were known to be acting illegally (Hollis and Sweetman, 1998). Unfortunately, after 50 years of decline, misguided regulations did to the Irish loan funds what even the Potato Famine failed to do, and the last fund closed in the 1950s (ibid.).

The History of German Financial Credit Cooperatives

The history of microfinance in Germany spans centuries and involves self-help, regulation, and supervision; this created the largest microfinance sector of any country (per capita) (Seibel, 2005). It comprises two networks associated with two people, Hermann Schulze-Delitzsch and Friedrich Raiffeisen. They were respectively associated with community savings funds, now referred to as *Sparkassen* (savings banks), and member-owned cooperative associations, now referred to as cooperative banks or *Volksbanken und Raiffeisenbanken* (Guinnane, 2011; Périlleux 2010; Seibel, 2005).

Community-owned financial institutions came into existence in the second half of the eighteenth century. Like the Irish charities, they learned quickly that charities are not sustainable and that there was a large demand from poorer segments of society for safe and available deposit facilities. Thrift Societies began in Hamburg in 1778, quickly followed by a communal savings fund (*Sparkasse*) (Seibel, 2005). As the movement grew, the increasing supply of savings created pressure to expand the lending business into the agriculture sector. The Prussian state provided regulation by passing the first Prussian Savings Bank Decree in 1838, and in 1884 the savings banks formed the German Savings Bank Association.

Unfortunately, like the Irish and so many microfinance movements throughout the world, the development of the German system was marked by crisis. The period 1846–47 was a time of starvation, during which many poor farmers were losing their land and microentrepreneurs were going bankrupt. Fortunately, as in the case of many Irish funds, crisis in Germany triggered a strengthening or a second wave in the microfinance movement. Working mostly with farmers in rural areas, Friedrich

Raiffeisen created credit associations (*Darlehnskassen-Vereine*). Hermann Schulze-Delitzsch created savings and credit cooperatives in urban areas now called People's Banks (*Volksbanken*), which worked more with craftspeople and other microentrepreneurs.

Although each found initial success, growth was very slow. Despite accepting charity early on, Raiffeisen too realized that this was not sustainable, and by 1864 established the first rural credit association in Heddesdorf, under the model of self-help without charity[3] (Seibel, 2005). In the mid-1880s, there were no more than 245 rural cooperatives and progress was not made until 1889, 'when both the rural and the urban networks of credit associations were brought under the law: the Cooperative Act of the German Reich, the first cooperative law in the world'[4] (Seibel, 2005, p. 3). By 1914, there were over 15 000 credit cooperatives in Germany; the publication of the first cooperative handbook in 1866 and subsequent republications until 1887 outlined lessons learned from the movement and led to similar cooperatives spreading all over the world[5] (Seibel, 2005). In 1934, when all financial institutions were brought under the banking law, both networks maintained their specific identities amongst the universal banks. The divide between cooperative banks, both rural and urban (*Raiffeisen* and *Volksbanken*), and savings banks, also both rural and urban (*Kreissparkassen* and *Stadtsparkassen*), has only recently undergone a melding process at the local level. But whether they remain one institution or two, the effects of their success have a wide reach. Seibel attributes their success to several distinct factors: self-help based on savings, local outreach with lasting relationships, evolution of the legal framework, establishment of regional national apex organizations, and delegated supervision through auditing federations (Seibel, 2005). This illustrates that local ownership and relationships both based on savings, with a supportive legal structure and supervision, are needed for a sound and successful model that can often withstand crisis (Patten et al., 2001).

For both the Irish loan funds and the German credit cooperatives, it is clear that they were successful at times when they relied on community deposits for funding instead of donors. It is also clear that their link to the

---

[3] Schulze-Delitzsch rejected the charity model from the outset.

[4] At the same time, joint liability was replaced with limited liability, allowing for system-wide growth (Seibel, 2005).

[5] The successes of the cooperatives varied, often by whether or not the community felt a sense of ownership and whether they were merely inspired by the German model or if the model was imported externally and there was no community sense of ownership. An example is the Indonesian MFI Bank Rakyat International (BRI), which was so successfully inspired by the German model that Patten et al. (2001) determined that it outperformed formal Indonesian banks during the East Asian financial crisis.

community and sense of local ownership gave them strength, and that supportive regulation was essential for growth or failure.

CONNECTION TO TODAY'S MFIs AND FINANCIAL CREDIT COOPERATIVES

For the purpose of comparison, I provide a brief examination to demonstrate that credit cooperatives of the past are in line with tendencies of
microfinance, and then go on to further show that they are most in line
with the stakeholder model. But first we must examine whether or not
credit cooperatives correspond to the features outlined earlier:

- *Small loan size:* Hollis and Sweetman compared several different
  early microfinance models. They set loan amounts from Irish loan
  funds at £1–10 in 1843 (the average being £3.3, just under the average
  per capita income of the poorer two-thirds of the population) and
  Irish credit cooperatives at £2–50 in 1910 (Hollis and Sweetman,
  1998, p. 1885). Data for Raiffeisen's cooperatives provided by Hollis
  and Sweetman show that their loan size typically varied from the
  equivalent of more than £250 to much smaller amounts, but that the
  mean loan amount was £5–15 in 1910 (p. 1882). These loan sizes are
  very much in line with the nature of microfinance loans; they are
  small for their context.
- *Purpose or mission:* The purpose of the Irish funds, cooperatives and
  German credit cooperatives was to be pro-poor financial institutions,
  although they may have had different foci, such as urban or rural.
- *Joint liability:* Each system required two co-signers to secure loans.
  However, they each also had a degree of depositor liability, which
  would mitigate the liability further in addition to remaining local in
  their geographic spread (Hollis and Sweetman, 1998).
- *Uncollateralized:* They each had uncollateralized loans.
- *Savings:* Each allowed and was funded primarily by depositor
  savings. In fact, they held a fairly conservative capital/loan ratio of
  10 percent for the Irish loan funds in 1843. Raiffeisen's credit cooperatives in 1907 and Irish credit cooperatives in 1910 both held 4.5
  percent (Hollis and Sweetman, 1998).
- *Skills training:* While they all provided implicit skills training through
  the creation of formality, the German credit cooperatives provided
  extensive explicit training. Seibel outlines how the provision of skill
  training is one of the key aspects of the German model's success
  (2005).

It is clear that historic credit cooperatives meet the standard features of modern microfinance and, because they accepted deposits and were, since they are deposit taking, not donor funded or private, they must therefore meet the requirements of the stakeholder model. They are more dependent on the factor of shared liability and savings, and require a strong relationship to the community. This limits the scope primarily to locally owned and locally based group savings and lending models, in addition to SACCO and ROSCA models rather than merely imported cooperatives. These are known as stakeholder models as opposed to the shareholder models of privately traded for-profit models and donor models for smaller NGOs or non-profit organizations. Examining the stakeholder models and their evolution through several centuries, it becomes clear that they are financially sound and stable.

There is a great need for the stability that stakeholder models offer. Périlleux argues that the recent financial crisis stresses the importance of saver protection and prudence in the banking sector and goes further to state that financial cooperatives are more adequate at addressing these needs than classical profit-maximizing commercial banks because the clients themselves are stakeholders (Périlleux, 2010). The personal investment in the institution as a community asset in addition to being a deposit holder has a strengthening effect for the institution as clients provide monitoring, evaluation, and funding. Hollis and Sweetman (1998) state that throughout history microfinance organizations that are depositor based have lasted longer and have served more borrowers than donation-based organizations because they too act as stakeholders.

A stakeholder-modeled institution reduces its exposure to moral hazard risks because assets are not foreign owned or donated; they are owned by their neighbors and clients, and clients are much more likely to report honestly, even if it is bad news, because they know their own savings could be at risk. For credit cooperatives like ROSCAs, SACCOs, and SHGs, which are stakeholder models, there is collective ownership of both liabilities and savings. This provides incentives to grow with prudence.

Cull et al. (2008) and Rosenberg (2007) argue that some microfinance institutions go public and fail because they do not see an alternative to commercialization, when they could have maintained slower but stable growth. It is my argument that stakeholder-modeled institutions with supportive governance structures and a strong reliance on savings can be that alternative, and in fact they have been a more stable alternative throughout history.

STABILITY OF THE ALTERNATIVE APPROACHES

There is evidence that stakeholder-based institutions fare better in times of crisis than their shareholder- and donor-based counterparts. Sweetman and Hollis (1998) examine this closely with regard to the Irish Potato Famine, showing that with the proper governance structures the loan funds could outlast a crisis of historical magnitude. Similarly, BRI of Indonesia was shown to have outperformed even commercial banks throughout the East Asian crisis (Patten et al., 2001). One reason for this could be that savings and community ownership act as ballast in times of turbulent crisis for microfinance institutions as well as for cooperative banks and the communities in which they are located.

Maintaining a sense of community ownership has helped these institutions to weather great crises and continue to grow. Strangely, in recent years many have seen this success and reasoned that instead of maintaining the structures and ethos that provided for that success, MFIs should pursue aggressive growth and a more shareholder-based model similar to commercial banks. MFIs from India to Mexico started to hold public offerings of their stock, with disastrous results. When Banco Compartamos went public in 2007 and reaped huge profits while still charging clients high interest rates, it caused a backlash against microfinance as a development practice (Périlleux et al., 2010). The impact was even greater when SKS Microfinance of Andhra Pradesh went public. It devastated the microfinance sector in the state due to oversaturation caused by the aggressive growth mentality of shareholder models, the effects of which were felt throughout the microfinance world (CGAP, 2010; Wright and Sharma, 2010). Instead of arguing, as Funk does, that 'micro-lenders can and should compete shoulder-to-shoulder with mainstream commercial banks, vying for billions of dollars on global capital markets' (Funk, 2007, in Cull et al., 2008, p. 1) it would be more valuable to urge commercial banks to behave like stakeholder-model banks. Banks could still remain profitable. However, they would need to be anchored in their communities and pursue slower, less aggressive growth that is balanced with higher rates of savings. Iceland witnessed an interesting example of this with Audur Capital (Tomasdottir, 2011). Amidst the utter collapse of the majority of its banking sector, one bank performed differently, quite frankly because it was designed to perform differently. It had a more modest and balanced approach to growth, and ironically like many MFIs, it had women at its core, only in this example they were running a bank. This may work best in countries with more open-minded cultures of capitalism or require many to rethink their cultures of capitalism. These structures would take a long time to alter, but the process could begin by embracing a few alternatives to standard commercial banks.

CONCLUSION

In conclusion, it is clear that microfinance as a tool is greater than merely the distribution of small loans; it encompasses an ever-growing number of financial services including financial literacy, loans, and savings. When microcredit and microfinance are used interchangeably, it is not merely incorrect; it is also damaging to the notion of what microfinance is – that is, a financial tool steeped in the tradition of self-help, rooted in communities, and not a 'magic bullet' of development.

Microfinance and cooperative banks have a shared history and shared features. Although they can serve different roles and customers, they have the same core framework and require supportive governance structures. Although specific governance structures differ between countries, core principles such as the legal possibility to hold savings and to offer competitive interest rates are necessary conditions to allow microfinance to exist within the respective banking sectors. However, it is the framework provided by the institution itself, namely the stakeholder model featuring a solid base of savings and community ownership, that allows them to succeed and withstand crises.

REFERENCES

ACCION US (2017), 'About us: We're more than just lenders. We're lending partners', accessed 8 July 2017 at http://us.accion.org/about-us.

Banerjee, A., T. Besley and T.W. Guinnane (1994), 'Thy neighbor's keeper: The design of a credit cooperative with theory and a test', *Quarterly Journal of Economics*, **109**(2), 491–515.

Boudreaux, K. and T. Cowen (2008), 'The micromagic of microcredit', *The Wilson Quarterly*, **3**(1), 27–31.

Consultancy Group to Assist the Poor (CGAP) (2010), Andhra Pradesh 2010: Global implications of the crisis in Indian microfinance, *Focus Note No. 67*.

Cull, R., A. Demirgüç-Kunt and J. Morduch (2008), 'Microfinance meets market', *Financial Access Initiative*, accessed 17 September 2012 at https://alicia-brindisi-79qu.squarespace.com/assets/publications/2008/microfinancemarkets.pdf.

Funk, S. (2007), 'Remarks by Steven Funk, founder and member of the Dignity Fund Board', *Microcredit Summit E-News*, **5**(1), July.

Guinnane, T.W. (2011), 'The early German credit cooperatives and micro-finance organizations today: Similarities and differences', in B. Armendariz and M. Labie (eds), *The Microfinance Handbook*, Singapore: World Scientific Publishing, pp. 77–100.

Hollis, A. and A. Sweetman (1998), 'Microcredit: What can we learn from the past?', *World Development*, **26**(10), 1875–91.

Hollis, A. and A. Sweetman (2003), 'Microfinance and famine: The Irish loans funds during the Great Famine', *Microfinance Gateway*, CGAP, accessed

17 September 2012 at http://www.microfinancegateway.org/library/microfin ance-and-famine-irish-loan-funds-during-great-famine.

Isern, J., J. Abrams and M. Brown (2008), *Appraisal Guide for Microfinance Institutions. Technical Guide, Resource Manual, and Appraise*, Washington, DC: CGAP.

Mersland, R. (2011), 'The governance of non-profit microfinance institutions: Lessons from history', *Journal of Management & Governance*, **15**(3), 327–48.

Patten, R.H., J.K. Rosengard and D.E. Johnston, Jr (2001), 'Microfinance success amidst macroeconomic failure: The experience of the Bank Rakyat Indonesia during the East Asian crisis', *World Development*, **29**(6), 1057–69.

Périlleux, A. (2010), 'Maturity mismatch and governance of microfinance cooperatives: Lessons from history', *CEB Working Paper No. 10-005.RS*, ULB – Université Libre de Bruxelles.

Périlleux, A., E. Bloy and M. Hudon (2010), 'Productivity surplus distribution in microfinance: Does ownership matter?', *CEB Working Paper No. 10/036*, July 2010.

Roberts, R. (2011), 'Munger on microfinance', *EconTalk*, 18 April 2011.

Rosenberg, R. (2007), 'CGAP reflections on the compartamos initial public offering: A case study on microfinance interest rates and profits', *Focus Note No. 42*, Washington, DC: Consultative Group to Assist the Poor.

Seibel, H. (2005), 'Does history matter? The old and new world of microfinance in Europe and Asia', paper presented at 'From Moneylenders to Microfinance: Southeast Asia's Credit Revolutions in Institutional, Economic and Cultural Perspective: An Interdisciplinary Workshop', Asia Research Institute, Department of Economics, and Department of Sociology National University of Singapore, 7–8 October 2005.

Tomasdottir, H. (2011), 'A feminine response to Iceland's financial crisis', *TED Talk*, accessed 8 July at https://www.youtube.com/watch?v=dsmgvrcH94U.

Wenner, M. (1995), 'Group credit: A means to improve information transfer and loan repayment performance', *Journal of Development Studies*, **32**(2), 263–81.

Wright, G.A. and M.K. Sharma (2010), 'The Andhra Pradesh crisis: Three dress rehearsals . . . and then the full drama', *MicroSave India Focus Note No. 55*.

14. The challenge of keeping public banks on mission

Christoph Scherrer

Many of the contributions to this volume have highlighted the beneficial aspects of public banks. However, it is undeniable that not all public banks perform to the highest standards, and quite a number have been captured by politicians, management and large debtors, resulting in misallocated or outright squandered financial resources. In response to these failures, but perhaps also because of pecuniary interests (the private competitors in banking) or ideological predispositions (neoclassical economists), many have called for the privatization of public banks; this is a call that has sometimes been heeded, especially in the 1990s. The failure of private banks on a grand scale in 2007/08 has somewhat muted these calls, but has not completely eliminated them; this is evidenced by the renewed efforts to create a European banking union without regard for the specificities of public banks (see Semenyshyn, Chapter 10 in this volume).

If there is a case to be made for public banks, and one finds many good arguments in support of public banks in this volume, then in defense of public banks it is necessary to discuss measures that prevent them from straying from their public service mission. This is the purpose of my contribution. My concern, however, is not so much about how to fight corruption, but rather how to prevent public banks from neglecting their public purpose, the so-called mission creep. In societies where corruption is pervasive, the misuse of public banks is not really surprising. Under such circumstances, it is the honest public bank that needs to be explained. As the German example shows, however, mission creep also happens under stable, mostly law-abiding circumstances. The German public banks can be proud of a long and successful historical record (see Mettenheim and Butzbach, Chapter 2 in this volume), and they operate in a context where corruption is present but plays a minor role (in the Corruption Perceptions Index of Transparency International, Germany traditionally scores highly, that is, has relatively low levels of public corruption). Nevertheless, especially among one type of public bank in Germany, the *Landesbanken*, which serve the state governments as well as the regional savings banks, many have strayed far from their original public purpose and incurred huge losses in 2007/08. While not the only public banks in Germany to be hit by the US financial crisis (the first victim of the crisis was IKB Deutsche Industrie AG), as a group they were the largest losers among the public banks, and therefore their case shall be scrutinized here. Furthermore, since not all *Landesbanken* (see Polikhronidi and Scherrer, Chapter 11 in this volume), especially not most of the large group of savings banks (see Semenyshyn, Chapter 10 in this volume), took on high risk before the crisis, a comparison of the risk-taking *Landesbanken*, the more prudent *Landesbanken* and savings banks promises to shed further light on the reasons for mission creep.

Having briefly described mission creep in the form of financialization among German public banks, I assess the contribution of their various stakeholders and regulators to this abandonment of the original public mandate. I discuss their behavior in light of principal–agent theory and sociological new institutionalism. As both theories fail to provide an adequate account of the confluence of the behavior of the various actors involved, I turn to the theory of hegemonic discourse. With the help of this theory I interpret the mission drift as part of neoliberal hegemony. Under neoliberal hegemony, public banks' original mandate faced a hostile environment. Placing the mission drift in this larger framework precludes any easy panacea for keeping public banks to their public purpose. I conclude with some ideas on what nevertheless could be done to build a publicly controlled and sound financial system.

THE EXTENT OF FINANCIALIZATION IN THE GERMAN PUBLIC BANKING SECTOR

Traditionally, public banks are mandated with asset formation and promoting the propensity to save among lower-income citizens, as well as supporting small and medium-sized firms and their respective regional economic development. Proprietary trading or sales of derivatives and other risky securities, which are generally subsumed under the term financialization, are commonly not considered to be part of their public mission. Nevertheless, many *Landesbanken* ventured into these activities. The extreme case was Sachsen LB (*Landesbank* of the state of Saxony), which purchased risky securities via off–balance sheet special-purpose vehicles of more than 1100 percent of its equity capital (for comparison, it was 114 percent in the case of the private Deutsche Bank; Hüfner, 2010, p. 5).

To what extent have savings banks and *Landesbanken* been involved in the process of financialization? Since this contribution only deals with a subgroup of the financial sector, the indicator 'trade with securities, mainly with derivatives' shall be used for an operationalization of the financialization concept. Additionally, the earnings of the executive boards shall be taken into account as an indicator of deviations from normal public service pay.

In Germany, savings banks are public-law institutions whose responsible bodies are municipal authorities. Their field of activity is only regionally limited, that is, within a certain area, they can operate all usual banking activities. A savings bank finances itself, essentially via saving deposits, and gives out loans to the local economy and population. It invests its liquidity reserves with its *Landesbank* (also with private banks since the 1970s), where they can potentially serve other purposes than regional economic development. Compared to the *Landesbanken*, the savings banks overall continue to cling to traditional, risk-minimizing behavior. The traditional deposit business with non-banking institutions still amounts to 70 percent of their total liabilities. Their central risk thus still rests with the loan business (Semenyshyn, 2011).

Savings banks, as a rule, feed a part of their gains into their reserve assets and distribute the other part to the locally responsible bodies of the savings banks or (dependent on the respective statutes) allocate it directly to charitable purposes or to their charitable foundations (Lepper, 2003).

The savings banks have survived well during and after the financial crisis. Nevertheless, they did not completely withstand the trend of financialization. First, they equally sold securities. Second, they participated in the creation of investment certificates through their control over the DekaBank. Third, some of them have advised their municipalities to adopt an active management with the help of speculative financial instruments (Richter, 2012). Fourth, via their associations, they are co-owners of the *Landesbanken*. Where they have taken direct influence, for example, regarding the Helaba, risk-minimizing strategies have been implemented (see Polikhronidi and Scherrer, Chapter 11 in this volume).

The *Landesbanken* display markedly more features of financialization. On the liabilities side of their balance sheet, they have been relying much more on capital market financing than other public and private banks (Deutsche Bundesbank, 2009, p. 42). On their assets side, they have also been engaged more intensively in the trade of securities and in the interbank business. Loans to non-banking institutions amounted only to 36 percent of the balance sheet in 2008 (Noack, 2009).

In 2007, the *Landesbank* of the state of North Rhine-Westphalia, the WestLB, was holding 41.7 percent of its securities for the purpose of trade. Securities represented 32.5 percent on the asset side of the bank. The trade volume of derivatives amounted to nine times the value of assets. At the Helaba, it accounted for 3.4 times the assets; at the Deutsche Bank, however, it amounted to 24.5 times, which is the extreme among German banks. Another example of entanglement in financialization is the fact that the Bavarian *Landesbank* conducted 93.7 percent of its trade in derivatives, not for hedging own risks, but exclusively for trade (Hardie and Howarth, 2009, p. 1024).

Equally advanced has been the degree of internationalization, which is in fact more progressed than among the private major banks. In 2007, 71.3 percent of the WestLB's assets were claims towards other countries. At Helaba, the *Landesbank* for Hessen and Thuringia, it was 52.2 percent, and at the Deutsche Bank it was 44.7 percent (Hardie and Howarth, 2009, p. 1027). The risks assumed in the trade and purchase of international securities led to considerable losses for the regional state banks when the crisis broke, due to which some of them lost their independent existence (see Polikhronidi and Scherrer, Chapter 11 in this volume).

The level of the remuneration for the executive board members of savings banks remains plainly under those of private big banking houses, but the chief executive of Frankfurt's Savings Bank, for example, received about €650000 in 2010 (Köhler, 2011). Each board member of WestLB, even at the time of state aid to the bank, earned more than €1 million (SZ, 2010; academically trained public servants earned on average about €45000, the German Chancellor €206000, the CEO of a company with at least 1000 employees €570000, and the CEO of Deutsche Bank at the time, Josef Ackermann, €9 800000; SZ, 2011).

THE ACTORS IN THE PROCESS OF FINANCIALIZATION

How could it happen that public banks are engaged to such an enormous extent beyond their public mission on markets for risky securities? Based on interviews conducted by Xeniya Polikhronidi[1] and three extensive studies of mission drift in the public banking sector of Germany (Gubitz, 2013; Kirchhoff, 1987; Seikel, 2013), the answer is that many actors were involved. These include the top management of the public banks, regional, national, and European public officeholders, regulatory agencies, private competitors, and the representatives of employees. To this list I will add the economic discipline.

---

[1] These interviews also informed the contribution of Polikhronidi and Scherrer, Chapter 11 in this volume.

Top Management

As explained in Polikhronidi and Scherrer in Chapter 11 of this volume, the charismatic first leader of WestLB, Ludwig Poullain, pushed the *Landesbanken* into areas previously occupied by private banks in the early 1970s. As the management literature tells us, management is mostly driven by concern for its own remuneration, autonomy and prestige, which can be best satisfied by expanding the business into supposedly profitable areas (Chen and Bozeman, 2013; Kirchhoff, 1987, p. 49). As principal–agent theory has pointed out, the agent, in this case management, can pursue these objectives even without the explicit approval of the principal, the owners, because of information asymmetry (Shleifer and Vishny, 1997). From sociological new institutionalism, we learn that management can be exposed to isomorphism via hierarchy, rivalry or professionalization (DiMaggio and Powell, 1983). For all three channels, empirical evidence can be found in the case of *Landesbanken* management with regard to a convergence towards the behavior of the private financial sector (see Polikhronidi and Scherrer, Chapter 11 in this volume).

The Owners: Governments and Savings Banks Associations

Over the longer run, especially after management failures, it is not so likely that mission drift could have occurred without support from the political level. And indeed, early on, state governments supported the expansionary course of *Landesbanken*. In some cases, they were actually the drivers to the point of dropping the public mission from the laws and charters pertaining to *Landesbanken*. According to statements in parliamentary hearings and interviews with *Landesbanken* board members and management, the public mandate played no role at most of these regional state banks in their business models or in their self-identification, except for the two institutions that did not incur losses during the crisis: Helaba and Nord/LB. None of the *Landesbanken* tied the bonuses for top management to the fulfillment of any specific public mandate; bonuses were only linked to usual management objectives. There is no further evidence that representatives of the respective governments criticized management for its expansionary business models (Gubitz, 2013, pp. 230–35, 238, 263).

From the viewpoint of principal–agent theory this can be easily explained, as the agent (in this case the politicians) is poorly overseen by the principal (in this case the electorate) and has ample incentives to expand the mission of a *Landesbank*: to obtain a shadow budget for political pet projects, to promote employment, to be able to offer lucrative positions to friends (or foes) or for the prestige that comes along with having an internationally recognized bank in the fold (Kirchhoff, 1987).

At the level of national politics, some similar motives were present. Politicians, like Finance Minister Karl Schiller (1966–72) and the Financial Secretary of State (later the long-term head of the Bundesbank) Karl Otto Pöhl, supported extending the mandate of public banks to include increasing competition in investment banking, that is, to break the oligopoly of the three major private banks (Blohm, 1988; Poullain, 2007). From their Keynesian macroeconomic reasoning, more competition would lead to a faster passing of interest rate changes to businesses (Kirchhoff, 1987, p. 53). Their exclusion as Social Democrats from the networks of the private banks may also have contributed to their enthusiasm for a larger role for the *Landesbanken*.

The European level also started to play a role in the decision to create a single market by 1992. The vision for such a single market was to eliminate any regional or national barriers to the free competition of private corporations. Therefore, the European Commission's Directorate General for Competition was readily available to follow up on a complaint by the private banks concerning the allegedly unfair advantage public banks would gain from their state liability guarantees (see Seikel, Chapter 9 in this volume). It also forced upon WestLB the legal status of a stock company, which removed the possibility to commit management to a specific public mandate (Kirchhoff, 1987, p. 149).

At the international level, the International Monetary Fund as well as the World Bank called for the privatization of public banks with some success (Hanson, 2004). More important for the German public banks was the new regulatory framework, the 1988 Basel Accord (also called Basel I), in response to the Latin American debt crisis (to which the savings banks had not contributed). This Accord carried the imprint of the Anglo-Saxon 'arm's-length' banking style and not of continental relationship banking (Oatley and Nabors, 1998). Basel I stipulated a higher capital base and a classification of credit risks. The higher capital requirements pushed the public banks to become more profitable because their owners were hesitant in providing additional capital. The new capital had to come from retained earnings. In those cases where the owners provided additional capital they were accused by the European Commission of granting competition distorting state aid (see Seikel, Chapter 9 in this volume). The classification of credit risk impacted the savings banks' style of relationship banking. This became even more pronounced with the regulatory response to the Asian crisis, Basel II, in 2004. As the creditworthiness of many small and medium-sized firms was not rated by independent rating agencies, they had to be classified as more risky, and therefore the savings banks had to hold more capital when they handed out loans to their traditional customers. The alternative left to them was to develop expensive internal risk assessment models (Gubitz, 2013, pp. 78–81).

These regulatory changes at the international level increased the importance of rating agencies. Once the state liability guarantee for *Landesbanken* was removed in 2005, they lost their AAA ratings. This loss increased their refinancing costs significantly. In order to at least keep investment grade ratings, the *Landesbanken* were under pressure to increase their return on equity, that is, to pursue more risky business. The ratings of the rating agencies of other financial products later played a decisive role in the downfall of some of the *Landesbanken*, because they trusted the ratings too much and invested much too little in their own capacity to assess risks (Gubitz, 2013, pp. 268–70).

As the more prudent savings banks are co-owners to different degrees of *Landesbanken*, one would have expected them to exert a moderating influence. The record is mixed. Where the regional associations of savings banks had been a dominant co-owner for a long time, they indeed kept the *Landesbank* closer to the original mandate (Helaba, LBB, and NordLB). Where these associations held only a minority stake, no limiting influence was noticed (Gubitz, 2013, p. 193). An evaluation report of the savings banks organization in 1987, for instance, demanded the increased involvement of the *Landesbanken* in the international and securities business, which have been identified as particularly promising and profitable (Blohm, 1988).

Financial Supervisory Authorities

The Federal Financial Supervisory Authority (BaFin), established in 2002 through the consolidation of different supervisory agencies, intervened selectively in cases when they had doubts about the qualification of a top manager, but it did not call into question the financialization strategies. In fact, BaFin actually considered securitization as a way to spread risk, and therefore thought it would lower the risks of loan default for an individual bank (Gubitz, 2013, p. 212). This agency was not necessarily captured by those it was charged to supervise (it was understaffed and also had difficulties paying the experts to check on the internal risk assessment models of the banks in the wake of Basel II; ibid., p. 210), but it was captured by the hegemonic discourse of finance at the time (see below).

The Private Competitors

As long as public banks were limited to serving people with low income or took on long-term risks for infrastructural work, the private banks did not lobby against them. But already in the 1920s private banks were trying to get rid of their public competition (Mura, 1987, p. 246). Once public banks moved into their lucrative investment banking, the private bank association started to mobilize against the presence of the state in banking. Because the German savings banks are municipal organizations and therefore enjoy strong support by local governments, the private sector was not yet successful in opening up this sector for private investments. It took the scandals of the *Landesbanken* and then, most decisively, the support of the European Commission to whittle away at the state support for public banks (see Seikel, Chapter 9 in this volume).

The private banks also influenced the mission drift of public banks in more indirect ways. Once workers became more affluent and wages were no longer paid in cash, private banks started to compete with the savings banks (and the cooperative banks) for working-class customers. They thereby reduced the profit margins of savings banks and made them more likely to support the profit increasing strategies of the *Landesbanken* of which they were part-owners. Better pay for managerial positions at private banks as well as private bankers' traditional social prestige left their imprint on the minds of public bank managers. Already in the 1980s, the managers of public banks showed little interest in the content of the public mandate and were instead focused on increased market share and profitability (Kirchhoff, 1987, p. 121). In the 2000s, public managers targeted ambitious profit goals using private competition as a benchmark. In some instances, top management for a *Landesbank* was even recruited from private banks (Gubitz, 2013, pp. 151, 165, 254).

Employees of Public Banks

From the perspective of stakeholder theory, it is a sad fact that the presence of employee representatives on the boards of public as well as private banks under the German codetermination law did not prevent excessive risk taking. Their absence on the board, as in the case of BayernLB, also did not preclude excessive risk taking (for more on employee representation on the boards of *Landesbanken*, see Gubitz, 2013, p. 199). Therefore, one can conclude that the employees of public banks played only a minor role in the drift towards financialization. As the main victims of the demise of some public banks, especially WestLB (a loss of 1500 jobs alone in 2012, *Der Spiegel*, 2012), one could have expected more resistance to risk taking.

As some of the traditional tasks of *Landesbanken*, especially their clearing-house functions, became automated and less labor-intensive, the expansion of business was welcomed by employees for its job creation. In light of these interests, it becomes understandable that employee representatives did not become a bulwark against financialization.

Business Customers

As already mentioned, large corporations favored a more active role for *Landesbanken*. They were interested in more competition to the big three private banks. This interest lost salience over time as these corporations were able to tap international financial markets by themselves or to make use of foreign banks that had settled in Germany. However, the original clients of savings banks and *Landesbanken*, smaller companies, had grown in the dynamic 1960s and started to internationalize in the 1970s. If the public sector banks did not want to lose these customers, they had to offer them a fuller spectrum of financial services (Kirchhoff, 1987, pp. 114, 118). This demand from the customer side certainly contributed to the expansion of *Landesbanken* activities, but cannot explain the immense extent of international and financial product trading exposure in the 1990s and 2000s (Gubitz, 2013, pp. 187–8).

THE HEGEMONIC DISCOURSE OF FINANCIALIZATION

While fingers can be pointed at certain individuals or groups of actors for being especially active in promoting the mission drift, the assessment of the motives of the various stakeholders shows that one cannot blame a specific group of actors for the overall drift towards financialization. The previous mentioned theories, principal–agent theory and sociological new institutionalism, are seriously challenged to provide an explanation for this phenomenon. Principal–agent theory is overtaxed by the multiple principal–agent relationships, and new institutionalism's isomorphism provides few clues about the origin of a norm. A plausible explanation can be found by turning to the theory of hegemonic discourse. In Ernesto Laclau's theorizing, discourse includes (in addition to verbal and written utterances) collective and individual practices (Laclau, 1990). Hegemony in the Gramscian tradition encompasses the dimension of consent in addition to coercion. It thereby opens up space for the role of ideas in any explanation of social power relations (Cox, 1983 [1993]). A Gramscian perspective does not remain at the level of analyzing the frames used in the debate (cf.

Boin et al., 2009); it also inquires into the other power sources of the actors in the field, such as their position in the economy and in the institutional set-up of any given society.

Financialization is embedded in neoliberal hegemony. It has a class-based origin and is fortified by the dominant state in the world economy, the United States of America. Neoliberalism's main objective was the defense of the rights of private property holders, especially moneyholders. It entails 'belief in competitive markets' and 'pro-market, limited state' (Schmidt and Thatcher, 2013). Neoliberalism gained traction in the 1970s when the Conservatives in the UK felt besieged by a strong trade union movement, when big business in the USA got tired of the environmental movement and powerful trade unions in the building trades and in transportation, who were insulated from competition by law, and when the US foreign policy establishment together with the US transnational corporations had enough of Third World insurgency. In other words, it is the ideology of a revolution from above intended to push back the claims of other social forces (Scherrer, 2014).

Neoliberalism's ideas not only resonate with the financial asset-holding class; they influence also other groups' meaning making of the world. The acquiescence of many ordinary people is also the result of the pervasiveness of neoliberalism in everyday life. In the realm of finance, an ever-larger proportion of the population is now dependent upon the capital markets for their retirement. Furthermore, many are tied to the financial system because they are debtors (Langley, 2008). The 'split identities of workers' (Boyer, 2010) as wage earners, consumers, pension fund holders and real estate speculators has also contributed to this acquiescence.

Since the beginning of the 1980s, public banks have thus been operating under an increasingly hegemonic discourse, which questions the previous role of the state in the economy in a very fundamental way. Within the academic discipline of finance, the efficient market hypothesis (EMH) became dominant. This hypothesis states that the prices for financial products, such as currencies, stocks or derivatives, will reflect their 'true' price the more freedom financial actors possess. Buyers and sellers act rationally in these markets on the basis of the information available to them. The result of their exchanges is efficient because the markets lead to the efficient allocation of resources, that is, capital, labor and land (Fama, 1970). The prominence of the efficient market hypothesis, despite its not very plausible assumptions, has been well explained by MacKenzie's performativity thesis (MacKenzie, 2006). The EMH was used to scientifically justify the liberalization of financial markets and the use of derivatives (Blyth, 2005). It not only lent academic support to the trading in derivatives at the *Landesbanken*, but also seemed to be plausible to the regulators (see above). During the crisis of 2007/08, the adoption of the EMH was singled out by a fast-growing group of critics as a major culprit of the crisis (e.g., Taleb, 2008). However, in the eyes of thinkers in favor of the EMH, a crisis would not disprove it; a crisis would reveal that high pre-crisis profits were due to high risks (MacKenzie, 2006, p. 67).

Given this neoliberal environment, it is not so surprising that most stakeholders in *Landesbanken* accepted or even promoted the adoption of the goals and behavior of private banks.

CONCLUSION: KEEPING PUBLIC BANKS ON MISSION

If public bank mission drift is seen in the light of neoliberal hegemony, then easy answers for stopping or reversing this trend are not at hand. Advice drawn from principal–agent theory comes easily to its limits, not least because the theory itself is part of the neoliberal hegemony. Its advice to align the interest of top management in private companies with the interests of shareholders by linking the pay of the former to the performance of company shares in the stock market did not prevent management from taking an ever-larger share of company surplus without necessarily improving the performance of the company. It actually drove financialization by giving the stock market a prominent role and encouraging short-termism (Lazonick, 2016). In relationship to public banks, the advice for more professional staff and less direct political influence and strict market orientation did not prevent colossal failures.

Sociological new institutionalism is less of a normative and prescriptive theory than principal–agent theory. Therefore, no concrete advice can be drawn from it. Hypothetically, one would have to look at what brought the current state of norms about, that is, the channels of isomorphism, and try to close them. However, there would be no theoretical guidance on why, how and by whom these channels should be closed.

Discourse theory is also not so known for prescriptions. However, it starts from the premise of a contested social realm (struggles for hegemony) and therefore takes into view counter-hegemonic forces. As the material promises of neoliberalism neither trickle down to large portions of the working class nor lead to economic stability, potential actors and counter-discourses are available. The question is how can they be strengthened and what has to be done concretely to keep public banks to their public mission?

Above I have shown that the savings banks stayed closer to their public mission than the *Landesbanken*. So what can be learned from savings banks? The major break on savings banks' drift towards financialization has been the regional principle, that is, their limitation to a specific region. Yet some of the bigger savings banks, for instance the savings banks in the city of Cologne, reached a size that also tempted them to forays into international finance and derivatives (*Kölnische Rundschau*, 2014). The savings banks associations' lack of resistance to WestLB expansion should also caution against too much optimism about savings bank prudence. The example of Helaba covered in this volume (Polikhronidi and Scherrer, Chapter 11) shows that besides the regional principle, another important principle is necessary for reining in excessive risk taking: the willingness to install a governance structure of many checks and balances. Yet even such a governance structure will not work if the key participants do not share an awareness of the risks involved. At Helaba, the institutional memory of near bankruptcy in the 1970s underpinned such awareness.

From the discourse analytical point of view, this awareness seems to be of utmost importance. If the key actors of public banks are not aware of the public mandate and do not identify with the public mandate, then staying within the public mandate cannot be expected. Therefore, a strategy for keeping public banks in public service needs to start with a general debate about the content of the public mandate and how public banks can contribute to it. As a place where systematic knowledge is produced and as a place where future practitioners get their training, academia could play an important role in this debate. It would require, however, that the neoclassical hegemony in the field of economics be dissolved in favor of a plurality of paradigms.

As long as private banks (or hedge funds or private equity companies) are seen as role models, little change can be expected. Practitioners in the public sector will continue to emulate their strategies. Therefore, a strategy for preserving public banks without limiting the speculative behavior of private financial actors will not suffice for keeping public banks on track. It also requires a change in European policies as well as the policies of the major international organizations dealing with finance, such as the International Monetary Fund, the World Bank, and the Basel Committee. Given the overall hegemonic capitalist structure, the US Treasury should not be left out. This requires a broad international coalition of the 'friends of a publicly controlled sound financial system'. As this is quite an ambitious task, the first steps are to defend the existing public banks, to discuss the content of a public mandate in banking, and to raise awareness, especially among the key actors in public banking, on how a public bank true to a public mandate can be beneficial to society.

REFERENCES

Blohm, B. (1988), 'Szenen einer Ehe. Im dritten Versuch soll die Fusion zwischen WestLB und Helaba klappen' [Scenes of a marriage. In the third attempt, the fusion between WestLB and Helaba], *Die Zeit*, 16 September 1988.

Blyth, M. (2003), 'The political power of financial ideas', in J. Kirshner (ed.), *Monetary Orders: Ambiguous Economics, Ubiquitous Politics*, Ithaca, NY: Cornell University Press, pp. 239–59.

Boin, A., P. Hart and A. McConnell (2009), 'Crisis exploitation: Political and policy impacts of framing contests', *Journal of European Public Policy*, **16**(1), 81–106.

Boyer, R. (2010), 'The collapse of finance but labour remains weak', *Socio-Economic Review*, **8**(2), 348–53.

Chen, C. and B. Bozeman (2013), 'Understanding public and nonprofit managers' motivation through the lens of self-determination theory', *Public Management Review*, **15**(4), 584–607.

Cox, R. (1983 [1993]), 'Gramsci, hegemony and international relations: An essay in method', in S. Gill (ed.), *Gramsci, Historical Materialism and International Relations*, Cambridge, UK: Cambridge University Press.

Der Spiegel (2012), 'WestLB baut 1500 Stellen ab' [WestLB cuts by 1500 jobs], 21 March, accessed 11 July 2017 at http://www.spiegel.de/wirtschaft/unternehmen/westlb-baut-wegen-zerschlagung-stellen-ab-a-822804.html.

Deutsche Bundesbank (2009), *Monatsbericht* [Monthly Report], September, Frankfurt.

DiMaggio, P.J. and W.W. Powell (1983), 'The iron cage revisited: Institutional isomorphism and collective rationality in organizational fields', *American Sociological Review*, **48**(2), 147–60.

Fama, E.F. (1970), 'Efficient capital markets: A review of theory and empirical work', *Journal of Finance*, **25**(2), 383–417.

Gubitz, B. (2013), *Das Ende des Landesbankensektors: Der Einfluss von Politik, Management und Sparkassen* [The End of the Landesbanken Sectors: The Influence of Politics, Management and Savings Banks], Wiesbaden: Springer Gabler.

Hanson, J.A. (2004), 'The transformation of state-owned banks', in G. Caprio, J. Fiechter, M. Pomerleano and R.E. Litan (eds), *The Future of State-Owned Financial Institutions*, Washington, DC: Brookings Institution Press, pp. 13–49.

Hardie, I. and D. Howarth (2009), 'Die krise not la crise? The financial crisis and the transformation of German and French banking systems', *Journal of Common Market Studies*, **47**(5), 1017–39.

Hüfner, F. (2010), 'The German banking system: Lessons from the financial crisis', *OECD Economics Department Working Paper No. 788*, ECO/WKP(2010)44, Paris: OECD.

Kirchhoff, U. (1987), *Zielwandel bei öffentlichen Unternehmen, aufgezeigt am Beispiel der Banken des Bundes* [A Change in the Goal of Public Enterprises, Illustrated by the Example of the Federal Banks], *Schriften zum Genossenschaftswesen und zur öffentlichen Wirtschaft, Vol. 20*, Berlin: Duncker & Humblot.

Köhler, M. (2011), 'Geheimsache Vorstandsgehalt' [Top secret: CEO's compensation], *Frankfurter Allgemeine*, 15 June 2011.

Kölnische Rundschau (2014), 'Sparkasse Köln-Bonn. Mehr Swap-Geschädigte als bislang bekannt' [Sparkasse Köln-Bonn. More swap victims than known so far], 13 October 2014, accessed 9 July 2017 at http://www.rundschau-online.de/253828.

Laclau, E. (1990), *New Reflections on the Revolution of Our Time*, London: Verso.

Langley, P. (2008), *The Everyday Life of Global Finance: Saving and Borrowing in Anglo-America*, Oxford: Oxford University Press.

Lazonick, W. (2016), 'The value-extracting CEO: How executive stock-based pay undermines investment in productive capabilities', *Institute for New Economic Thinking Working Paper No. 54*.

Lepper, M. (2003), *Die Verwendung und insbesondere die Ausschüttung von Sparkassengewinnen* [The Use and in Particular, the Distribution of Savings Banks' Profits], Baden-Baden: Nomos.

MacKenzie, D. (2006), *An Engine, Not a Camera: How Financial Models Shape Markets*, Cambridge, MA: MIT Press.

Mura, J. (1987), *Entwicklungslinien der deutschen Sparkassengeschichte* [General Lines in the History of German Savings Banks], Stuttgart: Deutscher Sparkassenverlag.

Noack, H. (2009), 'Konsolidierung als kompetenter Partner der Sparkassen' [Consolidation as a competent partner of the savings banks], in F.E. Stiftung (ed.), *WISO Diskurs. 2009. Die Zukunft der Landesbanken – Zwischen Konsolidierung und neuem Geschaftsmodell*, Bonn.

Oatley, T. and R. Nabors (1998), 'Redistributive co-operation: Market failure, wealth transfers, and the Basel Accord', *International Organisation*, **52**(1), 35–54.

Poullain, L. (2007), 'Die öffentlich-rechtliche Misere' [Public-law misery], *Handelsblatt*, 18 December 2007.

Richter, F. (2012), 'Speculating cities? The financialization of municipal debt management – evidence from North Rhine-Westphalia', unpublished Master's thesis, University of Kassel.

Scherrer, C. (2014), 'Neoliberalism's resilience: A matter of class', *Critical Policy Studies*, **8**(3) 348–51.

Schmidt, V.A. and M. Thatcher (eds) (2013), *Resilient Liberalism in Europe's Political Economy*, Cambridge, UK: Cambridge University Press.

Seikel, D. (2013), 'Der Kampf um öffentlich-rechtliche Banken. Wie die Europäische Kommission Liberalisierung durchsetzt' [The fight for public-law banks. How the European Commission enforces liberalization], Frankfurt: Campus.

Semenyshyn, H. (2011), *The Role of German Savings and Cooperative Banks in Providing Stability in the Time of Global Financial Crisis*, unpublished Master's thesis, University of Kassel.

Shleifer, A. and R.W. Vishny (1997), 'A survey on corporate governance', *Journal of Finance*, **52**(2), 737–81.

Süddeutsche Zeitung (SZ) (2010), 'WestLB und LBBW. Politiker geisseln Salär der Landesbank-Bosse' [WestLB and LBBW: Politicians lash out at Landesbank bosses' salaries], 17 May, accessed 8 July 2017 at http://www.sueddeutsche.de/geld/westlb-und-lbbw-politiker-geisseln-salaer-der-landesbank-bosse-1.162369

Süddeutsche Zeitung (SZ) (2011), 'Gehältervergleich' [Salaries compared], 9 November, accessed 11 July 2017 at http://www.sueddeutsche.de/karriere/gehaelterverg leich-in-deutschland-ackermann-schluckt-sie-alle-1.975186-5

Taleb, N.N. (2008), *The Black Swan: The Impact of the Highly Improbable*, London: Penguin.

Index

accumulation
  of capital 21
  compound interest 19, 21, 33, 37,
    39, 46
  of patient capital 33, 37, 46
agency problem 197, 208
agency theory 197
  see also principal–agent theory
agent-based banking 127
aggregate demand 55, 63
agricultural credit 119, 121, 123,
    129–30, 132
alternative banking/banks 1, 4–5, 8–9,
    29–38, 40, 45–7, 176, 187, 231
anticyclical 2, 5–6, 14, 17, 67–8, 71,
    75–80, 84, 88, 93, 95–6, 165
  policy 2, 6, 68, 77, 83–4, 93, 95, 163
arm's-length banking 248
asset liability mismatches 216
asset management company 92, 94
asset prices 57, 83
Asset Reconstruction Companies 215

bad loans 92, 212, 219, 221–4, 227
BaFin 178–9, 183, 249
  see also Federal Financial
    Supervisory Authority
balance of payments 103
Banco do Brasil 5, 56, 62, 68–9, 85, 93
  see also BB
BancoEstado 6, 84–9, 95–6
bank consolidation 84
bank credit portfolio 6, 15, 68, 91,
    93–4, 113, 117, 119–20, 123,
    127–9, 131, 166, 214
bank deposits 75, 117, 119
bank nationalization 116–19, 122,
    126–8, 131–2, 212, 214
bank outreach in India 126, 132
bank-based economic system 158
banking business intensity in India 124

banking group 31, 45–7, 158, 160,
    162–3, 166, 179–80
  law 86, 237
  policy 117–18, 121, 131, 133, 185
  services 17, 19, 30, 32, 34, 36, 117,
    123, 126–8, 132
  theory 30, 34–6, 38–9, 46
Banking Union 3, 8, 176–7, 180–83,
    186–7, 243
bankruptcy 16, 57–8, 69, 86, 169, 171,
    225, 254
Basel Accord
  Basel I 71, 248
  Basel II 92, 248–9
  Basel III 36, 40, 248
  Basel norms 213
BB 56, 62–3, 68–73, 75–80, 85, 86
  see also Banco do Brasil
BCB *see* Brazilian Central Bank
Belgium 185
big bank 5, 53–6, 60, 65, 92, 159, 162,
    180, 246
BNDES 3, 6, 56–7, 62–3, 69, 72–3,
    75–7, 85–6, 93, 97, 101–13
Board of Managing Directors 204, 206
Board of Owners 204–6
bond market 86, 130, 137, 142
borrower behaviour 144, 148
branch licensing policy 118, 121–2
branchless banking 123
Brazil/Brazilian 2–6, 13, 22, 53–65,
    67–76, 78, 80, 83–6, 90–96,
    101–13, 133, 142, 217
Brazilian Central Bank 5, 53, 56,
    58–62, 65, 67, 70, 86, 90, 92, 106
Brazilian Development Bank 6, 85, 101

Caixa 6, 91–6
Caixa Econômica Federal 5–6, 56–7,
    62, 68–9, 94
capital adequacy 122, 133

capital base 120, 248
capital drain 32, 45
capital market operations 32
capital markets 30, 32–3, 35–8, 56–7,
　　63, 85, 90, 106, 110, 112, 126, 139,
　　141–2, 147–8, 159–60, 166, 169,
　　171, 176, 179, 201, 240, 245, 252
　outflow 88
　requirements 71, 187, 248
　reserves 35–7, 40, 148, 166
capitalist economy 23–4, 55
capital-to-risk-asset ratio 224
cartels 161–3, 165
cash reserve ratio 121, 215
　see also CRR
casino capitalism 230
CDOs 170
CEF *see* Caixa Econômica Federal
central banks 29, 38, 55, 143, 147–8,
　　164
CFS 120–21, 214
　see also Committee on the Financial
　　　System
channeled credit 75–7
Chile 5–6, 83–8, 95
China 14, 64, 68, 101, 143, 212, 217,
　　220–21
　People's Bank of 143
clearinghouses 178, 251
Collateral Debt Obligations 170
commercial banks/banking 29, 32–3,
　　37, 39–40, 42–4, 70, 73, 76, 116,
　　118–19, 124, 126, 128–9, 132,
　　155, 160, 163, 169, 203, 214–15,
　　217–18, 221, 223, 230, 232, 234–5,
　　239–40
Commerzbank 159, 162, 167–8
Committee on the Financial System
　　120, 212, 214
　see also CFS
commodity prices 57, 64, 68
competition policy 3, 155, 161, 172
compulsory savings funds 6, 72, 90
construction banks 37–8
contagion 53, 57–8, 68, 76, 102
contingency theory 195–7, 199
cooperative banks 1, 4, 29, 31–4,
　　36–40, 42–5, 47, 158, 166, 176,
　　180, 183–4, 186, 236, 237, 240–41,
　　250

associations 232, 236
　and savings banks 179, 184
　service organizations 180
coordinated market economies 5,
　　29–32, 34–6, 45–7
corporate governance 34, 71, 121, 196,
　　204, 209
corporate imprudence 222, 227
countercyclical 1, 4, 84, 93, 95, 112, 146
countercyclical investment 3
credit
　access to credit 16, 32, 88, 90, 226
　allocation 15, 20, 22–4, 26, 65, 83
　associations 232, 237
　controls 86
　cooperatives 36, 56, 119, 230–32,
　　　236–9
　crunch 53, 56, 59, 89, 93, 146, 184
　cycle 68, 74–6, 80, 91, 93
　demand 22, 26, 83, 166
　expansion 53, 74–80, 93
　extension 91, 93
　flows 32, 71, 107, 130
　intensity 128–9
　limit 121, 130
　lines 4, 25, 57, 71, 78, 92, 112
　market 15–17, 20–22, 25, 27, 38,
　　　53, 59, 61, 63, 68, 71, 74, 83–4,
　　　90–91, 93, 215
　operations 14, 57, 60–63, 74, 76–80,
　　　92, 94–5
　policy 123, 217
　portfolios 60, 62–3, 68, 78–9, 91,
　　　93–4
　provision 70, 92–3, 96, 155, 165
　rating 137, 141–2, 148
　rationing 17, 32, 45, 222
　regulation 22
　risk 30, 34, 92, 248
　shortage 58–9, 95
　supply 21, 53, 56, 58, 159, 160
creditor 75, 106–7
CRR 121
　see also cash reserve ratio
currency devaluation 80, 107
cyclical 15, 27, 65, 163

debt(s) 6, 55–7, 60, 70, 87–8, 92, 94,
　　103, 106–7, 136, 181, 215, 223–4,
　　248

deflations 55–6
    instruments 87, 92
    securities 94
Debt Recovery Tribunals 215,
    223–4
debtor 4, 18–19, 79, 107, 243, 252
default risk 74, 159
defaulters, wilful 222, 224
deflation 55–6, 68
demand deposits 57, 59–61
denationalization 109, 113
deposit insurance scheme 176, 181,
    183–4, 186
    market 215
    requirements 75
    see also EDIS
depreciation 57–8, 88
depression 25, 54–5
deregulation 30, 45, 84, 86, 102, 108,
    121–2, 131, 214
    of interest rates 163
    of public banks 121
derivatives 1, 205, 246, 252
Deutsche Bank 137, 159, 162–4, 201,
    244, 246
developed countries 137–8, 146,
    148
developing countries 84, 117, 137–8,
    141–2, 144, 148
development
    bank(s) 3, 6–7, 21, 29, 32–3, 37, 45,
        56, 69, 80, 84–5, 101, 118, 120,
        136–48, 169
    finance 70, 123
    finance institution 123
        see also DFIs
    impact 136, 145–6, 148
    policy 6, 101, 110, 112–13
developmentalist state 103
DFIs 123, 132–3
direct agricultural credit 121, 129–30
direct investments 102, 109
diversified quality production 160
    see also DQP
dollar-denominated debt 106
domestic credit 29, 57
DQP 160
    see also diversified quality
        production
Dresdner Bank 159, 162, 167

earmarked credit 83, 110, 113
EBF 183
    see also European Banking
        Federation
ECB 176, 182–3
    see also European Central Bank
economic development 6, 19, 21, 73,
    75, 105, 107, 118, 158, 207, 213,
    244–5
    activity 58, 62–3, 80
    crisis 32, 37, 93, 102, 141
    growth 6, 40, 53, 64, 68, 75, 93, 96,
        106, 136, 143, 212
    policy 110, 163–4, 203, 214
    recovery 78, 107
    system 15, 84, 158, 200
EDIS 176, 181, 183–4, 186–8
    see also deposit insurance scheme
efficient market hypothesis 252
    see also EHM
efficient markets 35, 46, 252
EHM 252–3
    see also efficient market hypothesis
emerging countries 29, 35, 47
emission banks 37–8
EU 41–4, 139, 156–7, 167, 171, 177–8,
    181–2, 184, 186–8, 203, 208
    see also European Union
Europe 1, 7, 31, 37–8, 40, 42–4, 68,
    143, 146, 153, 155–8, 167, 172,
    177, 181–2, 185–8, 234–5, 243,
    246, 248
European Banking Federation 168,
    183
    see also EBF
European Banking Union *see* Banking
    Union
European Central Bank 143, 176,
    182–3
    see also ECB
European Commission 7–8, 155, 157,
    167–71, 176, 180–83, 185, 187,
    201, 248, 250
European Competition Commission
    146
European integration 156–8, 167,
    172
European law 155, 157–8, 167, 172
European multilevel system 156, 172
European Single Market 7, 176

European Union 8, 42–4, 137, 181, 183
  see also EU
eurozone 176, 188
exchange rate 58, 60, 69, 88, 109
expansionary monetary policy 17
exports 57–8, 60, 68, 102, 108–10, 145,
  160, 221
external debt statization 106
external financing 75, 105
externalities 16, 18–20
  see also positive externalities;
    negative externalities

fascism 33, 162, 164
federal banks 57, 69, 71–2, 90, 92
Federal Financial Supervisory
    Authority 178, 249
  see also BaFin
Federal Reserve 9, 55, 107
financial
  capital 161–2, 164, 201
  capitalism 159
  crisis 1, 5, 23, 53–5, 57, 59, 64, 67–8,
    74, 80, 84, 88, 91, 93, 95, 113,
    126, 130, 170, 176, 178–82, 185,
    187, 195, 201, 209, 237, 239,
    244–5
  development 13, 17, 116
  exclusion 3, 32, 46, 47, 127, 133
  inclusion 3, 6–7, 117, 122–3, 127,
    132
  instability 23, 26, 32, 45, 47, 54–5
  instruments 1, 4, 125, 245
  intermediation 6, 35, 116–18, 125–6,
    131, 133, 230–31, 235
  liberalization 6, 56–7, 85, 108, 117,
    120, 122–3, 126, 128–9, 131–2,
    176, 181
  market 1–5, 16, 22–3, 25–6, 54, 57,
    65, 166, 176–9, 181, 185, 187,
    251, 252
  policy 14, 102, 110, 185
  sector reforms 213–14, 219
  services 2, 14, 21, 27, 83–4, 171, 180,
    186, 203, 214, 225, 231, 233,
    241, 251
  stability 23, 45, 126, 131, 180, 217,
    233
financialization 1, 4, 9, 31, 45, 167,
  244–6, 249–54

FIPs 123
  see also financial inclusion plans
fiscal crisis 71, 103
foreign
  capital 56, 69, 90, 109
  credit markets 63
  currency 58, 60, 69, 88
  direct investment 109
  investors 57, 109
  trade 57, 61–3, 72, 88, 111
for-profit 123, 232, 239
France 31, 37, 185
Freiburg School 161

GDP 53, 57, 60, 73, 76–7, 80, 90, 129,
  160
  ratio 57, 76
Germany 3, 7–9, 13, 31, 33, 36–8, 136,
  140–41, 146–7, 155–6, 158–69,
  172, 176–81, 183–8, 195, 200–202,
  204, 206, 217, 230, 236–8, 243–6,
  248, 250, 251
  model of capitalism 155–6, 158,
    160
global financial crisis 126, 130, 195
governance structure 2, 8–9, 185, 195,
  199–200, 204, 208–9, 230–31, 239,
  240–41, 254
  theories 195
government bonds 38, 64, 90, 107, 119,
  215
  failure 15, 20
  transfers 111, 140
Grameen Bank 144, 232, 234
Gramscian perspective 251
gross advances 213, 218–20, 227
Growth Acceleration Programme 92,
  112
guarantor liability 159, 170, 177

hedge funds 31, 254
hedging 60, 144, 158, 163, 246
hegemonic discourse 9, 244, 249,
  251–2
hegemony 9, 251–4
Helaba 8, 159, 166, 171, 185, 195–6,
  200–209, 245–7, 249, 254
high interest rate 90, 225, 240
household credit 74, 77–8
housing loans 62, 76–7, 88, 91–5

illiquid 16, 133
IMF 1–2, 106, 107, 217
  see also International Monetary
    Fund
impaired loans 40, 44
impatient capital 31, 33, 40, 45
implicit savings 233
import substitution 6, 101–3, 108,
  113
inclusive economic policies 122
indebtedness 74, 90, 141, 56
India/Indian 2–3, 6, 8, 68, 116–27,
  129–33, 140, 144, 146, 212–23,
  225–7, 232, 234, 240
indirect agricultural credit 121,
  129–30
industrial financing 76, 123, 165
  policy 6, 113, 165
industrialization 6–7, 37, 69–70, 101–5,
  113, 138–9
inflation 23, 33, 64, 68, 70, 80, 85, 87,
  90, 103, 107, 109, 125
inflation stabilization plan 85
informal lenders 225, 235
information asymmetry 144, 247
infrastructure financing 122–4, 130
input legitimacy 147
instalments 213, 226
institutional liability 159, 169
institutional protection scheme 178,
  183
  see also IPS
insurance companies 31, 37–8, 117
Integrated Rural Development
  Programme 120
interbank market 56, 58–9
International Monetary Fund 1, 248,
  254
  see also IMF
internationalization 71, 86, 112, 165,
  246
investment banking 166, 248, 250
IPS 178, 183–4, 187–8
  see also institutional protection
    scheme
IRDP 120
Irish loan funds 9, 235–8
Isomorphism, coercive/mimetic/
  normative 198–9, 209
Italy 4, 185

joint liability 8, 176–7, 188, 225, 233,
  237–8

Karnataka 223, 226
Keynesian 13, 55, 161–3, 248
Keynesianism 161–2
Keynesian-Minskyan 25, 27
KfW 7, 140–44, 146
Kreditanstalt für Wiederaufbau *see*
  KfW

labor unions 29, 47
Landesbanken/Landesbank 7–8,
  136–7, 146, 155–9, 162–72,
  177–80, 184–5, 195–6, 200–201,
  205, 207, 209, 243–53
Latin American debt crisis 103, 136,
  248
Lehman Brothers 57
lender of last resort 5, 54–5, 64
leverage 16, 35–6, 54, 157–8
liability risk 34, 36, 39
liberal market economies 5, 29, 31,
  45–7
liberalization of finance 5–6, 8, 29–30,
  34, 36, 45, 56–7, 84–7, 95, 102,
  108–9, 116–17, 120, 122–3, 126,
  128–9, 131–2, 155–9, 163, 167,
  172, 176, 181, 201, 214–15,
  226
  process 56–7, 84, 86, 167
limited liability 233, 237
liquidation 56, 85, 206
liquidity 3, 5, 30, 34, 40, 53–65, 69,
  78, 80, 88, 90, 93, 119, 123, 132,
  164–5, 179, 184, 215–16, 245
  preference 59, 63, 78, 88, 90, 93
  problems 58–62, 93, 216
  reserves 245
  risk 30, 34, 132
  shortage 55, 63–4
loan default 144–5, 220–21, 249
  funds 9, 80, 235–8, 240
  portfolio 3, 61, 88, 93
  recovery 9, 225
  waiver 144, 219, 223, 226
lobbying 156, 183, 185–6
Lok Adalat 216
long-term
  assets 216

credit 37, 101, 107, 110–12, 178
liabilities 30, 170
lost decade 102
low interest rate 90, 225
Lula (Luiz Inácio Lula da Silva) 2, 73, 102, 110–11

macroeconomic policy 59, 64, 68, 106, 163
macroeconomic stability 138, 143
market
  distortions 101
  failure 4, 13–20, 22, 25, 32, 46, 54, 136
  imperfection 15–18
  logic 26, 172
  orientation 2, 167, 201, 253
  share(s) 34, 37, 46, 62, 85–6, 89, 165, 168, 180, 250
market-correcting 158, 172
Marxist 3
mature financial system 13–14
maturity transformation 16, 34
mechanistic organization 138
medium-sized bank 62, 93
mergers and acquisitions 56, 85, 90
MFIs 231–4, 238, 240
  see also microfinance institutions
micro, small and medium enterprises 112
microfinance 9, 61, 75, 83, 230–41
microfinance institutions 9, 230–32, 234–5, 239–40
  see also MFIs
Minsky (Hyman) 4–5, 14, 21, 23–5, 27, 45, 47, 53–5, 65, 67
mission creep/drift of public banks 3–4, 9, 137, 206, 243–4, 246–7, 250–53
Mittelstand 160–61, 166
mixed economy 167
monetary policy 17, 22, 64, 67, 70, 120, 181
monitoring mechanisms 8, 209, 226
monopoly in German finance 161–4
moral hazard 222–3, 239
mortgage banks 32, 37–8
mortgage securitization 32
MSMEs 112
  see also micro, small and medium enterprises

multi-paradigm 196, 199, 201, 207
multi-theoretical 8, 195–6

NABARD 225–6
  see also National Bank for Agriculture and Rural Development
Narasimham Committee 213, 215
National Bank for Agriculture and Rural Development 225
  see also NABARD
National Programme of Destatization 102
  see also PND
national savings 6, 117, 125, 131–2
nationalization 3, 6, 8, 85, 116, 119–20, 129, 131, 161–2, 164
  of banks 6, 120
NBFCs 123
negative externalities 16
neoclassical economics 8, 16, 18, 23, 27, 102, 243, 254
neoinstitutionalism 137, 196, 198–9
neoliberal hegemony 9, 244, 252–3
neo-Marxist 156
non-banking financial companies 85, 117, 123, 245
non-performing assets/loans 3, 8, 95, 122, 136, 212, 215, 219, 226–7,
  see also NPA
non-priority sector 213, 217, 219–21, 227
NordLB 159, 171, 201, 247, 249
North Rhine-Westphalia 158, 165, 168, 195, 200, 202–3, 205, 207, 245
NPA 136, 141, 144, 148, 212–27

OECD 31, 216
oil price shock 106–7
oligopoly 248
operational autonomy 122, 214
ordoliberalism 161
organizational learning 202, 208
organized capitalism 159, 166
output legitimacy 7, 147–8
oversight 133, 185, 188, 208
ownership structure 204, 206, 208

parafiscal 72, 75, 80
patient capital 5, 29–40, 45–7

payment banks 37–8
payroll loans 90, 92
peer monitoring 235
pension funds 31, 85–6
peripheral economies 14, 67, 102
PMJDY 123
 see also Prime Minister's People's
  Money Scheme; Pradhan
  Mantri Jan Dhan Yojna
PND 102, 106–8
Polanyi, Karl 5, 29, 32, 37, 45–6
political economy 7, 14, 29–30, 33, 36,
 155, 158, 172
politicization 136–7, 140–41
positive externalities 17, 19
Post Keynesian 15, 23, 36
poverty alleviation 119, 235
Pradhan Mantri Jan Dhan Yojna 123
 see also Prime Minister's People's
  Money Scheme; PMJDY
price stabilization 90, 109
Prime Minister's People's Money
 Scheme 123
 see also Pradhan Mantri Jan Dhan
  Yojna; PMJDY
principal–agent theory 2, 195–7, 199,
 244, 247, 251, 253
priority sector lending 119, 121, 129,
 219
private bank(s) 2–4, 7, 13, 15, 17,
 29–34, 36–8, 40, 45–6, 56, 58, 62,
 69, 71, 74–80, 85, 87–94, 96, 110,
 113, 116–18, 120–21, 123, 126,
 129, 131, 137–9, 144–8, 155–6,
 158, 160–64, 166–7, 179, 183, 185,
 207–9, 217–19, 221, 243, 245,
 247–8, 250–51, 253–4
 capital 17–18, 107
 credit 25, 53, 78, 88,
 investment 104–6, 112, 250
privatization 6–8, 13, 20, 56, 71, 84–5,
 90, 102, 108–9, 113, 121, 136, 171,
 185, 188, 243, 248
process 13, 108, 109, 185
procyclical 6, 25, 76, 80, 84, 95
productive sector(s) 73, 77, 87, 109
PROEF 71
PROES 71
profitability 1, 4, 25, 57, 62, 70, 90, 95,
 110, 120, 131, 212, 250

profit-maximizing 7, 29, 34, 46, 136,
 172, 230, 239
Program for Restructuring Federal
 Banks 71
 see also PROEF
Program of Incentives for the
 Reduction of the State Public
 Sector in Banking Activity 71
 see also PROES
propensity to save 244
proprietary trading 171, 244
provisioning 92, 120, 131, 212
prudential regulation 16–17, 26
prudential regulators 54
public bank(s) 1–9, 13, 15, 17–27,
 31, 37, 53–6, 59, 61–5, 67–73,
 75–80, 83–7, 90–91, 93–5, 110,
 113, 116–26, 129–33, 155–63,
 165–70, 172, 177, 181, 186, 188,
 195, 201–4, 207–8, 212–13, 217,
 219–22, 224, 227, 230, 243–4, 246,
 248, 250, 252–4
 credit 5, 69, 76, 80, 156, 158, 160,
  162, 168
 investment 105
 mandate 3, 7–9, 159, 244, 247–8,
  250, 254
 purpose 243–4
  see also public service
 service 9, 109, 157, 159, 167, 243,
  245, 254
public-law institutions 159, 245

rating agencies 137, 139, 142, 147,
 248–9
RBI 117, 122, 125–30, 212, 214–15,
 218–20, 223–4
real economy 2, 59, 63, 117, 179,
 187
real estate credit 76–7, 94
recapitalization 7, 133, 136, 140
recession 24, 55, 146
redistribution 116, 118, 120, 131,
 133
redistribution of finance 116
refinancing 55–6, 79, 124, 143, 148,
 159, 163, 169, 179, 249
regional banks 56, 73, 162
regional rural banks 117
 see also RRBs

regulatory framework 14, 31, 64, 86, 90, 92, 94, 248
   policy(ies) 158, 177
relationship banking 30, 35–6, 46, 248
renationalization 13
Reserve Bank of India 212, 214, 220–21, 227
   see also RBI
reserve requirements 59–61, 64, 119
resource allocation 15, 17, 20, 27, 83
   dependency 140–41, 143, 148
restructuring 2, 71, 85, 108, 112, 124, 144, 184–5, 215–16
retained earnings 110, 248
risk analysis 92, 148, 222, 227, 249
risk averse 57, 76, 126, 195, 202, 208
risk-minimizing 245
RRBs 117–19, 121
rural banking 61, 73, 75, 119, 123, 126, 127, 217, 219, 237
   poor 119, 225

SARFAESI Act 216, 222–3
   see also Securitization and Reconstruction of Financial Assets and Enforcement of Security Interest
savings accounts 38–9, 75, 77, 163
   banks 2, 4, 7–8, 29, 31–4, 36–40, 42, 45, 47, 87, 155, 158–69, 171–2, 176–88, 201–3, 205–9, 236–7, 244–51, 253–4
   deposits 60–61, 91, 178, 187
Savings Banks Finance Group 177–9, 185
SBI 116–17, 119, 214
   see also State Bank of India
SBLP 225
   see also self-help group bank linkage programme
securities business 179, 249
Securitization and Reconstruction of Financial Assets and Enforcement of Security Interest 216, 222
   see also SARFAESI Act
securitization of loans 1, 64, 179, 249
self-help group bank linkage programme 225
   see also SBLP

self-help groups 9, 214, 225–7, 232
   see also SHGs
self-monitoring 226–7
shared liability 233, 239
SHGs 225, 232, 239
   see also self-help groups
short-termism 90, 253
single supervisory mechanism 176, 181
   see also SSM
skill training 234, 238
SLR 119, 121
   see also statutory liquidity ratio
small and medium-sized enterprises 106, 155, 159–60, 166, 177
small banks 59, 60, 64, 183–6
small-scale industries 119, 214, 217, 219
   see also SSI
social and development banking 118, 120
social banking 33, 39, 47, 120, 122, 212, 217
   democracy 33, 162
Social Democratic Party 164, 203
   see also SPD
social development 83, 88, 95
   exclusion 45
   legitimacy 139, 146–7
   market economy 161, 188
   security 1, 73
socialism 33, 162
sociological new/neo institutional theory 195–6, 198, 244, 247, 251, 253
Spain 185
Sparkassen 38–9, 159, 165, 177, 179, 201, 204, 236
SPD 163–4, 187
   see also Social Democratic Party
special purpose banks 29, 31, 34, 36–7, 40, 42, 45, 180
SSI 119
   see also small-scale industries
SSM 176, 181
   see also single supervisory mechanism
stability anchors 6, 178, 180
stagnation 55, 61–3, 88, 125

stakeholder
  governance 6, 9, 30, 35–6, 46, 141,
    147–8, 230
  model 232, 238–41
  theory 195–7, 199, 250
State Bank of India 116, 214, 219
  see also SBI
state banks 8, 40–44, 71–2, 116, 140,
    155, 161, 163, 168–9, 177, 219–20,
    227, 246, 247
  guarantee 19, 146, 181, 186
  intervention 16–18, 20–21, 87, 103,
    223
  liability guarantees 7–8, 208, 248–9
  ownership 19, 20, 195, 208
  theory 156
statutory liquidity ratio 119, 215
strategic choice theory 195–7, 199
structural changes 172, 213, 227
  reforms 108, 120
subordinated debt 94
Supervisory Board 204–7
supply of credit 65, 91
swaps 60, 71, 92
systemic risk 179

take out financing 124, 130
Target Plan 103, 105
throughput legitimacy 147–8
Tier 1/2 capital 40, 94

time deposits 60–61, 178
total agricultural credit 129
trade unions 162, 164, 252
transnational corporations 252

unbanked persons 3, 119, 122–3, 223
uncollateralized loans 233, 238
United Kingdom 13, 38, 45, 47, 217
United States 1, 13, 22, 31, 38, 45, 47,
    55, 67, 104, 143, 181, 217, 232, 252
  see also United States of America;
    USA
United States of America 252
  see also United States; USA
universal banks 56–7, 69, 90, 123, 133,
    237
USA 216, 252
  see also United States; United States
    of America

varieties of capitalism 46, 167
volatility 1, 4, 5, 58, 74, 178, 221

Washington Consensus 13, 102
WestLB 8, 156, 158–9, 162–3, 165–71,
    185, 195–7, 200–209, 245–8, 250,
    254
working capital 76–7, 103
World Bank 101, 104, 140, 163, 248,
    254